EDUCATING THE MEXICAN AMERICAN

EDUCATING THE MEXICAN AMERICAN

Henry Sioux Johnson
William J. Hernández—M.

JUDSON PRESS, Valley Forge

Editorial Note: Because the editors have recognized that the use or omission of the hyphen in the term "Mexican American" may represent more than mere grammatical style, they have sought to follow the usage of each of the contributors to the book.

EDUCATING THE MEXICAN AMERICAN

International Standard Book No. 0-8170-0497-1
Library of Congress Catalog Card No. 73-124991

Printed in the U.S.A.

PREFACE

INCREASING ATTENTION IS CURRENTLY BEING DEVOTED to the development of ethnic studies programs in high schools, colleges, and universities throughout the United States. Concomitantly with the current interest in Mexican-American courses of studies in the public schools are the numerous requests for textbooks and materials with pertinent data that accurately reveal the stark outlines of the educational plight of Mexican Americans. There is an astonishing lack of "hard" data and research which would firmly establish the reasons for the cultural isolation and educational problems of Mexican Americans.

This introductory book of readings is designed to provide a vast array of hitherto unpublished contemporary materials and to give wide circulation to relatively sparse literature on the educational dilemma of Mexican Americans (Chicanos) in the Southwest.

In thirty-four articles, leading Mexican-American educators discuss the historical and cultural perspective of Aztlan ("lands to the north," the dwelling place of Mexican Americans in relation to Mexico). Included are their diagnoses and theories for change in the schools' curricular offerings, with emphasis on bilingual and bicultural programs for all students in the public and private schools of the Southwest. In this reawakening educational revolution, outstanding Mexican-American authorities plead for new understanding and patience in meeting the challenge of the twentieth century, Anglo-oriented, monolingual, and monocultural educational system.

This book depicts new ideas in curriculum and guidance to help Mexican Americans and Anglo-American students and educators to understand themselves and each other better and prevent them from becoming bitter, disillusioned, and from feeling disenfranchised. Such a compilation as this will help to bring forward some of the bold new ways of attacking old problems and to give them wider circulation and use to students, teachers, counselors, administrators, social workers, and researchers.

Henry S. Johnson is Professor of Mexican American Studies and Director of Intergroup Relations, California State College, Long Beach.

William J. Hernàndez—M. is Chairman, Mexican American Studies Committee, California State College, Long Beach.

LIST OF AUTHORS

Theodore Andersson
Chairman, Romance Languages Department
University of Texas, Austin

Joseph Bernal
Member of the Texas Legislature
San Antonio, Texas

Harold C. Brantley
Superintendent of Laredo School District
Laredo, Texas

Thomas P. Carter
Associate Professor in Sociology
University of Texas, El Paso

(Father) Henry J. Casso
Pastor, The Catholic Parish of The Holy Family
San Antonio, Texas
Prominent lecturer, active in Chicano student movement

7

Calvin D. Catterall
Past President, CASPP
(California Association of School Psychologists &
  Psychometrists)

Ignacio Cordova
Professor, Foreign Languages
University of New Mexico, Las Cruces

Marcos de Leon
Lecturer, Mexican American Studies, California State College,
  Long Beach
Teacher and coordinator with Los Angeles City Schools
Well-known lecturer and author of numerous articles
  on Mexican-American culture

Charles A. Ericksen
Formerly Assistant Director, Los Angeles
Foundations on Mexican-American Studies
Now Coordinator of U.S. Commission of Civil Rights, Urban
  Studies Project, San Diego
Former newspaperman and ghost-writer for radio and television
  programs

Jack D. Forbes
Professor, Cultural Anthropology
University of California, Davis
Consultant, Far West Laboratory for Educational Research
  and Development Center, Berkeley, California
Prominent author of several monographs and articles on ethnic
  minority groups in the U.S.

A. Bruce Gaarder
Chief, Modern Foreign Language Section
U.S. Office of Education

Manuel H. Guerra
Professor, in Spanish
Arizona State University, Tempe, Arizona
Author of numerous articles on bilingual educational needs of
  the Mexican American
One of original founders of the Mexican-American studies pro-
  grams in the Southwest

Augustus F. Hawkins
House Representative from Los Angeles
A black man recognized as an advocate for bilingual education

Henry S. Johnson
Professor, Mexican-American Studies
Director, Intergroup Relations, California State College, Long
   Beach

Herschel T. Manuel
Professor Emeritus of Educational Psychology
University of Texas, Austin
Prominent Mexican-American author

Edward V. Moreno
Past President, Association of Mexican-American Educators
Teacher and administrator, Ventura County Schools, California,
   and Los Angeles City Schools

Uvaldo Hill Palomares
Co-director, San Diego
Human Resources Development Center, Inc.

Alfonso R. Ramirez
Assistant Director, Valley Association for Superior Education
Edinburg, Texas

Manuel Ramirez III
Associate Professor in Psychology
Rice University, Houston, Texas
Leading researcher of Mexican American problems in U.S.

Armando Rodriguez
Chief, U.S. Office of Education, Mexican-American Unit
A recognized spokesman and leader of the Chicano movement
Educator and administrator in the San Diego City Schools for
   seventeen years
Formerly Chief, Bureau of Intergroup Relations for the state of
   California

Julian Samora
Professor in Sociology
University of Notre Dame, South Bend, Indiana
Author of *La Raza: Forgotten Americans,* a college textbook
Lecturer

Frank Sanchez
Formerly Special Assistant to the Dean, School of Letters and
 Science, California State College, Long Beach
Now Special Assistant to Chief, U.S. Office of Education, Mexi-
 can-American Unit
Administrative Assistant to U.S. Commissioner of Education

George Sanchez
Professor in History
University of Texas, Austin
Outstanding lecturer, consultant to public and private agencies
 problems of Mexican Americans
Author of recent book *Mexico: Today's World in Focus*

Vince Villagran
Community Relations Coordinator and teacher in the
Los Angeles City Schools

CONTENTS

PART 5
THE ROLE OF EDUCATIONAL INSTITUTIONS   295

Part 1
HISTORICAL AND
CULTURAL PERSPECTIVE

Who Am I?*

ANONYMOUS

AFTER I TELL YOU who I am you may not know me. You may not recognize me. You may deny that I exist. Who am I? I'm a product of myself. I'm a product of you and of my ancestors.

Now, one half of my ancestors were the Spanish who were Western European, but who were also part African and part Middle Eastern. They came to this country and met with the other side of my family — the Indians. The Indians also were a great race — people of a great culture. There were many kinds of Indians, as there were many kinds of Spaniards. They mixed, they married, they had children. Their children were called Mestizos, and this is what I am.

We came to California long before the Pilgrims landed at Plymouth Rock. We settled California and all of the southwestern part of the United States, including the states of Arizona, New Mexico, Colorado, and Texas. We built the missions, and we cultivated the ranches. We were at the Alamo in Texas, both inside and outside. You know, we owned California — that is, until gold was found here.

I think it was a mistake to let you into the southwestern states,

* This essay was written by a student in the seventh grade.

17

because eventually you took away our lands. When we fought to retain what was ours, you used the vigilantes to scare us away, to hang us, and to take away our lands. We became your slaves. Now we cook your food, we build your railroads, we harvest your crops, we dig your ditches, we stand in your unemployment lines — and we receive more than 20 percent of your welfare. But we've done some good things, too: We won more Medals of Honor during World War II than any other ethnic group. We've never had a turncoat, even during the Korean War. Yes, we have had outstanding war records. But, you know, we don't complain. By the same token, we don't get much attention, either.

We don't live in your neighborhoods unless we let you call us Spanish, French, or something else, but not what we are. We usually attend our own schools at the elementary or junior high level; and if we get to high school, we may go to school with you. However, even before we finish high school, more than 50 percent of us drop out, and you know we don't go to college. We make up less than 1 percent of the college students, yet we are 12 percent of the total school population. We don't use government agencies because our experiences with them have been rather poor; they haven't been very friendly or helpful. The Immigration Department has never really been our friend. The land offices help to take away our lands — we couldn't exactly call them friendly. The Farm Labor Bureau has never truly served us. The schools haven't really lifted us educationally. The police — well, they haven't been the most cooperative agency in the government either. You accept our Spanish words as long as we don't speak them, because if we do, you say they're "poor" Spanish — not Castilian; so our language can't be very good — it's almost like swearing. We are usually Catholics and sometimes Protestants, but in either case we have our own churches. You say we can leave our *barrios* to live near you — that is, only if we stay in our own place. When we attend your parties to meet your friends, you usually introduce us as being Spanish or something else that we are not. You are ashamed of what we are, and your attitude makes us feel that we, too, should be ashamed of what we are. When we go to school, we don't take part in your school activities; we don't think we're wanted. We seldom participate in sports; we don't run for student offices; we don't go to your school dances; we aren't valedictorians at graduations; we seldom win recognition as students, even in Spanish; we seldom receive scholarships; we are seldom given consideration in school plans; we are seldom given lead parts in school plays. The higher in education we go, the more obvious are the double standards; yet, we haven't given up.

Who are we? Some call us the forgotten people; others call us chili snappers, tacos, spics, mexs, or greasers. Some ignore us and pretend that we don't exist. Some just wish that we would go away. The late U.S. Senator Chavez from New Mexico once said, "At the time of war we are called 'the great patriotic Americans,' and during elections politicians calls us 'the great Spanish-speaking community of America.' When we ask for jobs, we are called 'those damn Mexicans.'"

Who am I? I'm a human being. I have the same hopes that you have, the same fears, same drives, same desires, same concerns, and same abilities. I want the same chance that you have to be an individual. Who am I? In reality, I am who you want me to be.

El Plan Espiritual de Aztlan*

ANONYMOUS

IN THE SPIRIT OF A NEW PEOPLE that is conscious not only of its proud historical heritage, but also of the brutal "Gringo" invasion of our territories, we, the Chicano inhabitants and civilizers of the northern land of Aztlan, from whence came our forefathers, reclaiming the land of their birth and consecrating the determination of our people of the sun, declare that the call of our blood is our power, our responsibility, and our inevitable destiny.

We are free and able to determine those tasks which are justly called for by our homes, our land, the sweat of our brows, and our hearts. Aztlan belongs to those who plant the seeds, water the fields, and gather the crops, not to the foreign Europeans. We do not recognize capricious frontiers on the Bronze Continent.

Brotherhood unites us, and love for our brothers makes us a people whose time has come to struggle against the foreign *gabacho* who exploits our riches and destroys our culture. With our hearts in our hands and our hands in the soil, we declare

* *El Plan,* published in the March, 1969, issue of *El Grito de Norte.* The paper grew out of a conference held in Denver, Colorado, in February, 1969.

the independence of our Mestizo Nation. We are a Bronze People with a Bronze Culture. Before the world, before all of North America, before all our brothers in the Bronze Continent, we are a nation, we are a union of free pueblos. We are Aztlan.

Aztlan, in the Nahuatl tongue of ancient Mexico, means "the lands to the north." Thus Aztlan refers to what is now known as the southwestern states of the United States.

El Plan Espiritual de Aztlan sets the theme: The Chicanos *(La Raza de Bronze)* must use their nationalism as the key or common denominator for mass mobilization and organization. Once we are committed to the idea and philosophy of *El Plan de Aztlan,* we can only conclude that social, economic, cultural, and political independence is the only road to total liberation from oppression, exploitation, and racism. Our struggle then must be the control of our *barrios,* campos, pueblos, lands, economy, culture, and political life. *El Plan* commits all levels of Chicano society to *La Causa:* the *barrio,* the campo, the ranchero, the writer, the teacher, the worker, and the professional. The following three points are the basic principles of *El Plan.*

Punto Primero: Nationalism as the key to organization transcends all religious, political, class, and economic factions or boundaries. Nationalism is the common denominator upon which all members of *La Raza* can agree.

Punto Segundo: Organizational Goals:

1. Unity of thought among our people concerning the *barrios,* the pueblo, the campo, the land, the poor, the middle class, and the professional is committed to liberation of *La Raza.*

2. Economic control of our lives and our communities can only come about by our own talents, sweat, and resources, and by driving the exploiter out of our communities and pueblos. Cultural background and those values which ignore materialism and embrace humanism will bring about the cooperative purchase and distribution of resources and production to sustain an economic base for healthy growth and development. Lands rightfully ours will be fought for and defended. Land ownership will be acquired by the community for the people's welfare. Economic ties of responsibility must be secured by the spirit of nationalism and the Chicano defense units.

3. Education (history, culture, bilingual education, and con-

tributions of *La Raza*) must be relevant to our people. There must be community control of our schools and our teachers.

4. Institutions shall serve our people by providing the services necessary for a full life and well-being on the basis of restitution, not handouts or beggar's crumbs. Restitution must be made for past economic slavery, political exploitation, ethnic and cultural psychological destruction, and denial of civil and human rights. Institutions in our community which do not serve the people have no place in the community. The institutions belong to the people.

5. Self-defense of the community must rely on the combined strength of the people. The front-line defense will come from the *barrios,* the campos, the pueblos, and the *ranchitos.* Those involved as protectors of their people will be given respect and dignity. They, in turn, offer their lives for their people. Those who place themselves on the line for their people do so out of love and *carnalismo.* Those institutions which are fattened by our brothers to provide employment and political pork barrels for the Gringo will fulfill their purpose only by acts of liberation by *La Causa.* The very young will no longer commit acts of juvenile delinquency, but will perform revolutionary acts.

6. Cultural values of our people strengthen our identity and give moral backbone to the movement. Our culture unites and educates the family of *La Raza* toward liberation with one heart and one mind. We must insure that our writers, poets, musicians, and artists produce literature and art that is appealing to our people and related to our revolutionary culture. Our cultural values of life, family, and home will serve as powerful weapons to defeat the Gringo dollar-value system and encourage the process of love and brotherhood.

7. Political liberation can come only through independent action on our part, since the two-party system is like an animal with two heads that feed from the same trough. Where we are a majority, we will control; where we are a minority, we will represent a pressure group. Nationally, we will represent one party — *La Familia de La Raza.*

Punto Tercero: Action:

1. There shall be an awareness of *El Plan Espiritual de Aztlan.* This shall be presented at every meeting, demonstration, confrontation, courthouse, institution, administration, church

school, tree, building, car, and every other place of human existence.

2. On September 16, the birthdate of Mexican Independence, there shall be a national walkout by all Chicanos from all colleges and schools, to be sustained until the revision of the educational system is complete. Its policy makers, administration, curriculum, and personnel must meet the needs of our community.

3. Self-defense against the occupying forces of the oppressors must be provided at every school, using every available man, woman, and child.

4. There must be a community nationalization and organization of all Chicanos to carry out *El Plan Espiritual de Aztlan.*

5. An economic program to drive the exploiter out of our communities and a welding of our peoples' combined resources to control their own production through cooperative effort must be realized.

6. The creation of an independent, local, regional, and national political party is necessary.

The liberation of our nation so that it is autonomously free — culturally, socially, economically, and politically — will enable it to make its own decisions on the usage of lands, the taxation of goods, the utilization of human bodies for war, the determination of justice (reward and punishment), and the profit of our sweat.

El Plan de Aztlan is the plan of liberation!

Spanish in the Southwest*

GEORGE I. SANCHEZ

THERE ARE CLOSE TO FIVE MILLION PERSONS with Spanish-Mexican antecedents in five southwestern states: Arizona, California, Colorado, New Mexico, and Texas. Most of these people still speak Spanish, and, in the main, considering the circumstances, remarkably good Spanish. Among those, there are many who speak only Spanish. This is a matter of considerable surprise to some observers because, among these Mexican Americans, there are many who have been exposed to the English language since the American occupation that took place some 125 years ago. When one compares this situation with that of European immigrants who came to this country much later — Italians, Poles, and others — most of whom have lost their original vernaculars, this would seem to be an exhibition of unprecedented cultural tenacity. Why have these Americans of Spanish-Mexican backgrounds been so stubborn in relinquishing *their* vernacular? What are the institutions and the forces that made this possible?

In the answer to these questions one would expect to find

* From a speech at the Occidental College Conference on the Education of Mexican Americans, 1963.

24

some sort of concerted effort on the part of Mexican-American people to retain their language, some sort of resistance to adopting English, some sort of cultural pride. Or, one would expect to find that the English-speaking dominant group, in its wisdom, had recognized the values inherent in the preservation of the Spanish language and had instituted programs to that end. That is, one would expect to find some laudable and positive cause for the persistence of this beautiful and important language, some wise head, institution, or policy that has conserved this natural cultural resource. Sad as it is to say, the major causal factor is none of these but one which involves factors that are far less noble, far less intelligent, and much more negative than positive. The conservation of the heritage of the Spanish language is an eloquent illustration that it is indeed an ill wind that does not blow somebody some good! But let us approach the matter cautiously, with circumspection.

In dealing with the conservation of Spanish in the Southwest, we must understand both the positive factors that have operated in the development of the Spanish language and its introduction and perpetuation in the area and the negative forces that have resulted in the failure to make the Mexican American a monolingual, English-speaking person. The former phase is, essentially, a matter of understanding historical antecedents; the latter is one of evaluating the factors that have resulted in the failure of the schools in their obstinate persistence to make English the only language of these Mexican Americans. This failure, more than anything else, has brought about the conservation of Spanish and has produced a bilingualism of a wide qualitative range — though, for the disadvantaged classes, the quality of the Spanish in this bilingualism is superior to the English. On the other hand, one must concede that there is a minority of persons of Spanish-Mexican descent whose English is excellent and whose Spanish is very limited or nonexistent.

SPAIN AND SPANISH

One usually thinks of Spanish as a Latin, a *romance*, language. It is that, of course; but what is often overlooked is that, in important ways, it is not Latin, and in some very important ways it is not even European. Spain has been a cultural crossroad from the earliest days of recorded history. Prehistoric men, Phoenicians, early Greeks, Carthaginians, and other early peoples blended their genes and cultures to form the Spaniard who was ruled by the Romans and then their conquerors, especially the Visigoths. During the various stages of this process, the languages of the people of Spain received infusions from all of the cultural contacts involved, especially from the Latin of the Romans. Then came the greatest invasion of all, that of the Arabic-speaking Mohammedans in A.D. 711.

For almost eight hundred years the Moors were in Spain, ruling virtually all of the Iberian Peninsula for a time. Then slowly they were pushed southward by the Christian armies. During this long period of conflict a remarkable process of acculturation took place. Though at times the conflict was bitter and bloody, there were long periods of stalemate when Christians, Sephardic Jews, and Moslems lived in comparative peace and tolerance. Cities controlled by the Mohammedans tolerated their subordinate Christian people; in turn, those controlled by the Christians tolerated their subordinate Arabic-speaking minority. In both instances, the Jew played a leading role as the businessman, the broker, and the financial counselor. The effect upon the Spaniard and upon the Spanish language wrought by this strange coexistence is incalculable. The Sephardic Jews and the Mohammedans brought to Europe the wisdom of the Middle East, of Egypt, and of North Africa. They brought institutions, technologies, value systems, instruments, and formal learning that, blending with what they found on the peninsula, produced the Golden Age of Spain in the fifteenth and sixteenth centuries.

While the effects of this process of acculturation are evident in many fields, such as architecture, religion, agriculture, educational institutions, political science, folklore, and value systems, nowhere is all of this so clearly symbolized as in the Spanish language. Today, we have at least four thousand words in Spanish that are not Latin but Arabic. Many of the words for luxuries — luxuries little known or completely unknown to the Iberian Christians before the coming of the Moslems — are Arabic. The finest of jewels are *lahajas;* pillows are *almohadas;* fine carpets are *alfombras;* and so on for a very large percentage of the Spanish words that have the initial *al,* such as *alguacil* (a police magistrate). While the Christian could say, *"Que Dios nos . . ."*

when he expressed a devout hope, he quickly adopted the Moslem prayer to Allah that is to the same effect and that has become the Spanish word *¡ojalá!* — "would that . . ." — which, expressing unreality, necessarily requires the subjunctive mood. For example, *"Ojala que estuviera," "Ojala que venga," "Ojala que tuviese."* Then there are those words which refer to a process, like *adobar* ("to conserve"). The word "adobe," now a good English word, comes from this verb; and one may have, in Spanish, an *adobe* of meat or vegetables just as one may have an adobe of clay and straw! *Carne adobada* (usually pork that has been steeped in hot peppers and other spices, and thus preserved) has long been a favorite food in New Mexico and in other Spanish-speaking areas which had no other means of preserving pork. The hand of the Jew was in this process; for, while beef and mutton may be preserved by drying (in dry climates), pork was a risky food, fresh or dried, before the days of modern technical inspection. But it would be a hardy bug, indeed, that could survive the long hours of immersion in the hot peppers and the spices (and the subsequent drying) that are devoted to the preparation of *carne adobada!* Even the most orthodox of Jews would concede that such meat is kosher!

There are many other Spanish words that are written and pronounced virtually the same way in Arabic and in Spanish. The words for shoes, trousers, neckties, socks, shirts, and many other articles are essentially the same in Arabic as in Spanish. Suffice it to note that while the foundations of Spanish are Latin, romance, the structure is a variegated one to which many tongues contributed.

SPANISH AND NEW SPAIN

When Spain, in the phenomenally expansive mood of its Golden Age, came to what today is Mexico, it did not come to a wilderness nor to a cultural vacuum. There were millions of people in the area that came to be known as New Spain who presented a kaleidoscope of cultures, languages, and degrees of civilization. Conservative estimates place their number at ten million, though there are authoritative sources that go far beyond this estimate. In the bibliography for this paper will be found sources that elaborate upon the facts of the indigenous peoples of New Spain at the time of the conquest. Those sources will reveal the magnitude, the wide scope of the cultural attributes of these peoples. More particularly, they will reveal the great linguistic variety that was represented. The Maya language, the language of the Aztecs, the languages of the Pueblos, the language of the Otomies — these and many others differed from each other as much as Chinese differs from English! Peoples living in close proximity to each other spoke vastly different languages. Some, like the Navajos, had linguistic relatives only far, far away. In the case of the Navajos (and their cousins, the Apaches), their closest relatives were in the interior of Alaska! These variegated tongues have had a tremendous influence in the development of Spanish in this part of the New World. It must be kept in mind that, in the three colonial centuries, less than one million Spaniards came to New Spain — only one million Spanish-speaking people among ten or more million native peoples who spoke diverse languages.

It must be remembered, also, that in New Spain the Spaniard came upon flora and fauna, processes, customs, and other phenomena for which he had no terminology and for which he had to accept native designations. While that strange, wonderful new bird, the turkey, could be described as *gallina de la tierra* (as my people in New Mexico still call it), or while the Spanish word *pavo* could be used (as it is in some places), it was very easy to fall into calling it a *guajalote,* a *cocono,* or some other Indian name. In many instances there were alternatives, as noted above. But what to call a "ringtail cat"? It had to be *cacomixtle* (which is now the proper English word "cacomixtle" for that beautiful creature). What to call a raccoon but a *mapache*? Try calling an opossum a *zarigüeya,* the correct Spanish word, in Mexico or in Texas! No one will understand you! The name is *tlacuache.*

In the nomenclature of birds and animals, regionalism and a great deal of confusion prevail because of the native linguistic variety and because of the application of Spanish names to creatures that were unknown in Spain. So, we find that the raccoon is a *tejón* (Spanish for badger) to some, *mapache* to many others — while *tejón* is still a badger in places like New Mexico! In many instances, however, alternatives were virtually impossible. A *quetzal* could hardly be called by any other name, nor could a mockingbird *(sinsonte),* though one can stretch things a little and call him a *burlón* (which really means "mocker" and has an unkindly connotation). While a "coyote" could be called a *lobo* ("wolf," as he is often called in English), he is hardly the wolf of the Eastern Hemisphere; so he is never called a *lobo* — and the double meanings of these two terms are highly significant. A secondary meaning of "coyote" refers to a man who is "sly" or "deceitful," while a *lobo* refers to one who is not only sly but thoroughly rapacious! And so it goes, the marriage of Spanish and the native languages of New Spain producing a most interesting and challenging variation in the already highly varied Spanish of Spain.

It would be laboring the point to dwell at any length on the many other contributions to Spanish by the Indian languages of New Spain. The names of plants *(mesquite,* for a simple illustration), the names of foods *(nixtamal, tamales, chile),* and the names of many objects in Mexican Spanish are Indian. The centuries of contact between the invaders from the Iberian Peninsula and that of the peoples they conquered gave a wondrous flavor to the language of New Spain. It is this well-seasoned and flavorful Spanish that is the heritage of the Americans of Mexican descent in the Southwest.

THE SPANISH-SPEAKING IN THE SOUTHWEST

Spanish-speaking people have been in the Southwest for 365 years. The villages north of Sante Fe, New Mexico, founded in 1598, take second place only to St. Augustine, Florida, settled in 1565, as the oldest settlements of Europeans on the mainland of what is now the United States. The New Mexico settlements, followed a little more than a century later by those in Texas and almost two centuries later by those in California, represent a colonial effort by Spain which left an indelible imprint upon the history and culture of the Southwest and of the United States as a whole. Still more important, that colonial endeavor left people here, from California to Texas, whose descendants constitute a part of the group that we now refer to, very loosely, as Spanish-speaking.

Note should be made of the fact that the colonial *hispanos* were not culturally homogeneous. The *nuevo mexicanos,* having arrived in the region as early as 1598, were different from their cousins, the *californios* and the *texanos,* who arrived much later.

The date of migration and settlement, with all its attendant cultural concomitants, geographic isolation, natural resources, the number and kind of Indians among whom they settled and mixed, and many such factors resulted in not one Spanish-speaking people but several, each with distinctive cultural personalities. The outlook on life and the schemes of values, the allegiances, the biology, and the very speech of these colonial settlers varied greatly — and though all were Spanish-speaking, they can be thought of as different peoples.

Until about the middle of the nineteenth century, the *californios*, the *nuevo mexicanos*, and the *texanos* went their separate cultural ways, held together only lightly, first by the slender threads of Spain and later for a brief time by the uncertain and flimsy bonds of independent Mexico. The annexation of Texas and the occupation of the rest of the Southwest by the United States changed the course of human affairs in this region. But the change was a slow one, unplanned and haphazard. The United States did not have the social institutions, the cultural know-how, to carry out an effective program of acculturation among her new citizens, the colonial *hispanos*. The new states and territories were left to shift for themselves in this regard, with an understandable lack of success. So the Spanish-speaking peoples of the Southwest remained Spanish-speaking and culturally isolated. They were unassimilated citizens, subject to the ever-increasing dominance of a foreign culture, the "American Way."

Even so, other things being equal, time alone would have had its influence. In due course, and with the casualties that accompany haphazard evolution, the *hispanos* would have become full-fledged Americans. However, not only were the social institutions inadequate for the task, but it soon developed that changing conditions made it impossible for time alone to bring about the assimilation of these colonial peoples. After 1870, the southwestern scene changed rapidly. The coming of the railroad opened up new economic fields and made the old ones more attractive. The region ceased to be the "Wild West"; it became instead a land of opportunity, a land where minerals and lumber, cotton and corn, cattle and sheep, and fruits and vegetables gave rise to new economic empires.

These developments, in themselves, did not hinder the process of acculturation. On the contrary, they should have gone far toward aiding it, just as analogous developments farther east quickly made Americans of the heterogeneous masses that thronged to America from Europe during the late nineteenth century. However, in addition to the fact that southwestern developments were based largely on rural-life activities and on the production of raw materials in contrast to the urban industrial situation in the East, this area was sparsely populated and, insofar as the "American Way" was concerned, culturally immature and insecure. Worse still, since labor for the new enterprises was not available from the East, the Southwest had to turn to Mexico and the Orient for its labor supply. As a consequence, the region, already suffering from cultural indigestion, added to its troubles by importing thousands of Mexican families and again postponed the day for the incorporation of its Spanish-speaking population.

Even thus enlarged by immigrants from Mexico, the Indo-Hispanic group could have been assimilated had the Southwest taken time to think out its cultural issues and to attack its fast-growing and increasingly complex socioeconomic problems, particularly those of this ethnic minority. But before 1910, almost no one seemed even to be aware that there were far-reaching issues and problems. Virtually no thought was given to the educational, health, economic, or political rehabilitation of these Spanish-speaking peoples. And after 1910 the opportunity had passed. Until then the issues and problems were still of manageable proportions; they were now to grow beyond all hope of quick solution.

The Mexican Revolution of 1910–1920 and World War I combined to bring many thousands of Mexicans to the Southwest. Large numbers came as displaced persons, driven across the border by the fortunes of a chaotic civil war. Even more people came as contract laborers, recruited by the trainload to work the beet fields of Colorado, the gardens and groves of California, the railroads of the entire West, the copper mines of Arizona, the cotton fields of Texas, and even the iron works of Chicago and the coal mines of West Virginia.

The consequences of this free-and-easy dipping into the cheap labor reservoir that is Mexico are not too difficult to observe. What, for brevity, may be called "cultural indigestion" can be documented by health and educational statistics, by pictures of the slums of San Antonio, and by all sorts of depressing socioeconomic data from all over the Southwest. Suffice it to say that once again in the Southwest, problem upon problem pyramided, for which sooner or later there must be a costly reckoning.

BIBLIOGRAPHY

Corda, Gilberto, Berta Babaza y Julieta Farias, *Vocabulario Espanol de Texas,* University of Texas Hispanic Studies, vol. 5. Austin: The University of Texas Press, 1953. (See pp. iv-v for listing of similar studies elsewhere in the Americas.)

Marden, Charles F., and Meyer, Gladys, *Minorities in American Society,* 2nd ed. New York: American Book Company, 1962. Chapter 6.

McWilliams, Carey, *North from Mexico; the Spanish-speaking People of the United States.* Philadelphia: J. B. Lippincott Co., 1949.

Sanchez, George I., *Forgotten People; a Study of New Mexicans.* Albuquerque: The University of New Mexico Press, 1940.

Sanchez, George I., *Mexico — A Revolution by Education.* New York: The Viking Press, Inc., 1936.

The Hamburger and the Taco:
A Cultural Reality*

MARCOS DE LEON

MY FATHER, LONG AGO, TOLD ME the story of an itinerant Protestant preacher in northern Mexico, who, while visiting his congregation in a rural section, came across one of his parishioners beating the "daylights" out of his wife. The minister, without any intention of meddling, went to the small *choza* to investigate the wailing and the crying as well as the thudding of blows that could be heard all over the community. No sooner had he entered the jacal than the woman turned on him and, in the vernacular of the area, berated him no end. *"Viejo metiche,"* she said. *"Si me pega es porque me 'quere.'"* "Meddlesome old fool," she said. "If he beats me, it is because he loves me." It should be observed that the verb "to love" as used by the woman does not lend itself to vulgarization in the English as it does in Spanish. You can well imagine this man of the cloth, confronted with this indignant and irate woman, yelling at the top of her lungs, *"Si me pega es porque me 'quere,'"* as if to say, "All I am doing is getting a beating which perhaps I deserve." Now, what would you have done if you had been confronted with such a

* Adapted from a speech given at the First Annual Conference on the Education of Mexican Americans in Los Angeles County, May, 1966.

problem? Certainly the minister must have known and recognized that here indeed was a problem of long standing: When two people do not get along together, it isn't something that happens overnight.

The story of the woman and the minister illustrates a dilemma — a problem of long standing. Its framework is in history. It began as an historical-cultural confrontation and eventually became an educational dilemma for our children. It appeared at the moment when the Anglo-Saxon and the Indo-Hispanic concepts of life began to interweave in the Southwest. It certainly must be admitted that the philosophy, objectives, and purposes of the school have been to perpetuate the values of the Anglo-Saxon community. There are some who could raise valid questions as to what or which segment of the Anglo-Saxon concept these values really belong. Judging by the number of young people dropping out of school all over the nation, it is certainly indicative of the need for a perpetual scrutiny of the function of the school in our communities.

However, it is to this institution — the school, provided with a specific Anglo-Saxon philosophy and whose purpose is assimilation at all costs, come what may — that the Mexican American child comes for his education.

It is imperative that we understand the importance and contributions of psychology in providing the basic philosophy, technique, and, above all, knowledge and information which should make our work with children more meaningful. There is, however, a crying need for reevaluating the validity of some concepts and approaches. In the many years of work in education, I have not come across any intent on the part of the school people in the Southwest or anywhere else to implement concepts from anthropology which would give us a sane answer to this educational dilemma of the Mexican American child. Culture-personality studies are not to be found as to how a child becomes a part of one culture and still learns the ramifications of a second one.

However, studies have been made on the importance of culture and the development of personality. This perhaps is the area of greatest importance to us. We cannot assume that our children, upon entering the school at the age of five, have lived those first five years in a cultural vacuum. Nor can we assume that when they leave the school every afternoon, they go to a community in which there is a cultural vacuum. This, then, is the challenge of the school! The school should provide for the educational needs of a personality who has been cradled in one culture and projected into a second one, who is at once a product of two cultures and two value systems.

The potential of cultural influence in a person's life is all-encompassing. Malinowski, who portrays a functionalist orientation, perceives it as the matrix of personality, the ethos of any people. Culture comprises a group's ideas, habits, values, attitudes, and institutions. It possesses physical and material aspects with sanctions in technology and economics. To give the group cohesion and direction, culture provides social institutions, education, and political structures; it sets up systems of belief relating men to the universe. Aesthetics is very much an integral part of culture, representing the graphic and plastic arts, folklore, music, drama, and dance. And finally there is language, the symbolism of abstract thought, the vehicle of knowledge, belief, legal systems, and tribal constitutions.

Anyone who has a social philosophy which has at heart the growth and development of children, and who has had experience in the schools with the Mexican American child, will readily recognize the educational frontier before us. Let us be frank with ourselves and admit that the ideology, the philosophy, and the methods utilized in dealing with this problem have until now been as inane as those used by Don Quixote in fighting windmills. The pioneering area to which I have made reference may readily be subdivided in a natural sequence: firstly, define and adopt a functional educational philosophy, in addition to the existing one, which concerns itself definitely with the cultural values of this child and those of his community; secondly, define the purposes and the functions of the school as they relate to this particular child and the community of which he is a part.

I have used the words "without precedent" in reference to this educational concern — and rightfully so. A review of the educational literature (which is at this moment coming off the presses like doughnuts) shows that there is not one serious effort being made to implement pilot studies dealing with the educational problems confronted by the *culturally different child*. As a matter of fact, the wording "culturally different child" never appears in any of the educational literature.

We use this expression because it is essential that the problem be pinpointed a little further. Every educational work, together with pilot studies or study efforts and concomitant programs, is guided and directed by the "culturally deprived" concept. There are already voices of rebellion against the concept which Francis Keppel, former United States Commissioner of Education, called a "myth." He said that this myth of considering the children of our slums to be of a lower order than children of other sectors of our economy is perpetuated by the use of such labels as "culturally deprived," "disadvantaged," "socially underprivileged," and "handicapped." However, Commissioner Keppel, by his omission of any reference to the "culturally different child," joins ranks with a good many of us in the education field in the social syllogism: "All Mexicans are poor and ignorant. Juanito is a Mexican; therefore, he is 'culturally deprived.' "

Juanito's cultural life may be visualized in five dynamic planes — two vertical and two horizontal models are necessary if Juanito happens to be closer to either the Anglo or Mexican concept of life. The vertical planes are defined as the "enculturative" process, in which the individual learns to implement his own culture from childhood to death; the horizontal planes of the cultural model indicate the "transculturative" process (or learning the other culture). (See Figure 1.) Both horizontal models are visualized as semicircles blending into one another, thus creating a third vertical plane. (See Figures 2 and 3.) All five of these concepts are to be placed on a continuum with Warner's model of society in function.[1]

Such a complex continuum has given rise to four types of cultural-linguistic personalities: the monolingual in Spanish, the monolingual in English, the bilingual, and then, to add to the teacher's headaches, there is the child who speaks a patois. Sometimes within this frame of reference Juanito may no longer be Juanito but Johnny, so that the "transculturative" process is applied in reverse. The concept of the differences between the first and second generations cannot be used as it was with the European. Juanito, moreover, is constantly in a state of transition from one culture to the other.

The premise for the frontier in educational philosophy and

the function of the school in the Southwest is a product of history. When the two concepts of life confronted each other, a social phenomenon began to unfold which affected both segments of the population. This two-way process affected the material aspects of culture and the general patterns of life for both groups. This historical "rubbing of elbows" of the two cultures involved food, art, music, religion, architecture, clothing, language ideas, values, attitudes, institutions, and economics.

Notwithstanding this pattern of cultural interaction, the ethos

Figure 1

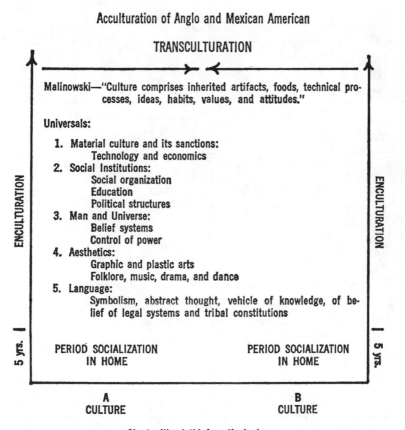

Acculturation of Anglo and Mexican American

TRANSCULTURATION

Malinowski—"Culture comprises inherited artifacts, foods, technical processes, ideas, habits, values, and attitudes."

Universals:

1. Material culture and its sanctions:
   Technology and economics
2. Social Institutions:
   Social organization
   Education
   Political structures
3. Man and Universe:
   Belief systems
   Control of power
4. Aesthetics:
   Graphic and plastic arts
   Folklore, music, drama, and dance
5. Language:
   Symbolism, abstract thought, vehicle of knowledge, of belief of legal systems and tribal constitutions

ENCULTURATION

ENCULTURATION

5 yrs.

5 yrs.

PERIOD SOCIALIZATION
IN HOME

PERIOD SOCIALIZATION
IN HOME

A
CULTURE

B
CULTURE

Chart without third vertical plane

Figure 2

Acculturation of Anglo and Mexican

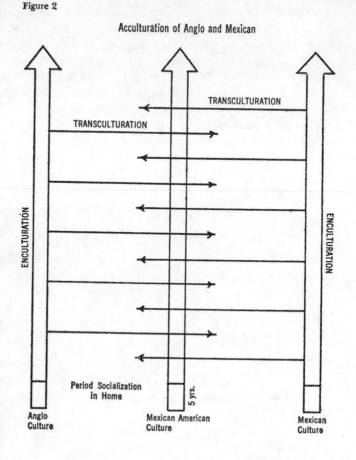

Chart by Luis Hernandez

and life character of both groups remained practically intact. Two distinct communities began to appear, each possessing its own unique interests, desires, wishes, sets of values, attitudes, aspirations, and languages.

ACCULTURATION

When we speak of two cultures meeting or throwing circles of influence over one another, we mean that people of two distinct or different cultures meet and that, as a result of this interaction, acculturation takes place.

Figure 3

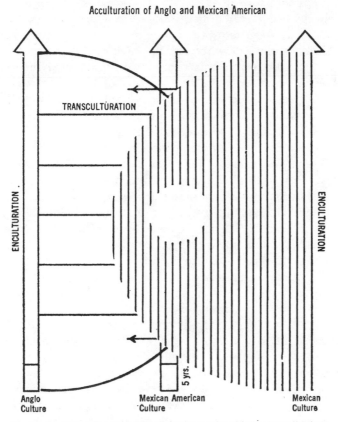

Acculturation of Anglo and Mexican American

The school as here shown must utilize the value systems of both cultures if it is to serve as a truly "educational" institution.

The process of acculturation, therefore, may be described as an all-encompassing social process with two vertical and two horizontal models in which readaptation and modification in the mode of life of either or both groups takes place, producing a third vertical concept in which the Mexican American can be found. Acculturation is an historic process, a social phenomenon that appears in history wherever major civilizations or cultures throw their tentacles around one another. The historical involvement of these two major civilizations, two distinct ethics and cultures, makes the Mexican American in the Southwest not a "minority" but an extension of the Latin American ethic in geography and history.

Let me bring this a little closer to home. Every Mexican American in the Southwest, and also in such states as Illinois, Michigan, Kansas, or wherever the Mexican American is to be found, is a product of this process — an undirected process carried on at random. What we would like to do is harness the process, give it direction, in order to educate individuals who are functional in both cultures and therefore give promise of better service to the community and the nation.

Europe long ago accepted this cultural pluralistic mode of life. There, individuals can be and often are bilingual or trilingual. Our cultural thinking, however, still dictates to us that such a personality be considered a *persona non grata*. The idea of a bilingual and bicultural personality, and therefore a culturally different child as dictated by our historical frame of reference, is still a novel one.

The Southwest is a cultural buffer area where the Spanish-speaking urban community portrays a high degree of mobility. Its members are relatively young. Its numbers are increasing by more than a normal birthrate and are supplemented by migration from Puerto Rico, Cuba, Mexico, and South America.

Many seem to understand wrongly that assimilation and acculturation are one and the same, or synonymous. By the frame of reference presented here, acculturation is an historical social process which can exist only where there is continuous interaction and influence of two specific civilizations or cultures over one another. Therefore, "enculturation" or "vertical assimilation" and "transculturation" or "horizontal assimilation" are but phases of the social concept of acculturation.

One may therefore classify acculturation into two practical categories: (1) Acculturation where historically two cultures exert relative or strong influence over one another, and due to the lack of a continuous migration pattern from one of the cultures, the transculturative link or phase ceases to exist and the enculturative process or vertical assimilation may be "complete" [2] or practically so; and (2) acculturation where cultures A and B exist in history and geography with strong concomitant influence over one another.

Let me elaborate on each one of these possibilities. First, acculturation where assimilation may be complete or practically so. Historically, the conquest of the Spanish peninsula by the Romans represents an ideal illustration. Even though the tribes of the peninsula did not willingly accept Romanization immediately, they eventually became so Romanized that to this day we say that Rome Romanized the peninsula even more than Rome itself. A further historical example of this process is the Spaniard in the New World. Although he influenced food, music, and every area of culture, nevertheless the Spaniard was absorbed by the Indian way of life in the Americas. The United States is another basic example where the European, after a span of immigration, became part of an assimilated group. Australia, at this particular moment, is undergoing a social phenomenon. Since her population is comprised of some ten million people and her geographic expanse is so vast, large numbers of Europeans have been brought to the country to help to populate it. Undoubtedly acculturation as here defined is taking place right now; and eventually, perhaps in a generation, these people will become, for all practical purposes, "Australians."

Examples of acculturation where transculturation or horizontal assimilation which produces the bilingual and bicultural personality took place are to be found in Spanish history. Upon conquest by the Moslems, a social group called the *Mozárabe,* began to appear. This group was, for all practical purposes, Roman and Spanish. The Mozarabs spoke the adulterated form of Latin, and eventually also Arabic. They served in the Moslem armed forces and in civil administration, becoming functionally bilingual and bicultural in personality.

The counterpart of the *Mozárabe* was the *Mudéjar:* As the reconquest of the Spanish peninsula rolled southward, there appeared another individual, the Mudejar. Whereas the Mozarab was Christian, the Mudejar was Moslem. He also became bilingual. He spoke both the adulterated form of Latin and his native tongue, Arabic. He also served in the armed forces, civil administration, and in every gamut of life that existed around him.

The third individual that I would like to mention historically is the Sephardic Jew, the Spanish Jew. This person became trilingual. Semantics fail to describe him. Two cultures acting on one another can be termed acculturation. But this Sephardic individual spoke three languages. He was trilingual for all practical purposes because he had to function in three cultural communities.

Another example is to be found in the Mediterranean area. The history of the western Greek is very close to us because he colonized the eastern part of the Iberian Peninsula. The Greeks also cradled themselves in the southern part of the Italian "boot." When the Roman Empire eventually came into being and the Greeks were rolled back, many of them stayed and became Roman citizens. In time, the Roman and the Greek became bilingual and bicultural. The Roman spoke Latin and Greek, while the Greek spoke Greek and Latin.

Modern European nations can give us another historical perspective. Those who have traveled or who may be able to do so in the future, will see that buffer areas exist between major civilizations in Europe (or any other part of the earth) where differing cultural conditions are near each other. Culturally, those who live in such buffer areas belong to both nations.

Finally, the pre-Columbian cultural complex of central Mexico with the Chichimec, Huastec, Totonac, Toltec, Tarascan, and the latecoming Aztec, and the complex in the South comprised of the Mixtec, Zapotec, Olmec, and Maya where people lived in the cultural shadow of one another to the point that one does not know where one culture began and the other ended, serves only to enhance the creation of a pluralistic concept of life among these people.

IMPLICATIONS OF ACCULTURATION

Let us return to the concept of the Southwest as a buffer cultural area for an example of the second type of acculturation. We shall attempt to define the implications of acculturation for the school.

1. The free movement of peoples from the Indo-Hispanic area is to be recognized not only as an historical continuum but also as an historical permanency. There are two hundred million individuals in the Latin American area, and there are two hundred million individuals to the north in the Anglo-Saxon area. If we are interested in the education of our children in the true sense of the word, the unavoidable two-way move-

ment of peoples makes it urgent for us to take this cultural mixing into consideration.

Eventually we have to recognize that the Indo-Hispanic people are here to stay. We find ourselves at the crossroads of two major civilizations, two concepts of life, which are back-to-back and dovetailing into one another. The only way we can eliminate this process is by constructing a wall from the Mexican Gulf to Tijuana, a wall fifteen feet wide and perhaps twenty-five feet high, putting machine guns every fifteen feet. Then take the Mexican American and scatter him throughout the entire nation, and in a generation or so the problem (if indeed he is a problem) would disappear. This is the only way that *vertical assimilation* could be accomplished in total. The alternative to such a totalitarian-like attempt would be to realize what Europe recognized through history. Cultural buffer areas do exist and people living within their boundaries belong to both civilizations culturally. *This is a cultural reality.*

2. The movement of people permits the coexistence of Hispanic and Anglo-Saxon communities, at times symbiotically and at times in conflict, but they are affected by the acculturative process whether they like it or not. What, then, are the purposes, objectives, and functions of the school when confronted with this bicultural complex?

Within a specific culture, the function of the school has been to perpetuate the values which that culture deemed right and appropriate to preserve. The assimilation process has been visualized as a vertical concept, functioning at the will of and controlled by a social stratification of that given society. However, a corollary to this thesis is that the assimilation process, as a function of the school, must be conceptualized as a horizontal continuum when two cultures, A and B, are affecting one another as in the process of acculturation.

The pedagogical principle of taking Juanito as he is, together with individual differences and innate abilities, must be coupled with his cultural experiences and heritage: He is the product of two cultures. Clearly, he must live and function within the scope of those two worlds.

When the school finally evaluates its present program and proceeds to construct one which is specifically geared to include the cultural values of the Mexican American child and his community, then its philosophy, policy, curriculum, methodology, personnel, evaluation, and procedures in testing and guidance must of necessity be changed.

To summarize the areas which are applicable to this problem of merging cultures, the following ideas are offered:

1. The purposes of education in American democracy as defined by the Educational Policies Commission of the National Education Association specify the function of the school. In order, however, that those purposes be implemented as the function of the school in any given Mexican American community, the underlying rationale must be redirected to recognize and accept the "culture within a culture" concept and, in effect, the principle of acculturation as an educational precept. The function of the school within this concept becomes twofold, perpetuating the core of values of the institutions of which the school is supposedly a functional part.

2. In order that the entire acculturative process, as it affects the Mexican American child, be facilitated and made a much more stable process, the following are imperative: (a) The school community idea must be given greater depth and meaning with better purpose and implementation. In many instances in our communities, the school and the community are like parallel lines in geometry — they never meet. (b) Not only must cultural awareness and image be strengthened, but the individual skills which will permit the child to become mobile and functional in both cultures must be imparted. Spanish, as well as English, should be taught as foreign languages as early as possible on the elementary level and continued through the junior and senior high schools. Units in the history, literature, music, art, regional dress, and food of Spain, Mexico, and the other Latin American countries should be developed within the structure of the curriculum. A great lesson was learned when the United States inherited Puerto Rico as a consequence of the Spanish-American War. The attempt was made to impose on the island the entire gamut of Anglo values through the schools. A contraculturative process was the result, and therefore it ended in complete failure. Today all subject matter is taught in Spanish in the elementary level with English entering as a foreign language in the upper grades and junior high; subject matter in the high school years is taught in Spanish and English.

3. A definite and specific effort must be instituted with the objective of supplementing the normal educative effort, preparing the Mexican American child, not as a "culturally deprived" personality, but as a *culturally different person,* to compete within the existing educational program.

4. Continuing programs of testing and guidance which are flexible and reliable, as well as valid, must be developed so that the potential of each child may be discovered as early as possible.

5. The vocational programs of the comprehensive high school must be expanded and modernized so as to give the individual, if he is not going on to any professional study, adaptability in the technologically changing community.

6. Schools must recruit bilingual teachers, counselors, administrators, and other personnel who have an understanding of and can identify with the Mexican American child and his community.

7. The community with the school must be involved on a policy-making level.

From all of this study there must be some practical application to the problem at hand. What we are after is a better educated individual, an individual who is mobile in our society, an individual who can be at home in Mexico City, in Buenos Aires, New York, or Washington, a bilingual and bicultural personality, who basically can be of better service to his community and to the nation.

NOTES

[1] Cf. charts on acculturation in W. Lloyd Warner and P. S. Hunt, *The Status System of a Modern Community* (New Haven: Yale University Press, 1942).

[2] The word "complete" in reference to assimilation falls short of strict accuracy since it is a dictum of anthropological thought that this process must be viewed as a relative continuum whether it be conceptualized as a vertical or horizontal phase. Furthermore, within this dictum, it is stated unequivocally that there is not one single individual who is capable of digesting or assimilating every facet of any particular culture. Thus follows the very intriguing question in education: Who are the culturally deprived?

The Mexican Heritage of the United States: An Historical Summary*

JACK D. FORBES

PRIOR TO 1821, when the modern Mexican nation won its independence from Spain, a Mexican was considered to be a person who spoke the Mexican or Aztec language (Nahuatl). In fact, the early Spaniards almost always referred to the Aztec people as Mexicans. This practice has continued in modern Mexico where the Nahuatl language is called "Mexicano" by the common people and where writers usually speak of the Mexican Empire rather than the Aztec Empire. The modern people of Mexico, who are said by scholars to be about 80 percent native Indian in their ancestry, are proud of their descent from the ancient Mexicans and trace the history of their people back to the builders of the magnificent cities of Teotihuacan, Monte Alban, and Chichén Itzá.

OUR ANCIENT MEXICAN HERITAGE

The Mexican heritage of the United States commences long before the time of Christ. About the year 4000 B.C., Indians living in southern New Mexico learned how to raise corn (maize)

* From Jack D. Forbes, *Mexican Americans: A Handbook for Educators* (Berkeley: Far West Laboratory, 1967).

as a result of contacts with Mexico (where that remarkable plant was first domesticated after what must have been a long and tedious process). Other crops, including squash and beans, were subsequently borrowed and still later (about A.D. 500) southwestern Indians began to develop the Pueblo Indian civilization. This advanced way of life, which still flourishes in Arizona and New Mexico, was largely based upon Mexican influences in architecture, pottery making, clothing, religion, and government.

In about A.D. 1000, according to some scholars, a people known as the Hohokam moved from northern Mexico into what is now southern Arizona. They brought many advanced traits with them, including the construction of monumental irrigation systems, stone etching techniques, and very possibly, new political concepts. The Hohokams constructed a large center at Snaketown, Arizona, and spread their influence widely, apparently establishing a colony at Flagstaff and trading their pottery as far as the San Fernando Valley in California. During the same general period, Mexican influences seem to have reached the Mississippi Valley, and advanced cultures developed there. The Indians of the southern United States developed a Mexican-style religious and political orientation and constructed small pyramid-temples, whereas the Ohio River Indians built fanciful effigy mounds, sometimes in the shape of serpents.

THE VITALITY OF MEXICAN CIVILIZATION

It is not at all surprising that ancient Mexico had a great impact upon the area of the United States. The Mexican people were extremely creative, industrious, and numerous (perhaps numbering twenty million in central Mexico alone in the 1520's). Great cities such as Teotihuacan were developed very early and at the time of the Spanish conquest Tenochtitlán (Mexico City) was perhaps the largest and certainly the most modern city in the world. In fact, our cities of today are not as well planned and are probably not as well cared for as was Tenochtitlán.

The ancient Mexicans excelled as artists, craftsmen, architects, city planners, engineers, astronomers, statesmen, and warriors. They also developed centers of higher education (called *calmécac* by the Aztecs), wrote excellent poetry, produced many historical and religious works, and were very interested in philosophical questions. One philosopher-king, Nezahualcóyotl, put forth the view that there was only one Creator-God. Mayan scientists developed a calendar which is more accurate than the one we use today.

Mexican traders *(pochteca)* traveled great distances, going as far south as Panama. They helped to spread Mexican culture and also prepared the way for colonists to settle in places such as El Salvador and Nicaragua and for the last Mexican empire (that of the Aztecs) to expand. By the 1520's the Mexican language was the common tongue of the region from north central Mexico to Central America.

THE SPANISH INVASION

In the 1520's the Spaniards commenced their conquest of Mexico. Although the Aztecs were conquered quickly, in spite of a noble defense of Tenochtitlán led by Cuauhtémoc (the present-day national hero of Mexico), the rest of what is now Mexico was subdued only very gradually. In fact, many Indian groups in northern Mexico and in the jungles of Yucatan-Guatemala were never conquered. Also, many of the Mexicans who were subdued never lost their identity and this explains why at least one tenth of the people of modern Mexico speak native languages, often in addition to *Mexican Spanish.*

The Spanish invasion did not bring an end to the vitality of the Mexican people. Most Spaniards came to rule, not to work, and the magnificent churches, aqueducts, and palaces of the colonial period are essentially the result of native labor and craftsmanship. Educated Mexicans helped to record the history of ancient Mexico and for a brief period a Mexican university, Santa Cruz del Tlaltelolco, flourished, training many persons of native ancestry. The conquering Spaniards, if of high rank, often married native noblewomen, and the common Spaniards married ordinary Indian women, in both cases contributing to the mixture of the Spanish and native Mexican races.

THE HISPANO-MEXICAN NORTHWARD MOVEMENT

The number of Spaniards who came to Mexico was always very slight, and the growth and expansion of the Spanish Empire depended upon the use of native and mixed-blood (mestizo) servants, settlers, craftsmen, miners, and soldiers (the Tlaxcaltecos, Mexicans of Tlaxcala, were particularly relied upon as colonists and soldiers). The conquest of the north would have been impossible without Mexicans, and every major settlement from Sante Fe, New Mexico, to Saltillo, Coahuila, had its Mexican district *(barrio* or *colonia)*. Many of the settlers taken by Diego de Vargas to northern New Mexico in the 1690's were called *"Espanoles Mexicanos,"* that is, "Aztec-Spaniards"; and Juan de Oñate, the first Spanish governor of New Mexico, was married to a woman of Aztec royal ancestry and their son, Cristobal de Oñate, was the second governor of that province. Every major expedition, including those of Coronado and DeSoto, utilized Mexicans, and in 1769, eight Mexican soldiers were stationed at San Diego, California, by Gaspar de Portolá. The northward movement of Spain into the southwestern United States was, therefore, a Spanish-Mexican affair. It was Spanish-led but depended for its success upon Mexicans and mixed-bloods. In California, for example, well over half of the Spanish-speaking settlers were of Indian or mixed ancestry and the forty-six founders of Los Angeles in 1781 included only two persons called Spaniards, and the wives of these two men were Indian.

THE CREATION OF MODERN MEXICAN CULTURE

Gradually the way of life brought to America by the Europeans became mixed with native Mexican influence, until the life of the common people became a blend of Spanish-Arabic and Indian traits, much as the culture of England after 1066 became a blend of French-Latin and Anglo-Celtic traditions. The Spaniards used the Mexican language for governmental, scholarly, and religious purposes for several generations and many Mexican words, such as *coyote, elote, jicara, tamale, chile, chocolate, jacal, ocelote,* and hundreds of others, became part of Spanish as spoken in Mexico. Roman Catholic religious practice was modified by many Indian customs, and devotion to the Virgin of Guadalupe has had a profound effect upon the Catholic faith.

Meanwhile, the Mexican people intermixed with diverse tribes and eventually began to absorb both the non-Mexican Indian and the Spaniard himself. This process of migration and mixture made possible the creation of the independent Mexican republic in 1821, after a ten-year struggle for freedom.

THE MEXICAN REPUBLIC IN THE NORTH

Independent Mexico was to have a lasting impact upon the southwestern United States. Many Mexican leaders were imbued with new republican and equalitarian ideals, and they sought to implement these reforms. Legislatures and elected local councils were established in California and elsewhere; the Indians and mixed-bloods were granted complete legal equality and full citizenship, and foreigners were encouraged to take up a new life as Mexicans. On the other hand, many persons found it hard to break with the authoritarian legacy of Spain, and republican reforms were often subverted. Foreign settlers did not always choose to become good Mexican citizens, as, for example, the Anglo-Texans who refused to set their slaves free or to obey Mexican land-title and tariff regulations.

The early Mexican governments were often beset by financial difficulties, and progress was difficult in the face of widespread illiteracy and an unequal distribution of wealth and power. Gradually, however, these negative conditions were overcome, and the Mexican people advanced along the road of democracy, albeit with backward steps from time to time.

In what is now the United States, Mexicans were active in the development of new mining regions (gold was discovered in California in 1842, for example), opening up new routes for travelers (as from Santa Fe to Los Angeles via Las Vegas, Nevada), founding schools (some twenty-two teachers were brought to California in the 1830's, and a seminary was established at Santa Ynez), establishing new towns (Sonoma, California, is an example), and setting up printing presses (as in California in 1835). The north was a frontier region and was, therefore, not in the forefront of Mexican cultural progress, but it did benefit from developments originating further south.

MEXICAN MINERS AND COLONISTS IN THE NORTH

Commencing in the 1830's, Mexican settlers began to move northward once again. Some two hundred craftsmen, artisans, and skilled laborers sailed to California in that decade, and soon overland immigrants from Sonora were joining them.

Thereafter a steady stream of Sonorans reached California, only to be turned into a flood by the discovery of gold in the Sierra Nevada foothills in 1848. The Sonorans were often experienced miners and their techniques dominated the California gold rush until steam-powered machinery took over at a later date. Chihuahuans and other Mexicans also "rushed" to California by sea and by land, and they, too, exercised an impact upon mining as well as upon commerce.

The United States-Mexican War of 1846–1848 did not alter immediately the character of the Southwest greatly, except in eastern Texas and northern California. The gold rush changed the language of central California after 1852 (when Mexican miners were largely expelled from the Sierra Nevada mines), but Mexicans continued to dominate the life of the region from San Luis Obispo, California, to San Antonio, Texas. Southern California, for example, remained a Spanish-speaking region until the 1870's with Spanish-language and bilingual public schools, Spanish-language newspapers, and Spanish-speaking judges, elected officials, and community leaders. The first Constitution of the State of California, created in part by persons of Mexican background, established California as a bilingual state, and it remained as such until 1878. Similar conditions prevailed in other southwestern regions.

ANGLO-AMERICANS BECOME DOMINANT

Gradually, however, Anglo-Americans from the East who were unsympathetic toward Mexican culture came to dominate the Southwest. Having no roots in the native soil and being unwilling to become assimilated to the region, these newcomers slowly transformed the schools into English-language institutions where no Spanish was taught, constructed buildings with an "eastern" character, pushed Mexican leaders into the background, and generally caused the Mexican American, as he has come to be termed, to become a forgotten citizen.

By the 1890's, on the other hand, tourists and writers began to rediscover the "Spanish" heritage, and "landmark" clubs commenced the process of restoring the decaying missions of the Southwest. A "Spanish" cultural revival was thus initiated, and soon it began to influence architectural styles as well as the kind of pageantry which has typified much of the Southwest ever since.

Unfortunately, the Mexican Indian aspect of the region's heritage was at first overlooked and the Mexican American people benefited but little from the emphasis upon things Spanish.

TWENTIETH-CENTURY MEXICAN "PIONEERS"

In the early 1900's a new group of Mexican immigrants began to enter the United States, attracted by job offers from agricultural developers who wished to open up virgin lands in southern California, Colorado, Arizona, and southern Texas. During World War I and the 1920's this movement became a flood which largely overwhelmed the older group of Mexican Americans (except in northern New Mexico and southern Colorado) and became ancestral to much of the contemporary Spanish-speaking population in the Southwest.

These hundreds of thousands of new Mexican Americans had to overcome many obstacles as they attempted to improve their life patterns. Anglo-Americans were prejudiced against people who were largely of native American, brown-skinned origin, who were poor, who of necessity lived in substandard or self-constructed homes, who could not speak English, and who were not familiar with the workings of a highly competitive and acquisitive society. Gradually, and in spite of the trauma of the Great Depression (when all sorts of pressures were used to deport Mexican Americans to Mexico), *los de la raza,* as Mexicans in the United States frequently refer to themselves, climbed the economic ladder and established stable, secure communities in the Southwest.

EDUCATIONAL PROGRESS

Educationally, Mexican American progress has been striking in individual cases, but the overall pattern has been slow. Generally speaking, whenever Anglo-Americans gained control over a particular state or region in the Southwest, they chose to import the kinds of public schools developed in the Middle West or East. Hispano-Mexican and bilingual schools were replaced by English-language, Anglo-oriented schools from which Mexican American children were sometimes excluded. After the turn of the century greater numbers of Spanish-speaking youth began to attend schools, but the latter were either irrelevant to the background, language, and interests of the pupils (as in

New Mexico) or were segregated, marginal elementary schools (as in much of California and Texas). Normally, secondary-level education was not available to Mexican American pupils except in an alien Anglo-dominated school (and even that opportunity was often not present in many rural counties in Texas and elsewhere).

During the post-World War II period, segregated schools for Mexican Americans largely disappeared, except where residential segregation operated to preserve the ethnic school. Greater numbers of Mexican Americans entered high school, and enrollment in college also increased, although slowly. Nevertheless, dropout rates remain high even today; and it is also true that the typical school serving Mexican Americans makes little, if any, concession to the Mexican heritage, the Spanish language, or to the desires of the Mexican American community.

A SIX-THOUSAND-YEAR-OLD HERITAGE

In summary, the Mexican heritage of the United States is very great indeed. For at least six thousand years Mexico has been a center for the dissemination of cultural influences in all directions, and this process continues today. Although the modern United States has outstripped Mexico in technological innovation, the Mexican people's marked ability in the visual arts, music, architecture, and political affairs makes them constant contributors to the heritage of all of North America. The Mexican American people of the United States serve as a bridge for the diffusion northward of valuable Mexican traits, serve as a reservoir for the preservation of the ancient Hispano-Mexican heritage of the Southwest, and participate directly in the daily life of the modern culture of the United States.

Part 2
EDUCATIONAL DILEMMA

Uprising in the Barrios*

CHARLES A. ERICKSEN

IN CALIFORNIA'S CITIES THE NATIVES ARE RESTLESS. The ethnic kin to the Cabrillos, Serras, Joaquin Murrieta, and Jose de la Guerra are confronting the power structure with demands for educational change. They want it now. They tell you that they do not intend to be stalled or sidetracked or bought off with a job or a raise, a new title or a fingerful of *atole*.

They are activist Mexican Americans. Their awareness of what the American educational system has done to the bilingual, bicultural Mexican American is acute. They know that in California he lags nearly four years behind the Anglo and two behind the Negro in scholastic achievement. They know that the worst schools in cities like Los Angeles, measured by dropout statistics, are those which are de facto segregated Mexican American schools.

The day when a lazy "educator" with a glib tongue dazzles Mexican Americans with double-talk about "language problems" and "responsibilities of parents" is past. They know better; they've done their homework. And although they don't claim to

---

* This paper was originally published in *American Education*, November, 1968.

have all the answers, they do know that solutions do not lie with the status quo.

Instant change is the only hope, or many thousands more brown children of the United States will be destroyed by the system, California's activist Mexican Americans tell you.

Who are these activists? They are Sal Castro, school teacher; Miguel Montes, dentist; Manuel Guerra, college professor; Esther Hernandez, housewife; Moctezuma Esparza, student. The list in Los Angeles alone could fill a book and encompass every trade and profession from newspaper boy to electrical engineer.

The commitment of each varies, of course. In part it is proportionate to the time each has left over from his obligation to his job and family; in the case of some who exploited or downgraded their own race *(raza)* to "make it," it is proportionate to their personal guilt. Or maybe it is in direct ratio to how much they have been Americanized and made aware of their individual rights.

Some send in a dollar. Some work at it twenty-four hours a day and go to jail for *la causa.*

The growth of Mexican American militancy in California has been rapid. Its focus is education. Dominated by youth, it moves in spurts.

In March, 1969, several hundred Mexican American students participated in a series of peaceful but widely publicized walk-outs from their high schools in East Los Angeles. Their orderly protests brought praise from some members of the Los Angeles Board of Education and after adult discussion had failed to do so, called the community's attention to urgently needed educational programs.

Underground newspapers, with Mexican American reporters in their teens and twenties, are sprouting in cities up and down the length of California. They take on the police, the alleged Tio Tomases of their communities, the growers, and the selective service system. But the main meat on which they feed is the educational system. In East Los Angeles there are two such newspapers: *La Raza* and *Inside Eastside.* They have been instrumental in exciting youth's passion for change.

In the past, regular community newspapers circulating in the Eastside and other Mexican American *barrios* throughout the Greater Los Angeles area studiously avoided social controversy.

Today they have changed. They report controversial matters, column upon column, because the community wants to know what it going on.

In Los Angeles, a few years ago, the first significant organization of Mexican American teachers was founded: the statewide Association of Mexican American Educators. It flourishes today, and its leaders speak out frequently and boldly. Most of its teacher members are in their twenties and thirties.

Soon after the teachers organized, the students did, too. Today the college and high school students from Los Angeles' Mexican American community have several organizations from which to choose. Most prominent among them are: the United Mexican American Students, the Mexican American Student Association, and the Brown Berets.

When the Los Angeles district attorney's office charged thirteen Mexican American activists with conspiring to cause the East Los Angeles high school walkouts (to walk out is a misdemeanor; to conspire to walk out is a felony), United Mexican American Students and Brown Beret members were among those arrested, as was a member of the Association of Mexican American Educators.

The action brought an immediate response from the Mexican American community and its leadership. Miguel Montes, a member of the California State Board of Education, termed the arrests "an imprudent attempt to keep students and teachers in line . . . unjust and highly partial application of the law."

Francisco Bravo, prominent medical doctor and president of the Pan-American bank, reacted to the arrests with an open letter to the district attorney: "I wish to take hard issue with you in this matter . . ." he began. Referring to "the continuing mental maiming of our children which has been in existence these many decades in our local educational system," Bravo explained, "while we wish to be responsible citizens, yet we must also ask . . . that our government be responsible and responsive to the needs and to the problems of our people. . . ."

On the issue of education, California's Mexican Americans speak with an unfaltering, united voice. Yet five years ago only a few dared to speak out, and they, with rare exception, were quickly discredited.

Why the sudden shift to militancy?

"The success of the Negro civil rights movement in America unquestionably had a lot to do with it," explains attorney Herman Sillas, a member of the California State Advisory Committee to the United States Commission on Civil Rights.

But Sillas sees other causes:

> Today's activist in the Mexican American community is the one who is most Anglo in his attitudes. He's more aware than his neighbors of his rights as an American and more sophisticated in his knowledge of the machinery of our democracy. In other words, he knows what happens to the squeaky wheel.

Sillas and other committee members spent two days in the heart of the East Los Angeles *barrio* last year, listening to the testimony of intense young Mexican Americans about civil rights problems in their community. Typical was the commentary by Rosalinda Mendez, a graduate of an East Los Angeles high school:

> From the time we first begin attending school, we hear about how great and wonderful our United States is, about our democratic American heritage, but little about our splendid and magnificent Mexican heritage and culture. What little we do learn about Mexicans is how they mercilessly slaughtered the brave Texans at the Alamo, but we never hear about the child heroes of Mexico who courageously threw themselves from the heights of Chapultepec rather than allow themselves and their flag to be captured by the attacking Americans.
>
> We look for others like ourselves in these history books, for something to be proud of for being a Mexican, and all we see in books, magazines, films, and TV shows are stereotypes of a dark, dirty, smelly man with a tequila bottle in one hand, a dripping taco in the other, a sarape wrapped around him, and a big sombrero.
>
> But we are not the dirty, stinking winos that the Anglo world would like to point out as Mexican. We begin to think that maybe the Anglo teacher is right, that maybe we are inferior, that we do not belong in this world, that—as some teachers actually tell students to their faces—we should go back to Mexico and quit causing problems for America.

According to Armando Rodriguez, chief of the U.S. Office of Education's Mexican American Affairs Unit, young people like Rosalinda, who organize and vocalize their bitterness, are our educational system's best friends.

He asks:

> What is an activist anyway? Our "conventional" activists are the ones who become involved in the PTA, who get wrapped up in community projects, or walk the precincts for one political party or another. Maybe they'll form a housewives' picket line around City Hall to get a street light on a dark block, or maybe they'll bake cakes to raise money for a new church building.

Whoever they are, whatever they do, they're working to bring about change. They possess special knowledge and have a special point of view. They introduce an idea to the community, and they campaign for it. This is a basic process of democracy.

Mexican American activists are no different than any other American activists. The issue of education is one that affects them most intimately. They themselves were most likely victims of our schools. They've seen the hopes and dreams of their brothers and sisters, their friends, their own children, diminished or destroyed by a system which for years has been indifferent to their needs.

They want a light in their block, too.

Rodriguez contends that these people are vital — just as a PTA is vital — if Mexican Americans are to get their full share of the American educational system.

"Remember," he says, "the Mexican American is not talking about destroying the system. He wants to improve it."

The federal government's awareness of the special needs of the bicultural student is also reflected in comments made by U.S. Commissioner of Education Harold Howe II, to delegates attending last April's National Conference on Educational Opportunities for Mexican Americans in Austin, Texas. Howe cited the need to help every youngster — whatever his home background, language, or ability — to reach his full potential. "Such a goal is a lofty one, and it is doubtful that the schools will ever achieve it perfectly," he stated. "What must concern us is the degree to which many schools fail to come within a country mile of that goal.

"If Mexican American children have a higher dropout rate than any other comparable group in the nation — and they do — the schools cannot explain away their failure by belaboring the 'Mexican American problem.' The problem, simply, is that the schools have failed with these children."

Howe pointed out that federal funds flow through Title I of the Elementary and Secondary Education Act into many school districts in which Mexican American children go to school. He said:

You and your fellow citizens with a particular concern for Mexican American children should bring every possible pressure to bear to ensure that Title I funds provide education which allows Mexican American children to have pride in their heritage while learning the way to take part in the opportunities this country has to offer. Title I funds are not appropriated by the Congress to promote 'business as usual' in the schools. They are appropriated, instead, to help the educationally deprived get a fair chance.

The Office of Education will join with you to help see that this fair chance is made a reality.

The California State Board of Education requires all school districts to set up advisory committees for Title I funds, which assist in assuring effective programs for the disadvantaged.

"The funds enabled us, for the first time, to focus on the needs of the disadvantaged Mexican American child — to zero in on some of his problems," says Wilson Riles, California's state director of compensatory education. "Students in our Title I programs have averaged about a year's gain for each year of instruction. Before Title I, they averaged about seven-tenths of a year's progress in a year."

The problem, Riles states, is in having insufficient funds to reach all of the eligible children with a saturated program. "We require districts to concentrate their programs. We try to reach the most severely deprived areas. Spread the money too thin, and you see no results."

Federal monies for migrant education projects also flow through Riles' office. Ramiro Reyes, who coordinates California's plan for the education of migrant children, says, "We're helping 50,000 children, and 85 percent of them are Mexican American."

Through special migrant education projects some school districts are discovering that they can structure a regular summer school program capable of attracting significant numbers of migrant children. Reyes cited the community of Mendota, in fertile Fresno County, as an example of this: "They had never had summer schools there before. They started when our program came in, and the youngsters turned out in droves. Many children of migrants from Texas were able to be absorbed into the program."

Another federally funded Title I program of importance to California's two million Mexican Americans is English as a Second Language (ESL). Manuel Ceja, consultant in program development in the state's office of compensatory education, sees ESL as the first step which districts take in recognizing that there is a problem and that other subjects should be taught bilingually, too.

"Many of today's ESL programs are stepping-stones to true bilingual programs," he says.

In September, Santa Monica started using some Title I funds

for a tenth-grade bilingual class in reading, mathematics, and English for recent immigrants as well as native-born Mexican Americans.

"We're watching Santa Monica closely," says Ceja. "We're looking to the day when we have Anglos in these bilingual classes, too."

Riles points out that there is a strong indirect benefit from the many federally funded innovative programs in use in California in the development of new techniques and strategies.

Armando Rodriguez cites one of these techniques:

> The English as a Second Language demonstration center in San Diego has been very successful in bringing the people into a more effective role in helping determine programs for their districts. Now San Diego's ESL program is moving in the direction of bilingual education.

Rodriguez points out that the federal government has made a national, legal, and moral commitment to bilingual education. He says:

> The commitment must be taken up by the States and implemented, regardless of how many dollars will be forthcoming through the new bilingual legislation, or when they will become available. There are sufficient monies available now through a variety of other Federal programs. It's up to local school districts to re-examine their priorities as to which are the most effective programs and to initiate bilingual teaching.

California's Miguel Montes of the California school board agrees that true bilingual programs must be given top priority. He sees them as intertwined with priorities for expanded preschool programs and projects to prepare teachers for the cultural differences of the Mexican American child.

Commissioner Howe says:

> The entire history of discrimination is based on the prejudice that because someone else is different, he is somehow worse. If we could teach all of our children—black, white, brown, yellow, and all the American shades in between—that diversity is not to be feared or suspected, but enjoyed and valued, we would be well on our way toward achieving the equality we have always proclaimed as a national characteristic.

Armando Rodriguez sees this as the challenge. "The more completely we develop this bicultural resource — the Mexican American — the better he will serve our nation. That's the goal: to educate the total Mexican American, not just parts of him."

When this happens, California's Mexican American activist will stay home and bake a cake.

The Mexican-American Child: Problems or Talents?*

MANUEL H. GUERRA

THE QUESTION WHICH MEXICAN AMERICANS POSE for themselves today resides in the realm of education. But on a larger canvas, it resides in the American conscience where the moral issue of social and economic injustice is being redressed. The inequities of unemployment, poverty, and education of minority groups in America are being corrected with new social awareness and responsibility. Indeed, the restlessness of world thought and social awakening finds its impetus in the American search for social progress and reform.

To understand the Mexican-American child, one must understand the Mexican-American community from whence he comes. To understand the Mexican-American community, one must understand the views of its leaders and the feelings and attitudes of its people. The Mexican-American community cannot resolve its problems by itself, because, by and large, they are not alone the problems of the Mexican-American community, but those of the entire society. In other words, what afflicts any group of

* Keynote speech at the Second Annual Conference on the Education of Spanish-speaking Children and Youth, November, 1965. Reprinted by permission of author.

citizens in America, concerns all. All citizens, regardless of their own race or national origin, share responsibility for the conditions affecting such groups as the Negro, Mexican American, Japanese American, and Puerto Rican. That is the American way. That is American citizenship alive in community action.

If it is true that the Mexican-American child has been neglected in California education, it is also true that the Mexican-American community has been the forgotten minority. The Mexican-American community resents this fact and feels badly about it. It also resents the fact that it has been placed in a competitive position with the Negro community for the acquisition of state and federal funds. Mexican Americans feel genuine empathy for the Negro, and they have proven their support by endorsing Negro candidates for office and Negro programs. No one understands better the plight of the Negro than the Mexican-American community, which for a century before the Negro came to California in any numbers experienced prejudice, bigotry, and political disenfranchisement. There is a tendency to forget that the Mexican Americans are indigenous to California and to think that their problems and numbers do not deserve the attention which the Negro community has received.

As a matter of fact, statistics tell a different story. There are two million citizens of Mexican-American descent in California, or 10 percent of the population. However, 33 percent of the dropouts in the schools today and about 17 percent of the juvenile delinquents are of Mexican-American background. Upwards of 40 percent of the inmates of penal institutions in California are of Mexican-American descent, and as much as 40 to 60 percent of the total drug addicts. Unemployment of unskilled workers among Mexican Americans runs very high, agricultural workers unemployed often high, and the people of Mexican-American origin on relief equally high. Just because the Mexican-American community does not dramatize its squalor, poverty, and misery and put a torch to East Los Angeles does not mean that the Mexican-American people are not frustrated and suffering. It does mean, like all Hispanic peoples, that they are a little more stoic and perhaps a bit more philosophical and fatalistic. The family plays a prominent role in Mexican-American life; Hispanic moral fibers weave strong bonds among family ties. In this respect, the Mexican-American community bears some resemblance to the Jewish home and culture. In money matters, the Mexican-American community bears more resemblance to the Negro culture.

What is the legal status of the Mexican American, and from what date does this citizen belong to the American republic? Although the Mexican American is indigenous to California, it was not until the Treaty of Guadalupe Hidalgo in 1848, concluding the Mexican-American War, that the status of the citizenship of those who reside north of the Rio Grande and Gila rivers was defined. As the present southwestern states entered statehood, some from territorial status, others like Texas and California from a republic status, citizens of Mexican parentage automatically became American citizens, with all the rights, privileges, and responsibilities thereof.

Mexican Americans who speak Spanish, whose customs or traditions originated in Spain or Mexico, whose religion is predominantly Roman Catholic, are seemingly identified with some foreign government or foreign loyalty, at least in the eyes of the non-Spanish-speaking masses. However, Juan de Oñate, the founder of Santa Fe, New Mexico, and Ponce de Leon, the explorer of Florida, had equal status with Roger Williams, of Rhode Island, or William Penn, of Pennsylvania. Moreover, Juan de Oñate and Ponce de Leon spoke Spanish, and Roger Williams and William Penn spoke English; the Spaniards were Catholics, and the Englishmen were Protestants. It is difficult for some people to think of Spanish and French as American languages on a par with English and to think of the people who speak them as loyal citizens of the United States. In fact, there has been a mistaken labor by state departments of education, in violation of the Treaty of Guadalupe Hidalgo between Mexico and the United States, to remake every Mexican-American child in the image of his Anglo-American counterparts. Spanish has been banned from the playgrounds and classrooms, Mexican-American customs and traditions discouraged in the community, and Mexican-American habits ridiculed in public. The cliché of a Mexican sleeping under a cactus plant is indeed a myth, but it serves to ridicule the institution of the siesta which modern psychiatrists are now recommending to preserve the heart and nervous system.

But if it is true that the Mexican-American minority is ridden with social problems, it is also true that there are many merits which must also be assessed. For example, in World War II and Korea, more of the Mexican-American servicemen were awarded the Congressional Medal of Honor than an equivalent percentage of any other group. At the height of psychological warfare in Korea, there were no cases of treason or desertion under fire involving Mexican-American combatants. It is noteworthy that many of these young men were the same kids who grew up in squalor and poverty in *barrios* across the tracks of cities and towns of the Southwest and who did not complete an eighth grade education. This fact argues well for the family and home of the Mexican-American community, which, despite its problems, gives its children a sense of loyalty which cannot be denied. More Mexican-American men and women serve in the armed forces of the United States than do members of any other minority group at the present time.

On the economic front, the Mexican-American community constitutes a vital and energetic labor market to help the wheels of industry and commerce to rotate. The Mexican-American community was largely responsible for the harvesting of fruits and vegetables before the importation of Mexican farm labor, and subsequent to the departure of the *braceros*. This community has one of the largest purchasing powers of any group for manufactured and other commercial products. And one only has to see the volume of advertising conducted by Channel 34 TV station in Los Angeles to understand this fact.

Moreover, not only do Mexican-American professionals administer to the needs of their own community, but to the needs of all society as well. In such fields as government, education, pharmacy, industry, commerce, medicine, law, architecture, nursing, engineering, law enforcement, and aviation, Mexican Americans serve the public with competence and dedication.

What about Juanito, the Mexican-American child, his image of his heritage and citizenship, and the adverse conditions in the community which affect him?

Mexican-American leaders have been stating throughout the Southwest that there is a need for the community to share positions of authority, responsibility, and leadership, and not relegate them to people of only one race, national origin, or social class. The reasons behind such a demand are obvious. The

Mexican-American community contends that there are many well-qualified professional men and women whose appointment or election to office would do much to raise the image of the Mexican American in society and to raise the standards of democratic representation. However, appointments of well-qualified people to positions of authority and importance from the Mexican-American community are few and far between. In many areas, these appointments are nonexistent; in other areas, they are negligible in number, and even less impressive in their importance and function. Both the Negro and Mexican-American people feel alike in this matter. How can Mexican Americans bring up their children to believe in their first-class citizenship when they see evidence everywhere of their second-class opportunities?

For example, everyone will tell you there is no discrimination against Mexican Americans in positions of authority, responsibility, or greater remuneration. The common assumption is that people are selected on the basis of their qualifications. Competition is great, and the best people are selected for the job, regardless of other arbitrary distinctions. Now, concerning the Mexican-American community, what does this mean? Does it mean there are no qualified Mexican-American applicants for these positions? Does it mean that they cannot compete successfully with their competitors? Does it mean they do not apply for positions? There are many competent and well-qualified Mexican-American professionals. They can compete successfully because in other states comparable with California they have already done so. They apply for positions and make known their availability. Nevertheless, the results are the same. Mexican Americans have a most difficult time acquiring a position for which they have good qualifications, if they succeed at all. Most of the time they simply are not considered seriously for the job.

The conditions of the California State College system may be an example. Perhaps few people would seriously doubt that the field of Spanish language and literature and competitive athletics are two areas where Mexican-American boys and girls demonstrate outstanding ability. Every year, the American Association of Teachers of Spanish and Portuguese awards a number of its highest medals to Mexican-American boys and girls who compete successfully in national examinations. Hardly a year goes by, in one of the many football, basketball, baseball, and track leagues and events, that Mexican-American boys do not achieve the highest honors, awards, and trophies. However, there has never been a football coach or athletic director of Mexican-American background in the history of any of California's eighteen state colleges. With one exception, there has never been a chairman of a foreign language department in any of the eighteen state colleges. Are there not qualified applicants? Do they apply for these positions? Is the competition so great in their area of strength that they are turned down for someone else?

The community college should serve the community. In a community with 100,000 Mexican-American citizens, there is only one Mexican American on the faculty of the community college, and he is on a part-time basis. Yet, there is a total of 240 people on the staff. Hence, he composes less than one-half of one percent of the faculty. Two state colleges have employed no Mexican-American scholars and teachers, despite the fact that both counties where they are located have 70,000 Mexican-American citizens.

What about administration? In the past eighty years, how many college presidents of Mexican-American origin have been appointed in California? Five? Three? One? The answer is *none*. There are over seventy junior colleges, twelve private colleges and universities, eighteen state colleges, and nine university campuses.

The Mexican-American community poses these questions: Why is there not a Mexican-American citizen on the state board of education? On the state college board of trustees? On the state university board of trustees? The Mexican-American community of California pays 10 percent of the taxes that support the schools, but it does not have a 1 percent representation on the boards, trusteeships, or commissions of education that are responsible to the public will.

What does this do to Juanito's image? What defeats the teaching of basic American democracy to Mexican-American children is not that they do not do their homework, but that society practices inequities that are inconsistent with the theory and principle of the schools. Mexican-American dropouts have been traced to this demoralization. What kind of image does Juanito, who may be portrayed as the average Mexican-American dropout, entertain?

The Mexican-American community is trying to arrest this problem. For example, the Youth Opportunities Foundation has initiated a scholarship drive to send deserving Mexican-American boys and girls to colleges and universities. Dean Atkinson of UCLA reports that of the seventeen students admitted this year (1965) all are doing better than the average freshman of the freshman class. This is a noteworthy statement, since many of these youngsters were denied admission elsewhere because of their low academic average. The foundation is also experimenting through its Fine Arts Committee with the bringing of Mexican-American artists and entertainers to the schools for performances and appearances. The celebrated jazz artist Eddie Cano co-chairs this committee with the author of this chapter, and already has brought his quartet to play at Lincoln High School, East Los Angeles Junior College, and the University of Southern California. Other celebrities include Vikki Carr, Trini Lopez, Val Martinez, Manny Lopez, and more. This is an effective way to keep boys and girls in school and to remind them that if others can make it, they can, too.

What is wrong with the Mexican-American child? Professor George Sanchez, of the University of Texas, once told the public of Alameda County in northern California that the Mexican-American child was not a problem because he came to school speaking Spanish; the real problem was that no one in the school could understand him. This point sums up the feelings of the Mexican-American community. This point escaped the attention of those attending the three-day conference, sponsored jointly by the California State Department of Education, Alameda County Schools, and the Union School District. Others who spoke did not represent the leadership of the Mexican-American community, nor did they have a knowledge of contemporary feeling and thinking. Professor Sanchez spoke in vain. When Juanito comes to school speaking Spanish, it is hoped that someone will be there who understands him. Yes, Juanito has problems, but his language is not one of them. The gifted child is the child with the gift of tongues, the bilingual and trilingual American, who is fluent in more than one language. In the past, the Mexican-American child has been made to feel ashamed of his Spanish language, Spanish surname, Mexican heritage, and Mexican parents. Arthur Tindell, Superintendent of Schools of the Whisman School District in Santa Clara County, California, once confided to this writer that Mexican-American children were being punished and made to stay after school because they were overheard speaking Spanish on the playground. What the non-Mexican American does not understand is that Mexican-American children return home belligerent, seeking a quarrel with their parents; they are confused, frustrated, and disappointed. The child develops an inferiority complex which he readily expresses in the neighborhood gang of other rejected children like himself. This undermining of parental authority, discrediting of his home culture, and dissociating the child from his identification with society are largely to blame for the high incidence of Mexican-American juvenile delinquency and dropouts in the schools.

No, the problem is not Juanito's knowledge of Spanish. Knowledge of any language is not a problem. His fluency in Spanish is a definite asset which the federal and state governments are spending millions of dollars to develop through the National Defense Education Act. If both this act and the Casey Bill governing foreign language instruction are properly understood, the objective of California education is eventually to make every child as bilingual as Juanito. Such programs afford the Mexican-American child an opportunity to share his knowledge with his classmates and to receive new recognition for a valuable asset. It helps Juanito to participate actively in school, and it raises the concept of what other children think of him.

It is unfortunate that a loophole in the Casey Bill has enabled some school districts to declare a dispensation from Spanish instruction on the basis that many youngsters come from Spanish-speaking homes. However, on that basis, no Anglos would have to study English, since most Anglos come from homes where English is spoken. Spanish may well be needed more for Juanito than for Johnny, because it is a matter of inculcating the child with pride in and respect for his own heritage. The Mexican-American community would like to see this loophole in the law closed, hopefully so that Spanish would be taught to all children.

Another area where Juanito has been penalized is the matter

of intelligence tests written in English. Sometimes the Spanish-speaking child does poorly on such a test because he cannot understand the questions. His poor score places him in a low percentile of the class or school, and he is promptly placed in a group of slow learners. However, in all likelihood he is not a slow learner; at least, not until he is forced to keep the slow pace with the retarded pupils in his class.

What is wrong? Why have Anglo and Mexican-American communities failed to communicate with one another? In 1952, the California State Department of Education held a conference in San Bernardino concerning the Spanish-speaking child. Afterward, a summary of the conference was published and widely distributed. Out of more than thirty participants, only two seemed to be Spanish-speaking. And one of these two later told me she did not speak Spanish; she simply had a Spanish surname! The Mexican-American community did not participate, and the conclusions reported in the document afterward were inconsistent with the feelings of the community as well as the basic concepts of modern sociology. The good intentions of highly professional people fell short of their goal because they forgot the role of the community and the school and the nature of the child they were studying. One must not lose sight of both the problems and talents of Juanito's language background.

In general, there seem to be six areas where Juanito's problems are most acute: (1) counseling the Mexican-American child, (2) reading and language arts among bilinguals and biculturals, (3) Spanish for the child of Mexican-American descent, (4) citizenship and social adjustment from Spanish-speaking homes to English-speaking schools and society, (5) fine arts and manual arts programs, and (6) competitive athletics.

First, counseling the Mexican-American child is a key problem today. It originates at the institution of teacher preparation where the counselor receives his training. At present, no curriculum which the counselor is required to take combines Spanish instruction with sociology of the Spanish-speaking community. As a matter of fact, future teachers, counselors, and administrators are not required to study a curriculum which prepares them for service among Mexican-American children. At present, in all state colleges of California less than 1 percent of the graduates ever take a course in Spanish or Mexican-American sociology. The sociology courses which many students are required to take combine the problems of many groups, including those of the Negro, Mexican American, and the Oriental American, as if their problems were similar or identical. This course at one of the three largest of the state colleges accommodates about 4 percent of the student body. In other words, the counselor, who has a key job of establishing a unique rapport with children, does not have the professional background that is necessary. In many instances, the counselor is actually antagonistic toward the Mexican-American culture, for he does not understand it. The State Department of Education should take under advisement the publication of a manual for counselors of Mexican-American children. The community should find its views in such a document and the leaders of the Mexican-American community should be joined by professional educators of Mexican-American descent in the drafting of such a document. Such a document should be made available to all school districts in the state of California.

Second, reading and language arts among bilinguals and biculturals have not received the attention which they merit. The bilingual child is often at a disadvantage because no approach respects the fact that he speaks Spanish. There has been little effort to use the Spanish language to teach English. Also, domestic conditions often short-circuit the child's concentration, motivation, or emotional stability. Poverty, disease, alcoholism, child abuse, and child abandonment are some of the reasons why Juanito does not read well. His inability to read frustrates his ambition and morale; so he compensates with antisocial behavior that will win attention. In other instances, he imagines there is a conflict of loyalties between his Spanish-speaking home and English-speaking school. Both factors represent two poles of authority in his life; both seem contradictory to his understanding of himself and society. A bilingual and bicultural child is often hypersensitive to the emotional conflicts of adjustment in which he sees himself as someone different from the vast majority of his English-speaking playmates and friends. During adolescence, no one wants to be different, and nothing strikes terror in a child's heart faster than the image of himself as someone who does not belong to his own society because of some disqualifying feature. Patience and sympathetic understanding will go a long way to help Juanito to read and to meet the other problems which this little child struggles to overcome.

Third, in the FLES (Foreign Languages in the Elementary Schools) programs today, many wonderful teachers have responded to the challenge. In no similar experience in American education have there been so many teachers who have contributed so much of their time to make a new program succeed. The success of the FLES programs has been due to the non-Mexican-American teachers, who, with open-mindedness, enthusiastic zeal, and the application of the concepts of good elementary education, have learned Spanish and how to teach it to children.

Fourth, the question of citizenship and social adjustment from Spanish-speaking homes to English-speaking schools and society seems, like the subject of language, never to have entered the picture. Eight merit or proficiency badges can be awarded to the Boy and Girl Scouts of America for their knowledge of the Spanish language and culture, but it is still not understood that Juanito's problem is his divided loyalty between his heritage and his citizenship, and the school must define for this child the true nature of his problems and his talents. His Mexican heritage is not inconsistent with the American way of life. Rather, like so many contributions by so many diverse racial and ethnic groups, America is made stronger, more beautiful, and wealthier by Juanito's gifts. The Mexican-American child should not be expected to grow up to be a good American if we make him ashamed of his parents and of his Spanish language. Mexican Americans must inculcate in their children a respect for their heritage and for the responsibilities of American citizenship. The two are fundamentally American in their moral, legal, and historical origin.

Perhaps one way to improve the citizenship status of the Mexican-American child is to improve textbook selections and publications. The Spanish and Mexican-American period of California history and Southwest history do not always portray a fair and impartial story of the Spanish conquest and discovery and of the later colonization period. Like stories of cops and robbers, the story of the "good" guys and "bad" guys is not always clear; Spanish colonizers often are not distinguished from English and Dutch pirates in the Caribbean, and the only outstanding means of identification is that one group speaks Spanish and the other English. The writers of most history books identify with the English-speaking group, although that group represents outlaws, thieves, and murderers. The established social order of the Christian world is represented by the Spanish-speaking group, which in this case becomes the villain or the outcast because it speaks Spanish rather than English. The case of Juan de Oñate is a similar case in point. Juan de Oñate, the founder of Santa Fe, New Mexico, founded the state of the forty-seventh star in the flag several years before the pilgrims founded Plymouth, Massachusetts. The governor's mansion, plaza square, and the cathedral are still standing in the heart of Santa Fe. But not enough is said about Oñate or his colony, which suffered hostile Indian attacks, famine, and disease.

For some reason or another little is mentioned about the printing press in Mexico City (the first in the Western Hemisphere) or the many fine libraries, some in California. No mention is made of Sor Juana Inez de la Cruz, the Tenth Muse, a child prodigy, poetess, mathematician, and physicist, who at the age of ten had devoured a library, and at thirteen engaged the doctors of the university in an open polemic in higher mathematics. She proved the Copernican theory and scientifically observed Halley's comet from the steps of the Cathedral of Mexico at a time when some people were committing suicide by jumping off bridges because they thought the apocalypse had arrived. Sor Juana has the unique distinction of being the first American feminist in the Western Hemisphere.

The name of Bartolome de las Casas, defender of the Indians, is seldom heard. He alone wrote letters to the king of Spain, appeared before the court, preached a gospel of love and kindness for the Indians, founded missions and convents, translated Indian languages into Spanish, and represented throughout his life a moral voice which reminded his compatriots of their Christian obligations and duties. To be noted are the marvelous chronicle of Cabeza de Vaca and his adventures throughout the Southwest, Coronado's letter to King Charles V describing the Grand Canyon, the letters of Christopher Columbus to the king of Spain, and the life of his son Diego, as governor of the island of Hispaniola. And we could go on and on.

Somehow, the reader gets two contrasting impressions of the

history of the Southwest. One is a sentimental and romantic picture, completely out of focus with history, with a false idealization of early California life. It dramatizes Ramona and her marriage place, sings "La Golondrina," and pictures the facade of one of the missions. California is depicted as a wilderness on a frontier far from culture. These are but stereotypes. However, in every mission the padres had libraries, and the rancheros had good libraries which they brought from Spain. There were people of refinement, education, and wealth; they read *Don Quijote de la Mancha* by Miguel de Cervantes. They did not eat with their fingers. They prayed to God in Spanish. The second impression omits the sentimental interpretation, out of preference for a pragmatic conclusion. The Mexican-American children of this state are all seen as being out in the fields cutting lettuce and picking fruit. There is nothing wrong with this, nor with the fact that they do not wear shoes. But too much of it gives the impression which a high official of government once gave to the MAPA (Mexican American Political Association) convention in Los Angeles a few years ago, when he said that the Mexican-American people are dropping out of school to pick lettuce in the fields and fruit in the orchards and that Mexican Americans do not have leaders because they do not complete school. The master of ceremonies reminded this gentleman that on the speaker's stand stood six Mexican-American citizens, one with a Ph.D., one with an Ed.D., two with LL.D.'s, and two social workers with B.A. and M.S. degrees, and that, strangely enough, all had gone to school. In other words, there must be a balanced picture which neither glorifies nor vilifies, but stays within the realm of reality. Perhaps it is time for Mexican-American children to know more about the Honorable Edward R. Roybal, Congressman of the 30th Congressional District; of Mr. Daniel Huevano, Assistant Secretary of the Army; of His Excellency Tellez, former mayor of El Paso, Texas, now Ambassador to Costa Rica; of the six Supreme Court judges of Mexican-American descent in California. The Mexican-American community has a right to feel proud of its leaders in every walk of life, from government to education, and most of all, of its war heroes of World War II and Korea. It is interesting to note that in South Vietnam, the first soldier to escape his Viet Cong captors was a Mexican American from El Paso, Texas. Surely there must be some value in all this — something better than a serenader with a guitar in his arms underneath a balcony, or a Mexican-American child prodding a burro in the desert while a jet plane zooms overhead.

Fifth, fine arts and manual arts programs are of vital concern to the Mexican-American community because many Mexican-American children demonstrate great talent which prepares them for jobs after graduation. Although fine arts and musical arts are competitive, there will always be opportunities for fresh and new talent. Special schools should prepare those children who have exceptional talent for vocations and professions. Society should restore the lost dignity of the man who works with his hands, and pass on to its children a respect for work and manual labor. There is a great need for skilled labor such as plumbers, electricians, carpenters, painters, bricklayers, barbers, X-ray technicians, and auto mechanics. Children who are poor performers in academic subjects should not be stigmatized, but should be assisted to find their places in society. Too much pressure on the value of a college education for everyone overlooks the minority child who would do better to go to a trade school in order to learn how to make a living. This breadwinner and good citizen should be just as much an integral part of our thinking as the child who is college material and college-oriented.

Sixth, both the Negroes and Mexican Americans of California have a similar experience in the area of competitive athletics. Both have found this area open to them. Both have achieved recognition in school, in the community, and in the national press for their abilities. There is hardly a school, conference, or league where youngsters of these two backgrounds do not excel. Furthermore, the ruggedness and competitiveness of athletics have provided these youngsters with a constructive outlet for their emotions. In the case of minority group children, competitiveness is not always a psychological part of their attitude. This is particularly true of the Mexican American whose Hispanic psychology of everyday life does not equip him for the competitive world of the Anglo-Saxon. Unlike the Jews who inculcate this competitive spirit in their children from early youth, Mexican-American children must acquire this impetus from some extrinsic source other than their homes. This lack of competitiveness has created a complacency and passiveness which is often mistaken as laziness. This is the unfortunate aftermath of the Mexican-American War which created in the mind of the conquered a feeling of surrender, impotence, and inferiority.

Thus, competitive athletics should be appreciated for their psychological values as well as for the merits of their physical training. However, the doors of coaching jobs and athletic directorships are still closed to these youngsters. State colleges and universities and private colleges and universities still do not employ qualified Negro and Mexican-American staffs. Professional sports are a different story; but the areas of education and coaching, where they could do so much good, still have a barrier which we can only hope will come down in the near future.

In summary, there is a relationship between the Mexican-American child in his Mexican-American community and society at large and the professional educator. In order to understand the Mexican-American child, it is necessary to understand the Mexican-American community — the views of its leaders, and the language and customs of the Spanish-speaking citizen. It is easy to underscore this child's problems and talents, one of which is often mistaken for the other. There is need to stress the necessity for the Mexican-American child to study Spanish in school and to receive from educators a reinforcement of his self-confidence and pride by inculcating an appreciation for his Mexican heritage. His lack of competitive spirit in some cases, his domestic instability, his reading problems, and his emotional problems are often compounded. But the Mexican American has demonstrated his athletic ability, his linguistic and artistic talents, and his loyalty as a citizen and as a soldier.

There is need for a new curriculum in guidance counseling of the Mexican-American child in the state colleges, teacher preparatory schools, and in-service workshops. The state department of education should publish a manual for guidance counseling of the Mexican-American child, written and edited by competent Mexican-American educators and citizens of the community. The importance of image building should be stressed among Mexican-American children to combat dropouts in the schools. Serious inequities still exist in positions of authority, leadership, and responsibility in education, government, commerce, and industry. There is a need for college presidents and deans of instruction who are of Mexican-American background. We have need of deanships, directorships, and chairmanships throughout higher education in the state not only because it is fair and just, but because Mexican Americans are competent and well-qualified; they not only serve their community, but they also raise standards in the community. Our society must make job opportunities available for minority boys and girls who do not excel academically, and for that reason, they should receive adequate vocational and manual arts training. Perhaps there is a job to be done by the Mexican-American community in the recruiting of children to the teaching profession. Future Spanish programs throughout the state are in a terrible need for competent teachers. Perhaps the Mexican-American community must accept greater responsibility for the education of its children by keeping its youngsters in school and giving them love and the advantages of stable homes.

The problems of the Mexican-American child need the cooperation of all segments of society. The Mexican-American community is ready to assist educational programs addressed to its children. But as much as it is concerned about its own children, it understands that the schools must be concerned with the best education for *all* children.

The Education of the
Spanish-Speaking in the Southwest:
An Analysis of the 1960 Census Materials*

JULIAN SAMORA

THE 1960 UNITED STATES CENSUS enumerates 3,464,996 persons of Spanish surname in the five southwestern states. If one takes into account the Puerto Rican migration to the mainland of the country, the number of Spanish surnames in other states, the number of Latin Americans, and the legal and illegal entrants across the Mexican border, the number of Spanish-speaking people in the United States is at least six million.

Table No. 1 gives a number of selected ethnic groups in the Southwest which will provide the basis for the following discussion.

During the past ten years there has been considerable population movement and growth in the Southwest. Considering the Spanish-speaking only, Arizona increased 51 percent, California 88 percent, Colorado 33 percent, New Mexico 8 percent, and Texas 37 percent. Of all the Spanish-speaking in the Southwest, 5 percent are in Colorado, 6 percent in Arizona, 8 percent in New Mexico, and 41 percent each in Texas and California. Thus, 82 percent are in the two states of California and Texas.

---

* An original paper presented at the Mexican American Workshop at Occidental College, January, 1963. Printed by permission of author.

Table 1

The Number of People in the Selected Ethnic Groups in Southwestern States, by State: 1960

State	Total Population	Spanish Surname	Negro	Indian	Japanese	Chinese	Filipino	Other
Arizona	1,302,161	194,356	43,403	83,387	1,501	2,936	943	474
California	15,717,204	1,426,534	834,642	39,014	157,317	95,600	65,459	20,723
Colorado	1,753,947	157,173	39,992	4,288	6,846	724	605	792
New Mexico	951,023	269,122	17,063	56,255	930	362*	192	458
Texas	9,579,677	1,417,811	1,187,125	5,750	4,053	4,172	1,623	2,123
Total	29,403,912	3,464,996	2,222,225	188,694	270,647	103,794	68,822	24,570

Sources: Table 15 in PC (1) 4B; PC (1) 6B; PC (1) 7B; PC (1) 33B; PC (1) 45B & Press Release—June 3, 1962, CB62—79 by the United States Department of Commerce.

Prepared for the Mexican-American Seminar, January 18–19, 1963, Phoenix, Arizona, by Dr. Julian Samora, University of Notre Dame.

Although the main subject of concern in this paper is education, a look at the related but peripheral characteristics of the population, such as income, employment, unemployment, housing, and occupations, reveals that in the most general terms more Spanish-speaking fall in lower-status categories than do the other groupings in the Southwest.

Those people who today claim that the Spanish-speaking are unindustrious, unambitious, and do not "take to education" need but to review the history of this population in the United States. The general situation is this: We find a people who came to this country in the early 1600's and 1700's; who established a folk society based on European traditions; who were isolated geographically and therefore culturally from the mainstream of western civilization; who lived a relatively "slow" life based on agriculture and the seasons; who had no particular need for education as we know it today; who, when conquered, were not assisted by the conquerors to make an adjustment to the new society; and who, when faced with the competition of the dominant society, could do little but withdraw into further isolation. When educational facilities were finally established, the Spanish Americans could not be expected to flock to the institutions, since essentially these were not an integral part of their culture. Even today, although facilities are generally adequate, the consequences of the long historical tradition are evident.

This whole picture for the Southwest was compounded by the influx of a large number of immigrants from Mexico who, generally speaking, were peasants, rural, uneducated, and of lower socioeconomic status and who also did not have the tradition of public education in their background. The latter immigrations, however, faced not only the same general problem of the previous group but, in addition, encountered the scourge of discrimination and segregation. Segregation in educational facilities has been well documented, particularly for the state of Texas where, in many instances, three public school systems have been maintained: one for the Mexican, one for the Negro, and one for the Anglo. In many areas of New Mexico and Colorado, discrimination was not so flagrant. Many communities have had their "Mexican rooms" for years and years. This is segregation on pseudopedagogical grounds, the reasoning being that Spanish-speaking children who come to school should be placed in a room by themselves in order to learn English. One community in Colorado had such segregation through the first four grades as late as 1950. A neighboring community in southern Colorado just abandoned their Mexican room last year after pressure was brought about by the local Spanish-speaking citizenry.

The biggest problem to date in the Spanish-speaking community with regard to education is the dropout problem. In the United States formal education has been considered important for enlightened citizenship, and in recent years education has also become the foundation for occupational opportunities and related socioeconomic status.

Among the Spanish-speaking, the optimum conditions for the pursuit of educational endeavors have seldom existed. The most common barriers have been inadequate facilities, forced segregation, cultural factors (such as language handicaps and little value placed on educational achievement), low socioeconomic status, and a lack of law enforcement by local officers. The results have been that over the years Spanish-speaking children either have not attended school, have attended irregularly, have dropped out sooner, or have received an inferior education.

In recent years two things have happened to improve the situation somewhat: (1) in most states the state allotment of school funds has been changed from the basis of an annual school census irrespective of school attendance to an average daily attendance basis, thus increasing the interest of school officials in actual school attendance; and (2) through the *Mendez Case* in Texas (1948) and other cases, the courts have restrained school districts and their officers from segregating pupils of Mexican or other Latin American descent in separate schools or classes.

The death blow to segregated schooling has not been dealt, however, as long as segregated housing continues, nor have the subtleties of discrimination ended. As late as April, 1962, a noted educator stated that in some schools in his state (Texas) the practice of multiple ability groups continued discrimination.

A comparison of the three populations in the five states (1950–1960) concerning the median school years completed (Table No. 2) reveals that the "all-white" population (which includes the Spanish-speaking) had a higher median for school years completed than the others, and the Spanish-speaking had

Table 2

Medians for Years of School Completed, Spanish Surname, All White, Nonwhite: Five Southwestern States 1950 and 1960

STATE	SPANISH SURNAME		ALL WHITE		NONWHITE	
	1950	1960	1950	1960	1950	1960
Arizona	6.1	7.0	10.6	11.7	5.5	7.0
California	7.6	8.6	11.8	12.1	8.9	10.5
Colorado	6.4	8.1	10.9	12.1	9.8	11.2
New Mexico	7.4	7.7	9.5	11.5	5.8	7.1
Texas	3.6	4.7	9.7	10.8	7.0	8.1

Table 3

Percent of Spanish Surname, Anglos, and Nonwhites, 25 Years of Age and Over, Who Have Completed Four Years of School or Less, and High School or More in the Five Southwestern States, 1960.*

STATE	SPANISH		ANGLO		NONWHITE	
	4 Years or Less	High School or More	4 Years or Less	High School or More	4 Years or Less	High School or More
Arizona	35.1	14.6	22.5	45.0	37.5	15.7
California	24.0	24.4	3.6	54.8	12.0	39.8
Colorado	24.0	18.3	3.2	54.6	8.3	44.6
New Mexico	29.6	18.9	3.7	56.9	39.2	19.0
Texas	52.0	11.7	6.3	46.3	23.6	20.9

*Data is based on 25 percent sample by Bureau of the Census.

Source: PHC (1) for the respective Standard Metropolitan Statistical Areas and unpublished Minor Civil Divisions results for Spanish Surname population.

the lowest median except in Arizona and New Mexico in 1950, when the nonwhites (in these cases predominantly Indian) had the lowest median. Note that in the ten-year period the non-white population has had a slightly higher increase in all states. Note, also, that the nonwhites in California and Texas (predominantly Negroes) show greater achievement than the Spanish-speaking.

Median school years completed is a crude statistic which does not discriminate very much. If we look at the data in another way, dramatic differences appear.

Table No. 3 gives the percentages of the three populations who have completed four years of school or less, and high school or more, in the five states for 1960.

Note the great differences between the Anglos and the other two populations. Texas has the most revealing record.

We have dealt with the educational statistics at the state level; now let us turn our attention to a smaller unit, namely, the Standard Metropolitan Statistical Area (hereafter called the SMSA).

SMSA ANALYSIS

Data on education for all the SMSA's (comparing Spanish-speaking, Anglos, and nonwhites) clearly shows the Spanish-speaking to be concentrated in the lower educational category "under four years," which category has been described by some educators as being "functionally illiterate." (See Table No. 4.)

The SMSA's in Colorado and New Mexico (with the exception of San Francisco in California) have the lowest percentages under four years of schooling for the Spanish-speaking. *In ten out of the fifteen SMSA's in Texas, 10 or more percent of the Spanish populations have under four years of schooling;* in eight out of ten California SMSA's 20 or more percent of the Spanish population (one out of five or more) is in the same category.

Such low educational performance cannot be explained away by ascribing the low educational status of the Spanish-speaking to their Mexican origins. It seems evident that if a border city like San Diego can keep its functionally illiterate population down to 20 percent, Bakersfield, Stockton, and Fresno (farther north) certainly should not have over 35 percent of their Span-

Table 4

Education: 4 Years or Less Compared to 4 Years of High School +
Completed, According to Spanish Surname, Anglo, and Nonwhite
by SMSA's in Five Southwestern States*

AREA	SPANISH SURNAME		ANGLO		NONWHITE	
	4 Years or Less	4 Years H.S.+	4 Years or Less	4 Years H.S.+	4 Years or Less	4 Years H.S.+
ARIZONA						
Phoenix	42.7	12.5	3.7	52.8	21.2	22.3
Tucson	29.4	18.3	2.4	59.3	30.2	18.6
CALIFORNIA						
Bakersfield	35.9	17.3	5.5	45.9	23.1	20.6
Fresno	42.1	12.6	6.9	46.2	19.1	29.6
Los Angeles and Long Beach	19.4	26.2	2.9	56.9	8.6	43.8
Sacramento	20.6	31.8	3.1	58.3	14.1	43.6
San Bernardino	29.0	17.8	3.4	52.9	12.8	31.7
San Diego	20.2	27.3	2.1	57.0	8.4	39.5
San Francisco	15.7	34.3	3.7	57.7	14.1	37.6
San Jose	25.4	22.2	3.8	60.2	11.7	51.2
Santa Barbara	30.0	20.1	2.6	61.3	16.1	34.5
Stockton	35.8	16.7	7.9	41.1	28.4	23.4
COLORADO						
Colorado Springs	11.9	36.7	1.6	62.2	4.7	52.8
Denver	17.4	24.8	2.4	59.5	7.0	45.4
Pueblo	22.8	15.1	6.7	56.8	14.7	29.6
NEW MEXICO						
Albuquerque	18.8	25.6	2.2	66.7	13.8	42.7
TEXAS						
Abilene	56.3	12.3	5.6	50.4	21.2	24.1
Austin	53.6	12.1	7.0	56.2	18.0	24.1
Beaumont	23.8	33.5	6.8	47.9	32.7	18.4
Corpus Christi	53.3	11.2	5.0	54.9	24.4	18.7
Dallas	40.0	18.8	4.5	53.1	18.8	23.7
El Paso	37.1	16.9	2.9	65.2	7.4	48.0
Fort Worth	28.4	25.5	4.5	49.0	17.7	22.6
Galveston	34.6	16.7	6.4	44.7	21.8	22.2
Houston	38.2	16.9	4.5	51.8	18.2	25.3
Laredo	47.0	15.7	7.5	59.9	—	—
Lubbock	67.8	4.9	3.8	53.3	18.8	18.9
Odessa	53.2	9.9	3.3	48.5	15.7	18.2
San Angelo	58.4	4.8	5.5	46.4	23.1	22.9
San Antonio	44.3	13.2	5.4	53.3	14.9	31.3
Waco	46.0	13.3	7.2	42.7	21.2	21.4

* For the population 25 years old and over, from the 20 percent sample.

ish populations in this category. Perhaps rurality is the explanation for such low educational status, but the Spanish-speaking have been predominantly urban since 1950. In Tucson, Arizona (farther south), 29 percent of the population is functionally illiterate, whereas Phoenix has 43 percent in the same low educational category. In Texas why should Lubbock (not a border SMSA) show 68 percent in this low educational category, when Beaumont-Port Arthur can show 24 percent? El Paso, a border city, shows 37 percent functionally illiterate, whereas Laredo, another border city, shows 47 percent. Also, if El Paso's better showing is to be explained by the fact that the lower educational status migrants from Mexico do not stop there, then how could Albuquerque, New Mexico (directly north and with a heavy concentration of Spanish), show only 19 percent in the low-status category? Further, it seems clear that Texan cities do less for the education of the Spanish generally as they move northward; e.g., Corpus Christi (53 percent), Austin, the state capital (54 percent), Abilene (56 percent), and San Angelo (58 percent). In addition, if a city like San Antonio has had a large Latin population for several decades, how can its over four out of ten Latins with less than four years of schooling and only five out of one hundred Anglos in the same category be explained? San Antonio has done a remarkably better job for Negroes (15 percent) than for Spanish. The same is true on the high school levels.

Comparing Spanish and Anglo in the "under four years schooling" category, the differences are dramatic and follow the patterns noted above. However, specific note may be taken of the following:

1. Sixty-four percent *more* Spanish are functionally illiterate compared to Anglos in Lubbock (only 15 percent more of nonwhites than Anglos). The *differentials* in other cities (Spanish and Anglo):

50 percent plus: San Angelo, Abilene.

40–49 percent: Odessa, Corpus Christi, Austin.

30–39 percent: Phoenix, Bakersfield, Fresno, Dallas, El Paso, Houston, Laredo, San Antonio, Waco.

20–29 percent: Tucson, San Bernardino, San Jose, Santa Barbara, Stockton, Fort Worth, Galveston.

2. "High School Plus" differentials (favoring Anglos):

40–49 percent: Phoenix, Tucson, Santa Barbara, Pueblo, Albuquerque, Austin, Corpus Christi, El Paso, Laredo, Lubbock, San Angelo, San Antonio.

30–39 percent: Fresno, San Bernardino, San Diego, San Jose, Denver, Abilene, Dallas, Houston, Odessa.

Nonwhites in the Southwest generally are far better off in terms of educational achievement than the Spanish-speaking.

The educational problem of the Spanish-speaking is a complicated one for which no easy or ready-made solution is available. Two facets of the problem are readily apparent: (1) the default of the school system, and therefore the community, in providing equality of opportunity in education for ethnic groupings, and (2) the lack of motivation for continuing education on the part of the Spanish-speaking.

THE DEFAULT OF THE SCHOOL SYSTEM

The American school system, whether public or parochial, functions best when conforming middle-class administrators and teachers professing middle-class values address themselves to middle-class students who possess the same value orientation or are in the process of acquiring it. The lower-class and the minority students who do not fit in the mold are less likely to be educated and more likely to become "dropout statistics."

If it is true that the schools reflect the norms and values of the community, perhaps it is equally true that community prejudices are also reflected through acts of commission as well as omission. Few school systems can, or do, gear their curricula to the needs of a minority of the population. Few know, empirically, what the needs are. It is easier and safer to prohibit the speaking of Spanish on the school ground and in the school (the need being to learn English) than to take the imaginative step of teaching both English and Spanish to both Anglos and Spanish-speaking, beginning in the elementary school. As a consequence, the "educated" Spanish-speaking person who has survived the school system is likely also to be one who has been stripped of his native language, or at best speaks and writes it imperfectly. To the enlightened this situation is a waste of human resources; to others, including some school teachers, the burden of proof is on the shoulders of the minority: "If you want to be American, speak American!"

In the Southwest many teachers of American history begin with the Pilgrim Fathers rather than presenting the cultural and historical heritage of their own area, which predates the Pilgrims. The basic question being raised is this: Is there anything about the Spanish-speaking in the Southwest that is important and desirable and that could be used by the school system to bring recognition and higher status to members of that group in the eyes of their peers and the community? The answer, of course, is yes. Do school systems take advantage of these cultural-historical experiences and contributions? Aside from a few instances, the answer, unfortunately, is no.

In brief, the available literature and other sources suggest, with regard to the failings of the school system, such factors as inferior facilities and teachers, inadequate counseling, lack of encouragement from the staff, and differing curricula and programs resulting in inferior education.

In one southwestern city a study revealed that some schools differed in terms of academic versus vocational curricula. But even in the vocational curriculum in the school that was predominantly Mexican American, there were twelve courses in upholstery but none in machine shop.

LACK OF MOTIVATION

There appears to be a consensus among most observers, professional and nonprofessional, that the Spanish-speaking lack sufficient motivation to stay in school. It is further observed that the most important contributing factors are the different cultural settings including the value orientations, lack of supportive behavior from family and peer groups, and lack of understanding of the role that the school can play in economic and social mobility. Then there are the more commonplace stereotypical reasons that they are lazy, shiftless; they don't care to get ahead; and they lack (inherent) ability. Many cases can be pointed out to support the above contentions.

The writer has often sought explanations for lack of motivation in the culture and the social structure of the group under consideration. At the same time he has often been puzzled by the disproportionate dropout rate of this population in comparison with its desire for an education. Talk to the man in the street, at the tavern, in his home, at meetings, and in the field, about the importance of an education. Listen to his aspirations for himself and for his children. He invariably will speak regretfully of his lack of education and how it has kept him from getting a decent, steady, and "easy" (inside work) job or how it has hindered any opportunity for advancement. He will also tell you of his plans for his children (which you know, statistically, will never come true).

If the very great majority of the Spanish-speaking enroll their youngsters in the elementary schools, if these children in great proportion continue through the eighth grade, and then if the tremendous dropout occurs at the end of junior high school or the beginning of senior high school, is the lack of motivation to be sought as having its genesis within the group or outside of the group? The writer submits the opinion that this lack of motivation originates in the school and community where the child, in the process of gaining an education, internalizes attitudes of inferiority, futility, and frustration. If the child looks about him and wonders about his occupational, educational, and status opportunities, about the section of town and the house in which he lives, about his role models, about his socioeconomic status and the opportunities open to him, he is likely not to be inspired to great effort. If, too, neither his family, peer groups, school, nor community come forth with continuing efforts of encouragement and support, dropping out of school and getting a job is probably his own logical answer to his situation.

If there is much motivation in the early elementary grades, as is suggested by high enrollments, what happens to it in the eighth, ninth, and tenth grades? This is a question that demands research rather than assertions and opinions.

TRACT ANALYSIS

Table No. 5 considers six SMSA's in terms of high- and low-density population areas. In a comparison of the median school years completed in these areas, all but one low-density tract has a higher median than the high-density tracts. The range of the differences between the tracts is from one grade (Albuquerque suburb) to seven grades (Phoenix and El Paso fringe). Most tracts in the Southwest differ by more than three grades. The data for the Spanish-speaking by tract reveal about the same pattern, i.e., almost every low-density tract has a higher

Table 5

Educational Status of Spanish Surname and Total Population by Selected Tracts in Six SMSA's in the Southwest.

	Central City		Fringe		Suburb	
Phoenix Tracts:	High	Low	High	Low	High	Low
% Spanish	76	14	59	11	66	22
Md. School years total	5	10	5	12	7	9
Md. School years Spanish	4	8	5	9	5	—
% Elementary School (6-13)	101	110	107	102	107	113
% High School (14-17)	45	82	20	82	53	70
Los Angeles Tracts:						
% Spanish	88	22	80	20	54	9
Md. School years total	7	12	6	11	10	12
Md. School years Spanish	7	11	4	9	9	10
% Elementary School (6-13)	107	100	95	100	101	100
% High School (14-17)	76	107	85	95	92	110
Pueblo Tracts:						
% Spanish	63	20	50	19	50	8
Md. School years total	8	10	8	11	9	13
Md. School years Spanish	8	8	8	10	7	—
% Elementary School (6-13)	105	103	95	94	94	94
% High School (14-17)	69	97	96	111	70	89
Albuquerque Tracts:						
% Spanish	79	11	78	27	65	35
Md. School years total	8	13	7	13	9	10
Md. School years Spanish	7	—	7	10	8	8
% Elementary School (6-13)	105	115	106	88	111	108
% High School (14-17)	109	207	52	131	151	112
El Paso Tracts:						
% Spanish	86	22	95	14	85	32
Md. School years total	7	13	6	13	9	12
Md. School years Spanish	6	10	5	11	4	12
% Elementary School (6-13)	104	99	116	104	113	95
% High School (14-17)	63	83	62	105	92	108
San Antonio Tracts:						
% Spanish	95	32	71	7	83	33
Md. School years total	4	12	10	5	5	8
Md. School years Spanish	4	6	8	4	4	4
% Elementary School (6-13)	102	87	100	106	87	105
% High School (14-17)	52	68	44	78	47	78

median than the high-density tracts. In only six instances do the median school years completed by the Spanish equal that of the total population. Since tracts are supposed to be fairly homogeneous areas, it is a little surprising to find such large differences between the two populations in median school years completed, as occur in some tracts.

If one takes the number of children in the tract who are enrolled in *elementary* school as a percentage of the number of children who are between the ages of six and thirteen, no general pattern of differences between high- and low-density tracts is revealed.

The number of children enrolled in high school, as a percentage of those between fourteen and seventeen years of age, shows very important differences between tracts. The data are suggestive of a very heavy dropout rate in high-density tracts after the age of thirteen. Although a general attrition could be expected from elementary school to high school, it is to be noted that in Phoenix (fringe) the attrition in the high-density tract is 87 percent and only 20 percent in the low-density tract. In more than one-third of the comparisons, there is more than 40 percent attrition in the transition from elementary to high school.

The differences between high- and low-density tracts in the percentages enrolled in high school vary as much as 98 percent (Albuquerque, central city). The general pattern is for a substantially higher enrollment in high school in the low-density tracts.

Ya Basta, The Siesta Is Over*

FATHER HENRY J. CASSO

MEXICAN AMERICANS EVERYWHERE ARE TRYING TO COME TO GRIPS with such awesome issues as: Success, A Dollar a Day, The Culture of Poverty, What Price Dignity? School on the Streets, The Double-Edged Sword, Forward Together, Is the Gate Closed? and The Etiquette of Power.

To behold this great forward thrust is greatly disturbing, for there are in these many pressures that are pushing Mexican Americans ever forward in the search for greater educational opportunity and greater educational achievement, the need for a clearer vision of the goals sought and a commitment to these goals. As Mexican Americans reflect upon what has been accomplished, it hardly seems possible that this has happened in only two years. It is difficult to believe that the Mexican American's quest for quality education began as recently as two years ago! Spontaneously the quest has been taken up, particularly by the youth. Mexican Americans are dealing with an educational institution that is geared to the exclusion of minorities — yet in

* An original paper by Fr. Henry J. Casso, printed by permission of the author. Paper prepared for the UNIAS Conference on Increasing Opportunities for Mexican American Students in Higher Education, May, 1969.

such a short time the minorities are already trying to become inclusive.

Higher education does not yet have the tools, neither does it have the commitment nor the awareness to be able to shift into another gear. An awesome reaction is beginning to set in that may threaten the student movement across the country — the danger that legitimate requests will be confused with radicalism. Initiative that is being exerted, especially on behalf of youth for improvement, will be misinterpreted as a desire to overthrow the educational system. Having convinced the American people that there is wisdom in providing higher education and that there is value in assuring that higher education can be obtained by all who desired it, a new trend in the opposite direction is occurring. Now there are discouraging accounts of cutbacks, of heads of national programs who speak publicly of withdrawal of funds for programs and scholarships, and of men in high government places who answer questions about the need for more funding on the national level for the things the educational system stands for, with a shrug of the shoulders and a faraway look. Apparent, too, in many states is the frustration experienced by the would-be student who encounters a proposed increase in university and college tuition. Frustrations that are caused by natural design can be tolerated by students. Frustrations that are caused by human design and are never resolved are the ones that soon become pressure points. Eventually they must erupt, and the direction the blowup takes cannot always be determined.

Mexican-American problems in college are related to a lack of program and initiative at the elementary level.

What has been done about these problems? In 1966, the National Educational Association held a conference which reported that the greatest challenge in the Southwest was the improvement of education for the Mexican-American child, the bilingual and bicultural child. The report admitted that educators are aware of the work that has to be done but do not have the tools whereby that awareness can be put into action. A possible solution, they felt, lay in attacking the problem of language, especially a national thrust on the concept of bilingualism. And for those who are grappling with definitions, bilingualism may be defined educationally as teaching the language of the land in the language of the home. This definition has immediate application to the Mexican American.

At a statewide conference in Texas in 1967 on "The Educational Opportunities of the Mexican American," it was resolved that one of the priority goals was the recognition that there was a serious statewide educational problem in relation to the Mexican American and that this problem had to be brought to the surface.

In 1968, the National Conference of Educational Opportunities was held in Austin, Texas. An important moment came when Commissioner Harold Howe, in his address "The Cowboy and the Indian," said:

> I would like to talk about the educational problem and it is basically just one problem; helping every youngster, whatever his home background, whatever his home language and whatever his ability to become all he has in him to become.

What must concern us is that the schools fail to come within a country mile of that goal, and if Mexican-American children have a higher dropout rate than any other identifiable group in the nation — and they do — the schools cannot explain away their failure by belaboring the Mexican American himself. The conclusion can only be that the schools have failed with these children. The Mexican American in the educational system of this country assuredly has been cheated. He finds that he and his friends have an 80 to 90 percent dropout rate. In California, a state that is supposedly one of the most enlightened and progressive in the country as far as education is concerned, there is a 50 percent dropout rate in the high schools alone. But the fact is that for more than a hundred years this nation and its educators and national educational institutions have stood mutely while this travesty has been taking place. How many people would continue to go to a doctor who had lost eight or nine out of every ten patients? How many would go to a lawyer who lost eight or nine of every ten cases? How many corporations would be allowed to continue in business if year after year they came up with an 80 to 90 percent deficit? Yet, the nation stands mute, while all but 10 or 20 percent of this vast minority have been dropping out of school! Worse yet, these children have thereby been allowed to drop out of every other institution in American life.

What are the educational systems doing about it? In 1968, Armando Rodriguez made a tour of five southwestern states and attended a total of 101 meetings, speaking to and receiving observations from 1,765 persons, among whom were members of state boards of education, commissioners, and all kinds of community people. As a result of observations made and results recorded during the survey, his conclusions included these:

1. There is a serious shortage of educational programs directed toward the needs of Mexican Americans in all five southwestern states.

2. A serious problem relates to the transmission of information concerning existing programs in their areas or in adjacent areas.

3. School districts lack imagination in devising or adopting new or innovative programs for Mexican Americans.

4. All communities evinced great interest in doing something about the problem, but lacked a sense of direction and knowledge about what to do.

5. Very few Anglo educators are prepared to handle the educational problems of Mexican Americans.

6. There is a great desire for information about promising educational programs for Mexican Americans.

7. An almost total lack of coordination among federal, state, and local agencies that deal with needs of Mexican Americans creates a critical problem.

The awesome truth is: This is the best that the educational system in the Southwest has done to take care of the problems of Mexican Americans.

Another cause for dismay and grave concern in the last two years is the student walkout across the Southwest and in some other areas. It happened in Los Angeles, in San Antonio, Elsa, Edcouch, Kingsville, Milwaukee, Tucson, and Denver. The youngsters are beginning to realize that they believed in a system that said, "Son and daughter, get a good education, finish high school, and you will be able to compete in the national scene." Then, all of a sudden these young people realize, as they look at their top fellow students, the valedictorians, the salutatorians of their classes, that they cannot compete. There is the need for counselors with *carino*. There is the need for bilingual education, the need to be able to speak Spanish on the school grounds, the need for a history in which they can see themselves, history as it was in the Southwest, and the need for an updated curriculum. On one hand, teachers are saying, "You're not going to make it, kid," and on the other hand, the kids are saying, "We want to be able to compete." The students are discovering, likewise, that the vocational courses to which many of them have been relegated have not been training them with marketable skills.

A greater tragedy occurs when young Mexican Americans think they are getting a good education because they are in high school; there they see, often too late, that the education which they have received is inferior in quality and is one that will not enable them realistically to compete. One can only speak of this historically as "The Great Rape of the Mind," a travesty of American education. Society has stood mutely while hundreds of young Mexican-American children in the first grade have been relegated to the mentally retarded classes in the Santa Ana Unified School District.

The National Advisory Committee on Mexican-American Education has pinpointed six major issues:

1. The existing educational programs for the Mexican American have been woefully inadequate and demand serious evaluation.

2. Instruments are lacking for measuring the intelligence and achievement potential of Mexican-American youth.

3. A very small percentage of Mexican-American students who could qualify for college actually enroll.

4. Legal restrictions in various states discourage instructions in languages other than English.

5. There is an exceedingly high dropout rate of Mexican Americans in public schools.

6. Society has not recognized nor accepted the need for a multilingual, multicultural school environment.

These issues were followed by four imperatives:

1. The preparation of teachers with the skills necessary to instruct Mexican-American pupils in such a manner as to insure success. This included bilingual capability.

2. Instruction in both English and Spanish so that the mother tongue is strengthened concurrently with the pupil's learning a second language and then his using both languages.

3. Instruction of preschool Mexican-American pupils so that they are more nearly ready to take their places with others by the time they enter school.

4. Complete programs for adults in both basic education and vocational education.

These points call for action. First, get the educational associations to adopt resolutions that will result in programs and designs to implement them. Second, get the national political parties to endorse the resolutions not just with words, but with appropriate action. Third, take an active part in the student movement.

One of the greatest accomplishments of this movement is the destruction of the stereotype that the Mexican American is lazy, disinterested, and unconcerned about education. How can society say young people are not interested? With few exceptions, every conference to this date has been put on, thought up by, and funded by the students, not by the institutions of higher learning. This is the most beautiful thing that is emerging: the young people (who were formerly stereotyped as less-than-dynamic) are putting on positive programs to get themselves into the educational system.

Other achievements in the movement are found in the concepts that have emerged, especially those pertaining to bilingualism and biculturalism. There is real insight in the recognition that a man does not have to divorce himself from his own personality, his family, his language, or his religion to become a good American. Another contribution is the breakdown of the concept of America as the melting pot of the downtrodden people of the world. Perhaps the biggest contribution is the preservation of the virtues of the Mexican American. Young people offer a remarkable set of virtues for this country at a time when the country seems to need them most: warmth, loyalty, close family ties, humanitarianism, love of community, justice, honesty, compassion, and religion. These are the things that have kept America united as a nation. And one may wisely ask: "If our country really values these things, why do we not all work together with vigor to spread the awareness that these are the things that have made our society great?"

Another contribution to the movement is the display of potential leadership for tomorrow. The Mexican-American youth on our campuses are the real nucleus that can provide leadership for the millions of Mexican Americans in this country. It is from this nucleus of educated Mexican Americans that others in the Spanish-speaking countries to the south of our country — 260 million or more — will look for leadership. A linkage between the North, Central, and South American countries can be built by a bridge of understanding. It is to be hoped that the many ties that bind America may be strengthened — ties of historical, cultural, linguistic, and religious understandings.

Few people are aware of a very important contribution that Mexican Americans have made to American education. One of the basic problems in the education of Mexican-American students has to do with the poor performance of bilingual children in general ability (I.Q.) and achievement tests. This, of course, poses a challenge to the whole system of testing in our schools. Finally, another contribution of the movement which has not yet been articulated on the national scene is the question: "Is education a right or is it a privilege?" If it is a right, society must go in one direction; if it is a privilege, then it must go in another. This writer assumes the position that education is a right. It is a right to the best education available in the best institutions in the land.

Youth is on the move. It has raised the flag. It is saying *"Ya basta,* the *siesta* is over."* All Mexican Americans should join with them in this current. Young MECHA *(Movimiento Estudiantil Chicano de Aztlan)* students are great people, because there are fine, promising young people in Colorado, Texas, Arizona, California, and New Mexico. Let all Mexican Americans keep their face to the wind, their eyes on the sun, and continue to work for that beautiful tomorrow!

Part 3
GUIDANCE AND
CURRICULAR PRACTICES

Why Juanito Doesn't Read*

MANUEL H. GUERRA

IF JUANITO DOESN'T READ, should we blame the child, his teacher, or his environment? There are many reasons why the Mexican-American child in California seems to be a slow learner, but unfortunately the reasons are not readily admissible or adequately understood by the classroom teacher. Juanito's real problem has not been identified or defined.

There have been few scientific studies by competent linguists concerning the problems of bilingualism of the Mexican-American child, probably because language backgrounds differ widely. In order to understand Juanito, it is necessary that the investigator speak Juanito's mother tongue proficiently, understand the customs, attitudes, and inclinations of the Mexican and his effort to adapt to the California scene.

Our state colleges and teacher education institutions are not preparing teachers to deal sympathetically with the problems of minority children, especially those requiring bilingual adjustments. Our teachers in California have been trying valiantly to carry new responsibilities without adequate skills. If we really

* From *California Teachers' Association Journal*, October, 1965. Reprinted by permission of the publisher and the author.

want to help Juanito, we must understand the morphology, the syntax, and the phonemic system of the child's bilingual problem. It seems reasonable and logical that our teacher education institutions should direct attention to these subjects for all candidates who expect to teach in California.

The social and economic problems of the Mexican-American child are now coming into focus with new emphasis on compensatory education. Lack of cultural opportunities, substandard conditions of home life, and the insecurity, misery, discomfort, and even squalor associated with poverty are being attacked at their sources. The McAteer Act of 1963 set up a pilot compensatory education program throughout the state, followed by federal anti-poverty programs which are beginning to show constructive results.

These harmful economic and social forces dissipate energies, short-circuit ambition, create anxieties and fears that rob the child of a conducive state of mind for reading. Often the child is exposed to the misfortune of parent abandonment or the detrimental influence of alcoholism, narcotics addiction, wife beating, abusive language, or child maltreatment. If Juanito comes to school from such an environment, it is not surprising that he does not read.

The correlation between testing and the ability to read puts Juanito behind the eight ball from the very start. The language problem inherent in the test itself reduces his chances and automatically puts him in a class category from which he cannot escape. Juanito consequently believes in his second-class capabilities, and he seeks the company of others who may be more retarded than he.

What holds true in second-language learning in the elementary grades also holds true in learning to read in English. A high I.Q. is not a requisite for foreign language learning; children with average I.Q.'s learn a second language successfully. Any child with a high I.Q. has a better prognosis to learn any subject or skill than one with a low I.Q. But I.Q. is not a criterion of success in itself; the way it is ascertained and the importance it is given have not helped the Mexican-American child. It has rather perpetuated a myth about Juanito's low reading ability and postponed a truly scientific and constructive approach.

As I have enumerated, Juanito's linguistic and cultural differences, his social and economic environment, and the unrealistic testing procedures which stigmatize him have impeded his growth and have placed him in a group which is barred from full effectiveness and success.

In the case of the Mexican-American child, bilingualism is concerned with a study of structure and phonemics unlike that required for any other group. This basic fact has escaped sociologists, psychologists, and linguists. Sociologists tend to combine the problems of minority groups and to study them as a single phenomenon. They also maintain the "acculturation" theory of fifty years ago. The first does not recognize the individuality of ethnic groups, and the second is inconsistent with the reality of the current civil rights movement.

For example, both Negro and Mexican-American peoples wish to preserve their heritage and culture, and the differences of their contributions to the American society enhance our way of life with great vigor, beauty, and diversity. Their contributions to the mainstream of American life stem from their individual talents and skills. "Acculturation" still implies "absorption" and "assimilation" into the Anglo-Caucasian majority group — in the sacred name of Americanism. Understandably, the Negro and the Mexican American resist this homogeneity, feeling a need to identify themselves proudly with their national origins. The Mexican prefers tortillas and beans to Boston brown bread and green peas — but he still considers both good American tastes.

If the sociology professor continues to look upon the Mexican-American child in the same way he approaches the problems of Negro children, he will deal with unreality. If the child psychologist does not understand the thinking processes of the Mexican-American child, his studies will be ineffective. If the linguist studies no more than the morphological and phonemic problems of the Mexican-American child, his view will be myopic.

Juanito's mind must deal with a basic conflict of loyalties between the English-speaking culture of his school and the Spanish-speaking heritage of his home. What confuses him — and in his juvenile immaturity this seems irreconcilable — is that differences of language and culture must be incompatible with the American way of life to which he emotionally yearns to belong.

To Juanito, his citizenship status and identity on the one hand, and his domestic heritage on the other, belong to two separate images of himself which he cannot integrate.

Juanito's segregation is self-imposed. He censures his Anglo-American side or his Mexican-American side for this reason or that, and his automatic criticism of himself is the most severe penalty he could possibly sustain. He cannot give himself completely to either side, so he withholds himself from both. Lack of understanding in school, discrimination in society, and the racism of ethnocentric gangs poison his sense of security.

Juanito is keenly sensitive to his problem. As any American child, he wants to belong to the large society and to be respected by it. He is embarrassed because his parents are "different." Unless pride in his culture should develop, he will reject either his parents and their authority or his teachers and monolingual classmates. His emotional turmoil cannot be understood without genuine empathy for him. If the upheaval is not corrected, the child who has not learned to read will seek compensation and understanding in gangs of Mexican-American youth who, like himself, view themselves as social rejects. The child becomes a logical candidate for juvenile delinquency.

The problem of Juanito is not insurmountable; he needs only to learn that respect for his Mexican heritage is consistent with good American citizenship.

If Juanito is taught that his knowledge of Spanish is an asset, not a liability, which he may share with teacher and classmates, he will develop a new sense of worth of himself and a new source of security and status.

There has been little communication between the Mexican-American community in California and the professional educator concerning the problems of the Mexican-American pupil. Mexican-American parents often have social adjustment problems even more acute than those of their offspring; hence they shun parent-teacher conferences and school activities. School authorities, often unaware of conflict, neglect consulting with the silent minority. Organizations which offer liaison service where needed now exist and stand ready to help.

I have pointed out that Juanito's failure to read is based on reasons which are linguistic, environmental, and emotional. But I believe that psychocultural reasons predominate, that the child feels a confusing conflict of loyalties which exist only in his imagination. Lack of empathy throughout society, indifference of teachers, and prejudice on the playground tend to convince the child that his California community rejects him.

Juanito needs friends; he needs a sense of dignity and self-respect. Given these, he could be among the best readers in his class.

Motivation and the Mexican-American*

HENRY S. JOHNSON

THROUGHOUT THE HISTORY OF PSYCHOLOGY, the general problem
of motivation has been given much thought. No aspect of human
behavior has proved more resistant to analysis and measurement than that of motivation. Only in recent years has there
been a serious effort to provide adequate means of measuring
human motives. Research studies by Cattell (1961), Frymier
(1962), and Farquhar (1963) (see Bibliography at end of
chapter) have only recently opened the avenues for the objective measurement of motivation. Such motivation tests direct
attention to the fact that educators and psychologists are concerned with factors other than the sheer mastery of subject
matter.

A review of available literature suggests that there is a definite need, revealed by high dropout rates, delinquency, and unemployment, to foster a better understanding of the motivational
factors that affect the achievement performance of all pupils
and particularly of Mexican Americans. In a recent article,
Sheldon (1961) demonstrated that in contrast to the numerous publications on the relationship of ability and achievement

* An original paper prepared by the author.

of Anglo-American and Mexican-American pupils there is still a marked paucity of scholarly literature comparing these two ethnic groups on certain nonintellectual factors. Both Demos (1960) and Cline (1961), in their studies of Anglo and Mexican Americans, have indicated that the motivational structures applicable to ethnic groups should be measured to ascertain their full force as a cause of academic retardation. In short, the research reviewed was consistent in showing that the measurement of motivation would make it possible for teachers, administrators, and other educational specialists to assist Mexican-American students to survive in the alienated monolingual, monocultural schools they are forced by mandate of the school board to attend.

PROBLEM

This study has sought to identify those aspects of motivation that may account for the differences in the academic performance of Anglo-American and Mexican-American pupils. The purpose was to determine whether differential motivational characteristics exist between eighth grade low, middle, and high achievers of Anglo-American and Mexican-American descent, when achievement status is determined by average teachers' marks for all subjects taken in the seventh and eighth grades. It was hypothesized that certain factors of motivation might be associated with academic success or with minority-group membership. The study attempted to answer the question: Does the Mexican-American student possess the necessary motivational traits to succeed in his school work?

PROCEDURE

The total population for the study consisted of 620 eighth grade students. These students were enrolled in the two junior high schools serving a community of 30,000 people. The grade-point average (GPA) for the entire two years of junior high school was calculated for each student to provide low, middle, and high achievers. A student who ranked in the lowest thirty-six percentile range was defined as a *low* achiever. A student whose GPA fell at or between the thirty-seventh and sixty-fourth percentile range was referred to as a *middle* achiever. The remainder, of course, were ranked as *high* achievers.

Students identified in this manner as low, middle, or high achievers were then categorized on the basis of surnames into respective Anglo-American or Mexican-American ethnic groups. The total sample for the study consisted of 214 Anglo-Americans and 224 Mexican Americans.

Three instruments were used for the measurement variables within the areas of intelligence, achievement, and motivation. A fourth instrument, the Student Information Sheet, was constructed to obtain data relating to certain pupil and parental characteristics.

Intelligence quotients were obtained by administering the California Test of Mental Maturity (CTMM), Junior High Level, Short Form, 1957 edition. Achievement in reading, arithmetic, and language art skills was secured by administering the California Achievement Tests (CAT), Form W, Junior High Level, 1957 edition. Motivational traits were measured by the School Motivational Analysis Test (SMAT), 1961 research edition.

Socioeconomic level was determined by means of the occupation scale of the Warner's Revised Index of Status Characteristics (1949), using the information available in the school files and checking against the pupil's responses on the student questionnaire.

Means, standard deviations, analysis of variances, and F ratios were the statistical tools used in the study. The BIMD 14 program, a three-way 2x3x2 general linear design, was employed. The three factors were *(a)* ethnic group — Anglo-American and Mexican American; *(b)* achievement level (GPA) — low, middle, and high; *(c)* sex — boy and girl. All major statistical computations were done on the IBM 7094 computer at the Western Data Processing Center located on the University of California, Los Angeles, campus. Bartlett's test, as described by Guilford (1956), was used to test the homogeneity of variance within each cell. Whenever the F test rejected the homogeneity hypotheses, Kramer's (1956) multiple range test procedures were used.

RESULTS

Sex. The data by sex show significantly larger numbers of Mexican-American than Anglo-American pupils in the low-achieving groups (boys two to one; girls four to one). In the high-achievement groups the ratio is a little less than two to one in favor of the Anglo-American pupils. Only in the middle-achievement levels are the ratios between the ethnic groups approximately equal.

Age. As would be expected, low achievers, regardless of their ethnic background, tend to be significantly older than middle and high achievers. Surprisingly, Mexican-American pupils as a group tend to be younger than Anglo-American pupils at each achievement level. The significant interaction F value of 4.85 for the ethnic x sex effect shown in Table 3 gives further support to this finding.

Table 1

Comparisons of Mean Score Differences Between Anglo-American and Mexican-American Eighth Grade Pupils

Selected Variables	Sex	Ethnic Grouping						t Ratio [a]	f Ratio [b]
		Anglo-American			Mexican American				
		N	M	S D	N	M	S D		
CAGP[c]	Boys	107	8.3	0.4	101	8.3	0.5		
	Girls	107	8.3	0.4	123	8.2	0.4		
	Both	214	8.3	0.4	224	8.3	0.5		
SES [d]	Boys	107	4.7	1.2	101	5.3	1.1	5.92**	
	Girls	107	4.7	1.2	123	5.0	1.1		
	Both	214	4.7	1.2	224	5.1	1.1		9.28**
Father's Education	Boys	107	11.2	3.1	101	9.9	2.7	12.74*	
	Girls	107	11.3	3.3	123	9.6	3.5	18.07**	
	Both	214	11.2	3.2	224	9.7	3.1		
Mother's Education	Boys	107	11.8	6.2	101	9.8	2.7	20.69**	
	Girls	107	11.8	1.8	123	10.0	2.7	19.46**	
	Both	214	11.8	4.6	224	9.9	2.7		36.02**
SMAT Total	Boys	107	242	6.8	101	242	5.2		
	Girls	107	243	5.6	123	242	6.2		
	Both	214	242	6.1	224	242	5.7		

a—modified t ratio computed by Kramer's (1956) multiple range analysis test.
b—F ratio computed by BIMD 14 program on a 2x3x2 factorial linear design.
c—CAGP abbreviation for chronological age grade placement.
d—SES—abbreviation for socioeconomic status as determined by Warner's method.
* $P < .05$; ** $P < .01$.

Socioeconomic status. In spite of the very significant F values seen in Table 4, an inspection of the means in Table 2 does not show the socioeconomic variable to be unequivocally associated with the ethnic factor or with level of achievement. Only at the middle achievement do the Anglo-American pupils as a group

Table 2

Comparisons of Mean Score Differences Between Anglo-American and Mexican-American Eighth Grade Pupils

		Low			Middle			High	
	$\overline{\text{AA}}^a$	MAᵇ	t Ratio	AA	MA	t Ratio	AA	MA	t Ratio
Boys:									
N	27	47		47	30		33	23	
CAGP	8.3	8.4		8.2	8.3		8.2	8.2	
SES	5.3	5.4		4.5	5.3	4.84**	4.4	4.8	
Father's Education	10.0	9.9		11.8	10.0		11.2	10.7	
Mother's Education	9.6	9.4		11.6	9.1	15.00**	12.1	11.4	
SMAT Total	244	242		242	242		241	243	
Girls:									
N	13	50		33	38		61	35	
CAGP	8.5	8.3		8.3	8.2		8.3	8.2	
SES	5.1	5.2		4.7	4.8		4.7	5.0	
Father's Education	9.4	8.6		11.2	10.8		11.9	9.9	
Mother's Education	9.9	8.6		11.6	9.6		12.4	10.2	14.94**
SMAT Total	243	242		244	242		242	242	
Both:									
CAGP	40	98		80	68		94	58	
N	8.4	8.4		8.3	8.2		8.3	8.2	
SES	5.2	5.3		4.6	5.1	4.11**	4.6	5.0	
Father's Education	9.7	9.1		11.4	10.4		11.7	10.1	
Mother's Education	9.7	9.0		11.6	9.4	19.28**	12.3	10.8	12.37**
SMAT Total	243	242		243	242		242	242	

a—AA: Anglo-American
b—MA: Mexican American
** $P < .01$

possess significantly higher mean SES scores than the Mexican-American pupils. Further analysis of the data reveals the fact that the significant mean differences are confined to the middle-achieving boys in both ethnic groups.

Parental education. As noted in Table 2, the mothers of middle- and high-achieving Anglo-American pupils reported sig-

Table 3

Summary of the Analysis of Variance of the CAGP, SES, and SMAT

Source of Variation	SS	df	MS	F Ratio
Chronological Age Grade Placement:				
Ethnicity	24.06	1	24.06	
Achievement Level	225.60	2	112.80	5.94**
Sex	0.56	1	0.56	
Ethnic x Achievement Level	4.72	2	2.36	
Ethnic x Sex	92.03	1	92.03	4.85*
Achievement Level x Sex	12.35	2	6.7	
Ethnic x Achievement Level x Sex	11.38	2	5.69	
Within Groups	8,086.78	426	18.98	
TOTAL	8,457.48	437		
Socioeconomic Status:				
Ethnicity	11.67	1	11.67	9.28**
Achievement Level	17.40	2	8.70	6.92**
Sex	0.27	1	0.27	
Ethnic x Achievement Level	1.38	2	0.69	
Ethnic x Sex	1.40	1	1.40	
Achievement Level x Sex	3.64	2	1.82	
Ethnic x Achievement Level x Sex	2.68	2	1.34	
Within Groups	535.40	426	1.26	
TOTAL	573.84	437		
SMAT Total:				
Ethnicity	8.75	1	8.75	
Achievement Level	50.00	2	25.00	
Sex	0.00	1	0.00	
Ethnic x Achievement Level	76.00	2	38.00	
Ethnic x Sex	20.25	1	20.25	
Achievement Level x Sex	48.00	2	24.00	
Ethnic x Achievement Level x Sex	46.00	2	23.00	
Within Groups	15,054.50	426	35.34	
TOTAL	15,303.50	437		

* $P < .05$
** $P < .01$

nificantly more schooling than their ethnic counterparts. The highly significant F values in Table 4 bear out this observation. Only in the low-achieving groups are the mean differences between the two ethnic groups in parental education not significant. None of the achievement groups show any significant mean differences between the two ethnic groups for father's education level even though a significant F is seen for this variance effect in Table 4.

Motivational traits. As revealed in Table 2, none of the mean differences in motivation between the two ethnic groups at each of the achievement levels is significant beyond the 5 percent level. The results of the motivation test summarized in Table 1 reveal insignificant mean differences between the two ethnic

Table 4

Summary of the Analysis of Variance of the Father's and Mother's Level of Education

Source of Variation	SS	df	MS	F Ratio
Father's Level of Education:				
Ethnicity	4,716.32	1	4,716.32	
Achievement Level	23,461.13	2	11,730.56	6.50**
Sex	3,216.38	1	3,216.38	
Ethnic x Achievement Level	2,695.32	2	1,347.66	
Ethnic x Sex	885.13	1	885.13	
Achievement Level x Sex	760.57	2	380.28	
Ethnic x Achievement Level x Sex	517.82	2	258.91	
Within Groups	769,027.81	426	1,805.23	
TOTAL	805,280.48	437		
Mother's Level of Education:				
Ethnicity	207.99	1	207.99	36.02**
Achievement Level	275.73	2	137.86	23.87**
Sex	2.13	1	2.13	
Ethnic x Achievement Level	32.48	2	16.24	
Ethnic x Sex	13.79	1	13.79	
Achievement Level x Sex	10.28	2	5.14	
Ethnic x Achievement Level x Sex	17.43	2	8.71	
Within Groups	2,442.70	423	5.77	
TOTAL	3,002.53	434		

* $P < .05$
** $P < .01$

groups. One may surmise from the findings that the overall differences in motivational level between the Anglo-American and Mexican-American groups are negligible in nature.

CONCLUSIONS

It was noted that at the two extremes of the achievement continuum significantly larger numbers of Mexican-American pupils were found in the lower-achieving groups. If one of the important objectives of teachers' marks is to raise a pupil's motivation level to learn more effectively and efficiently in school, then the skewed or bias distributions at the lower-achievement strata clearly indicate that teachers' marks favor the Anglo-American students.

On the motivation test no significant overall mean differences between the ethnic groups were found. Similar nonsignificant findings between ethnic group membership and achievement level were also revealed. Unless these were chance results, factors other than differences in motivation, such as parental education, socioeconomic status, and a bias grading system, may have accounted for the significant differences in academic performance between the Anglo-American and Mexican-American eighth grade pupils in this study.

BIBLIOGRAPHY

Brown, Charles M., "Acculturation and School Achievement." Unpublished Ph.D. dissertation, Los Angeles: University of Southern California, 1956.

Cattell, Raymond B. et al., "Prediction and Understanding of the Effect of Children's Interest upon School Performance." Co-operative Research Project No. 701, 1961.

Cline, Marion, "Achievement of Bilinguals in Seventh Grade by Socio-Economic Levels." Unpublished Ph.D. dissertation, Los Angeles: University of Southern California, 1961.

Demos, George D., "Attitudes of Student Ethnic Groups on Issues Related to Education." Unpublished Ph.D. dissertation, Los Angeles: University of Southern California, 1959.

Farquhar, William W., "Motivation Factors Related to Academic Achievement." U.S. Office of Education Co-operative Research Project No. 846, Michigan State University, January, 1963.

Frymier, Jack R., "A Study of Several Factors Related to Motivation and Achievement of Fifth Grade Students." Paper presented at the Annual Meeting of the American Educational Research Association in Atlantic City, February 21, 1962.

Guilford, Joy Paul, *Fundamental Statistics in Psychology and Education*. 3rd ed., New York: McGraw-Hill Book Company, Inc., 1956.

Kramer, C. Y., "Extension of Multiple Range Tests to Group Measures with Unequal Numbers of Replications," *Biometrics*, vol. 12 (1956), pp. 307–310.

Sheldon, Paul M., "Mexican-American in Urban Public Schools: An Exploration of the Drop-out Problem," *California Journal of Educational Research*, vol. 12 (1961), pp. 21-26.

Sweney, Arthur B., and Cattell, Raymond B., *Handbook for the School Motivation Analysis Test*. Champaign, Illinois: The Institute for Personality and Ability Testing, 1961.

Warner, W. Lloyd et al., *Social Class in America*. Chicago: Science Research Associates, Inc., 1949.

Identity Crisis
in Mexican-American Adolescents*

MANUEL RAMIREZ III

SOCIAL SCIENTISTS HAVE LONG BEEN CONCERNED with the plight of the bicultural person in our society. They have described him as a person caught between the merciless demands of two cultures. His inability to comply with the requirements of both groups results in a failure to establish an identity, which then results in disorientation and stress.

One of the first researchers to study the bicultural man intensively was Professor Irvin L. Child, of Yale University. His studies of second-generation Italians in Hartford, Connecticut, revealed that these people were ambivalent in the face of conflicting claims. They were constantly faced with two alternative courses of action, one Italian and the other American. If they called themselves Italians and accepted the values of their ethnic group, they were ostracized by the non-Italians in the community. On the other hand, if they called themselves Americans and rejected the Italian culture, they were considered traitors by the members of their group. Madsen's studies of the Mexican-Americans in south Texas uncovered evidence of a similar con-

* Published with permission of the Bureau of Intergroup Relations, California State Department of Education.

flict. He found that the Mexican-American is, on the one hand, being pressured by the Anglos to abandon his folk culture; and, on the other, he is being encouraged by some of the members of his group to ignore the Anglos and retain the old ways. Again, as with the Italians of Hartford, the Mexican-Americans of the Rio Grande valley are being faced with a difficult and almost impossible choice.

Since the bicultural individual is constantly forced to choose between his loyalty to two different groups, he is constantly under stress. Conflicting values in an individual give rise to an uncomfortable sense of insecurity and instability. The bicultural man, then, in his desire for stability, searches for ways which will reduce his discomfort. Many times his solutions are costly. Professor Spindler, for example, has found that the Menomini Indians, who have been forced to undergo cultural transfer too rapidly, have developed an extensive peyote cult in order to relieve the threat to their identities which results from abandoning the old ways.

Another investigator, Professor Hallowell, studied a group of Ojibwa Indians who have acculturated too rapidly. His results revealed that these people were under so much stress that they never matured psychologically. Dr. Vita Sommer's work with bicultural individuals at the Los Angeles Veterans Administration Mental Hygiene Clinic shows that culture change results in loss of identity which eventually leads to emotional disorders.

The bicultural individual faces so much frustration in having to choose between loyalties so often and under such difficult conditions that he usually attempts to resolve the conflict by choosing one group and rejecting the other. Professor Child found that the young male Italian eventually resolved the conflict by reacting in one of two ways: (1) *The rebel reaction.* This was characterized by the desire of the individual to establish himself as an American. The rebels usually attached American labels to themselves and tried to dissociate themselves from the labels of the Italian culture. The rebels, he found, paid a heavy price for their decision. For example, all of the rebels he interviewed admitted having conflicts with their parents. (2) *The in-group reaction.* These individuals demonstrated a tendency to strive for affiliation with Italians. They attached Italian labels to themselves and were overtly hostile to the symbols of the American group. The in-grouper paid a different price, but it was nevertheless heavy. Although he had a strong loyalty to the family group and his relationship with his parents was pleasant, he usually had difficulties relating to non-Italians. Madsen's study revealed a similar trend among the Mexican-Americans. He found that these people were divided into a conservative group which adhered to the traditional folk culture and had a complete lack of admiration for the Anglo ways, and an Anglicized group that was trying to abandon the mother culture and emulate Anglo behavior. It seems obvious, then, that most bicultural individuals faced with severe conflicts find it necessary to become either Identifiers (remain loyal to their ethnic group and reject the Anglo ways) or Anglicized (accept the Anglo ways and reject their identification with their ethnic group).

The author recently conducted a study of Mexican-American junior high and high school students in Sacramento, California, which was an attempt to determine members of the Identifier and Anglicized groups. In addition he was interested in pinpointing problems being experienced by members of the two groups.

In order to determine the extent of identity with the values of the Mexican-American culture, the experimenter administered the Mexican Family Attitude Scale (Ramirez, 1967) to two hundred Mexican-American junior high and high school students. The scale reflects the following values which usually differentiate between Mexican-Americans and non-Mexican-Americans: (1) Loyalty to the family group. (2) A feeling that relatives, no matter how distant, are more important than friends. (3) Respect for adults. (4) Belief in strict child-rearing practices. (5) Consideration of the mother as the most-loved person in existence. (6) A present-time orientation. (7) A need to defend one's honor, at all costs, whenever threatened.

From the original group of two hundred, twenty subjects were selected for further study. Ten of these were adolescents who rejected Anglicized values and ten identified strongly with them (Identifiers). These twenty people then filled out the Bell Adjustment Inventory Student Form. This is a personality inventory which identifies the areas of life in which the adolescent is experiencing problems of adjustment. It covers six areas: (1) family, (2) health, (3) sex role, (4) adequacy of relationship with people outside the home, (5) feelings about oneself, and (6) hostility and suspiciousness of others. The results obtained showed striking differences in the problems being experienced by members of the two groups. The Anglicized adolescents reported having experienced many disagreements with their parents. They had a tendency to answer yes to the following items on the adjustment inventory: (1) my parents fail to recognize me as a mature person and treat me as if I were still a child; (2) my parents do not understand me; (3) frequently, I have had to keep quiet or leave the home in order to keep the peace. These same adolescents, however, reported having very pleasant relationships with people outside the home. They were outgoing, friendly, and trusting of others. The adolescents of the Identifier group, unlike the Anglicized group, reported having pleasant relationships with their parents. Their relationships to others outside the group, however, were quite different. They had a tendency to answer yes to the following items: (1) there are many people in the world I can't afford to trust; (2) people do not understand me; (3) you must watch your step around people or they will take advantage of you; (4) I feel self-conscious when I recite in class; and (5) I hesitate to volunteer in class recitation. The members of the Identifier group are well adjusted at home but feel alienated from people on the outside. It appears, then, that both groups of adolescents are paying a steep price for their one-sided identities. They are confronted with opposing sets of values. The decision for members of either group is whether to retain the values of their parents or to reject them for those of authority figures outside the home, such as teachers, employers, and policemen. The following excerpts from interviews conducted by the author with representatives of the two groups will further reveal the unhappiness which accompanies both of these patterns of adjustment:

Paul is a member of the Anglicized group. This is what he had to say:

> I don't want to be known as a Mexican-American, but only as American. I was born in this country and raised among Americans. I think like an Anglo, I talk like one, and I dress like one. It's true I don't look like an Anglo, and sometimes I am rejected by them; but it would be worse if I spoke Spanish or said that I was of Mexican descent. I am sorry I do not get along well with my parents, but their views are old-fashioned. They still see themselves as Mexicans, and they do not understand me. Many

times we have arguments, but I ignore them. In fact, I had to move away from my home because of our disagreements. I wish those people who are always making noise about being Mexican-American would be quiet. We would all be better off if they just accepted things as they are. I just want a good education. I don't want to be poor or discriminated against.

Roberto, who is an Identifier, has a different opinion:

I am proud of being a Mexican-American. We have a rich heritage. Mexico is a great country which is progressing fast, and it has a wonderful history and culture. My family is the most important thing in the world to me. I owe my parents everything and I will never complain when they need me. I don't want to be like the Paddys because they don't care about their families; they just care about themselves and making money. They don't like anybody who is different. At school the teachers would ignore you if they knew you weren't going to college and most of us Mexicans couldn't afford to go. The things I learned at school were against what my parents had taught me. I had to choose my parents because now they are old and they need my help and understanding. I know most people—even some Mexican-Americans—look down on us because we are Mexicans and I hate them. It is unhealthy and unnatural to want to be something you are not.

So much for the two divergent groups. Let's examine the interview of a Mexican-American adolescent, Rosa, who was fortunate to form an identity within both cultures. She states:

I am happy to be an American of Mexican descent. Because I am a Mexican I learned to be close to my family, and they have been a source of strength and support for me. If things ever got too bad on the outside, I could always come to them for comfort and understanding. My Spanish also helped me a lot in my education and will also open a lot of doors for me when I look for a job. As an American I am happy to live in a great progressive country where we have the freedom to achieve anything we want. I feel all I have achieved I owe to the help of my parents, the encouragement of my teachers, and the chance to live in a country like this one. I feel very rich and fortunate because I have two cultures rather than just one.

Rosa, then, has achieved an ideal adjustment. She views both the Anglo and Mexican-American cultures favorably. She has, in fact, combined the best from each to form a richer, more beautiful culture. How can we insure that more bicultural adolescents will achieve such a desirable identity? Perhaps the following recommendations would be appropriate in considering solutions to this problem:

1. There is need to establish more efficient lines of communication between parents and school personnel; otherwise we will continue to have both groups working against each other, and the adolescent will be caught between the demands of both

groups. Schools with large Mexican-American populations should hire Mexican-American personnel who speak Spanish and are aware of conflicts which can occur. Unless both parents and school personnel become aware of and respect each other's values, conflicts will continue with the Mexican-American student suffering the consequences.

2. An attempt must be made to eliminate the *barrio* schools. Observations made by the author have led him to conclude that *barrio* schools are conducive to power struggles between school personnel on the one hand and students and parents on the other. Both groups are out to acculturate each other, and the result is that both become alienated and become more dogmatic about their value systems. Elimination of de facto segregation in an atmosphere of acceptance of cultural diversity does not force the bicultural student to take one extreme route or the other, but to accept both.

Counseling programs for the bicultural student, which are geared to help him anticipate those value conflicts which are inevitable, should be instituted in our schools. The more understanding a student achieves about his problems the better he will be able to cope with conflict and stress when it arises.

It will be necessary, then, to establish an accepting, helpful environment which will aid the bicultural student to achieve an identification within two cultures. In this manner he can select the best of both without having to reject one or the other.

BIBLIOGRAPHY

Bell, H. H., *The Bell Adjustment Inventory.* Consulting Psychologists Press.

Child, Irvin L., *Italian or American?* New Haven: Yale University Press, 1943.

Hallowell, A. I., "Values, Acculturation and Mental Health," *American Journal of Orthopsychiatry,* vol. 20 (October, 1950), pp. 732–743.

Madsen, W., "Value Conflicts in Cultural Transfer," in Worchel, Philip, and Byrne, Donn, eds. *Symposium on Personality Change.* New York: John Wiley & Sons, Inc., 1964.

Ramirez, M., "Identification with Mexican Family Values and Authoritarianism in Mexican-Americans," *Journal of Social Psychology,* (in press).

Ramirez, M., and Taylor, C., "Sex Role Determinants in Attitudes Toward Education among Mexican-American Adolescents." Research in progress. Project is being supported by a grant from the U.S. Office of Education of the Department of Health, Education and Welfare.

Sommers, V., "The Impact of Dual-cultural Membership on Identity," *Psychiatry*.

Spindler, G. D., "Personality and Peyotism in Menomini Indian Acculturation," *Psychiatry*, vol. 15 (1952), pp. 151–159.

The Retention of Mexican American Students in Higher Education with Special Reference to Bicultural and Bilingual Problems*

MANUEL H. GUERRA

THE HIGH DROPOUT RATE OF MEXICAN AMERICAN STUDENTS in junior high and high school is of grave interest to us.[1] But equally distressing is the high dropout rate of Mexican American students in higher education.[2] Once the boy or girl from the *barrio* enters college or the university, some educators seem to think that the job has been done; equal opportunity has been redeemed; the objective has been reached. It is the purpose of this paper to explore the subject and to determine whether the system which we have employed in this vital field of American education is consistent with modern needs, or if the system is outmoded and inconsistent with the problems of the *barrio* and the ghetto. It is the purpose of this paper, moreover, to explore the bilingual and bicultural deficiencies and merits of Mexican American students and to examine these facts toward the recommendation of a system which recognizes contemporary needs and future planning, rather than an educational system which looks back in retrospect to justify its reason for being.

* Paper prepared for the Conference on Increasing Opportunities for Mexican American Students in Higher Education, May, 1969. Published with permission of the author.

Perhaps the most salient factor which impresses the objective person is the radical contrast between the traditional mind in American education and the consistent criticism of American education. Perhaps we should restate this idea as the polarization of authority and the challenge of that authority. Or perhaps an even better way to express the contrast is to note the growing disenchantment with the educational structure and system by minority citizens and the reactionary justification of that structure and system by a growing majority of Anglo-Saxon middle-class citizenry. Such alienation of mind and spirit is inherent in our social climate.

This alienation pervades the educational milieu because the pluralistic differences of American society have *not* found the spiritual and intellectual bonds to unite basic separateness of race, national origin, religion, and culture. Thus the "American dream" which was thought to be a uniting factor entertained by all Americans was, in reality, an illusion and a myth. It did not extend equality to many citizens of black, brown, yellow, and red pedigree. The myth solicited total commitment but, in practice, denied many citizens their inalienable rights.

This "American dream" or moral and legal ambivalence has been repudiated by minority citizens today. Blindness of WASP (White Anglo-Saxon Protestant) authority and institutions has created in the nation what so many militants refer to as "The Establishment." The defenders of the status quo, in their noble character, discharge their responsibilities of government with sensitivity and imagination, and in their ignoble character substitute authority and force for understanding and reason. The "American dream" could never unite the American people as a whole because it was never an American dream in the first place. It was never a product of our popular conscience, with as much respect for people of low station as for people of means. The materialistic fibers of this false dream can never override the idealistic concept of man in the American mind, for this is where the national treasury of the United States really resides.

But what does all this have to do with the retention of Mexican American students in college or the university? Simply this: The traditional and prosaic philosophies dominate our college and university campuses. Educators are the products of a highly conservative system in which both time and discipline have molded temperament and attitudes. It is difficult for educators to reevaluate, reappraise, and readjust to changing times.

In America, institutions have developed their own sterile bureaucracies and machinery, and those of higher education are the most outstanding examples of fossilized and prosaic life. Institutions have sought survival and perpetuation in a world of high taxes, declining enrollments and alumni contributions, and a rising cost of living. Their stubborn resistance to change and exploitation of available resources strengthens a structure where new ideas cannot penetrate. If new ideas should be entertained, they pose a threat to the welfare of the institution which fears that new ideas bring change and reform and a different way of doing things. Add to this inflexibility sectarian biases in some schools, ultraconservative boards of trustees who do not encourage young administrators with young ideas, and many faculties whose scholarly ideals have degenerated into petty partisan politics or flights of fancy to the academic tower.

This ambience of the academic community is where the Chicano from the *barrio* brings his problems and hopes, his frustrations and anxieties, his talents and fears. The question remains a rhetorical one. Can the educator in higher education respond to the challenge of the Chicano student? Can the administration and system adjust themselves to the intense need for curriculum change and understanding of minorities? Will the tenets of American education and the principles of public education triumph in a victory of reason and understanding against chaos and confrontation?

It would seem that we should listen to the critics from the minority community who bring their bill of particulars in a spirit of good faith, and we should study their recommendations with soul-searching introspection as well as pragmatic suggestions for reform or addenda.

The Chicano student is caught in a vise of higher education today. On the one hand, the problems of the educational establishment which I have just outlined have created an arbitrary barrier to reason and effective democratic communication. On the other hand, the Chicano brings new problems and the need for new understandings at a time when there is less money, expanded enrollment, and an entrenched reaction to his cultural well-being through admission to college.

Indeed, what we have said, in effect, throughout America in our colleges and universities and throughout our admission requirements and standards, is that any black student or Mexican American, or anyone for that matter — for we are truly universal and democratic — can attend our college and university if they meet our entrance standards. These entrance standards have been traditionally designed by a committee of WASP's, who think like the white middle class, come from the white middle class, and represent the interests of the white middle class. Those who conform to their standards and criteria of what the college seeks and desires are admitted to the holy city. Even today the chancellor of the University of California at San Diego speaks about an experimental college[3] for minority students in order that the "holy cow" of academic standards will not be lowered or damaged, despite an admission of concern for the welfare of minority students.

What is deplorable in this intellectual point of view is that the criteria for admission do not come under a new scrutiny to determine whether they make allowances for the merits and demerits of the minority students now entering in new numbers or, better yet, to determine whether the university is really serving the needs of the community which supports it, whether the university is really knowledgeable about the needs and demands of the community, and to what degree it accepts its reason for being and the major responsibilities it is constantly espousing. Equal to the concern for the maintenance of academic standards should be the concern for the development of a new curriculum that is commensurate with the needs, heritage, and desires of people of a minority background.

As both a scholar and a citizen, I would oppose an experimental college that is tax supported if it is not really "experimental" and if its innovation does not include the thinking of the professional minority community, or a consensus of community needs. Rather than the old academic standards, it should focus on new educational goals which are more concerned with modern realities than the academic trappings of prestige without virtue.

This "experimental" college, like the experiments in the South with black children, reveals to us the nefarious conflicts of the Anglo-Saxon conscience which is deeply committed to a point of view that does not respect American racial and ethnic differences. The hypocrisy of this mind and spirit is just as twisted as the church goer on Sunday who becomes a sinner on Monday. Not only does this frame of mind adhere to a racism of superior and inferior Aristotelian classes, but it endeavors to conceal and disguise its inhumanity to man in the respectability of self-righteous rhetoric, bureaucratic and authoritarian pronouncements, and the anonymous and depersonalized findings of respectable academic committees. If this is what the Chicano militant is tired of, if this is what he seeks to change, if this is what he considers his adversary, then his redress is far more than the benefits of self-improvement. American education in general will owe a debt of gratitude to these young Americans and scholars who bring a new focus and enthusiasm where there is myopia and bankruptcy.

Indeed, admission standards have been designed to keep people out, not bring people in to the learning process. Examinations and tests in both government and private industry have traditionally done the same thing.[4] The irony of government projects which were intended to help minority people is seen in the fact that employees of minority background were excluded because they were unable to pass examinations which had little relevance to the job itself.

In the educational area, the matter of intelligence testing among Mexican American children strikes a sensitive nerve, because in the southwestern states where many Mexican children reside, intelligence tests harmfully stigmatized in more ways than one those children the testing ostensibly was trying to help. Many boys and girls were placed in M.R. (mentally retarded) classes because of their low language scores. Language is supposed to be an area of intensive and modern study, for purposes of improvement. It has instead been used for testing and classifying for purposes of stereotyping and segregating.[5]

Rather than including people in the process of learning and employment, here, as in government and industry, testing and standards serve the purpose of excluding people. Those who make and give the tests are the most vociferous defenders of the system, which they always deny has good intentions with bad results. But it is peculiar that the same people who make and give the tests are Anglo-Saxon middle-class educators or technicians, seldom black or Mexican American professionals whose expertise might have guided the criteria toward realistic evaluations. The fact that the Anglo professional believes that he understands the black child and the Mexican American child, although he has never studied black culture or Mexican American culture, is evidence of the two weaknesses of the Anglo professional: first, his naïveté that all American children are the same; and second, his posture to defend his ignorance rather than to correct it.

The member of the conservative-minded academic community which views with alarm the growing number of minority students on campus reacts according to his emotional habits and background. Very often this person believes quite emotionally that people of color, most of whom live in the ghettos and *barrios*, mow the lawns and wash the dishes of the schools, often speak a language that is different from his own, and are, indeed, colorful and funny, inferior and subordinate. Perhaps this point of view is reinforced by one of several Protestant religious sects which fail to apply Christ's teachings to the color line. Indeed, what is most alarming to the conservative-minded educator is that minority students do not conform to the behavior and appearance of the blond and blue-eyed Anglo-Saxon. Different hairdos, dress, language, customs, and traditions bother him considerably. To him they are un-American, since to be an "American" is to be a WASP.

What is even more distressing is the false posture and mask of self-righteousness of the conservative-minded educator. Miguel de Cervantes said it quite well in his immortal *Don Quijote de la Mancha, "Detrás de la cruz está el diablo"* (Behind the cross hides the devil). Indeed, like the humanist without humanity, the academician would like us to respect his academic standards without a careful perusal of their merit. I mentioned institutional bureaucracy and outmoded values. However, nowhere in business and industry can an institution survive inefficiency, waste, and archaism. Government regimes are defeated at the polls for the same reasons. But in higher education, myth, trivia, and rhetoric have developed a world of escape rivaled only by *Alice in Wonderland*. Faculties exhaust hours discussing parking problems; students spend hours on fraternity and sorority parlor games; and administrators issue memoranda to the czars of department chairmanships. Meanwhile, minority students are bombing a dormitory, refusing to fight in Vietnam, and the community is burning in the same ghettos where rats attack little children sleeping in their cribs.

The burning question refers to the nature of these "academic standards" and their relevancy to minority students today. Questions: Are these the same academic standards that were developed in the last century when the institution first opened its doors? Are these the same standards that were developed by a faculty committee after World War I? After World War II? Were the criteria of these standards developed in conjunction and cooperation with student or community advisers, or do they represent the point of view of a dominant group within the faculty? What minority opinion is represented in the faculty criteria? Does the college or university employ any professionals and scholars from a minority background? Do these have any policy-making duties?

Admission standards are correlated with academic standards. One is concomitant and predicated upon the other. It is the finding of this study that the terms "academic standards" and "admission standards" in the colleges and universities of the United States largely do not take into account the opinion and values of the minority community which they serve. At least three reasons can be given for this policy: First, these standards intellectually discriminate against minority peoples for whom WASP's have historic contempt, disrespect, or suspicion. Second, the administrators are well-intentioned professionals, but with a gross ignorance of minority problems and a reputation of recorded misjudgments, blunders, and oversights in the area of minority education. Third, both administration and faculty are composed of ultraconservative and pseudoliberal staff who are committed to a point of view that seeks to retain the status quo, oppose educational reform and innovation, and use force and authority rather than reason and compromise.

Whereas the discriminatory point of view of the academic standards is rather philosophical and passive, the discriminatory "admission standards" are not, and they open education to minority people with reluctance and resistance. Concessions are made only when minority students are willing to conform to the criteria of Anglo-Saxon, middle-class, Protestant values. The intransigence of this point of view is just as alarming and contributory to violence and confrontation on our college campus as the irresponsible and hostile acts of a flaming militant. Perhaps it is even more alarming, because the student radical who commits an illegal act is immediately identified both in behavior and person. However, authority in the hands of people who mismanage it and wear the mask of respectability is not always as easily recognizable, and often we must wait for a painstaking investigation before the other party to the violence is correctly identified.

The admission requirements of junior colleges, at least in California, admit more people of minority background than those of any other institution. However, the dropout rate is proportionately the highest, too. Usually, a high school diploma, being at least nineteen years of age, and a residence requirement of some sort admit the student to any of California's junior colleges.[6] But colleges differ in professional training, library facilities, faculty and staff, location, and curriculum standards. Some colleges emulate the courses of the state university in both textbooks and requirements. This is true of a number of colleges, of which Foothill College, Los Altos, is one. Others are more independent and gear instruction to the needs of students.

In the junior college area of American education we come to grips with minority problems. The reasons are: (1) More minority students attend junior colleges. (2) Many minority students can afford this schooling. (3) Junior colleges are located near the homes and large cities where minority students live. (4) Instruction is more flexible and geared to the needs of the community and the minority student. (5) Instruction is often technologically geared to the nonacademic interests of the minority student. Perhaps we should add that as more minority students graduate from high school, costs of tuition and fees increase, and dormitory facilities continue to be congested in state colleges and universities, more minority students will attend junior college where the learning process after high school will be a terminal two-year course rather than a four-year diploma.

Perhaps our appraisal of junior college education should also state that more teachers of minority background may be found in junior colleges than in other schools. This is also true of presidents and deans. Because of the number of minority students and faculty in junior colleges, and the closeness of community and college in the tax-supported school system, junior college education will continue to play one of the most important roles in the education of Mexican American youth of the future.

The state college and state university systems are also tax-supported institutions. In the past they have not responded to the needs of the Mexican American community, and today they reluctantly accept responsibilities in practice which they have espoused in promises to the public who support them. For example, despite Ph.D. degrees, research, and publications of many administrators and scholars who have lived and taught in a community of two million[7] Spanish-surnamed citizens, this same intellect questions the existence of Mexican American studies, the inequities in every field of social endeavor, and the academic propriety of Mexican American curriculum. Everywhere can be heard the doubt and suspicion that valid courses of Mexican American research and intellectual activity may be found. The arrogance and pedantry of academic councils which traditionally look to Greece and Rome, science and technology, and real estate and business administration refuse to accept the inequities of history books which give our children an unbalanced picture of the Spanish discovery and colonization of America. The teacher-training curriculum should prepare young professionals for their responsibilities to the Spanish-speaking youngster, and the linguistic departments should use modern and realistic research and instruction concerning bilingualism and biculturalism. Indeed, not even the august Modern Language Association of America and its conservative leadership have ever considered the Mexican American and Puerto Rican bilingual and bicultural problems and talents as legitimate subjects of research and scholarship.

It is documentary testimony that in this nation of erudite scholarship and financial capacity there have not been any Ph.D. theses in any of our great universities on the subject of Mexican American bilingualism and biculturalism. I submit as a loyal member of the Modern Language Association of America that our concern for castles in Spain, the *voceo* of Argentina, and the rivalry of Latin American versus Peninsular Spanish studies have enjoyed considerably greater interest, status, and prestige than the problems of the Spanish-speaking students of the United States. In some instances, colleges and universities have made

Mexican American students feel ashamed of their Spanish Mexican heritage and have mocked their pronunciation, vocabulary, and idioms with the commentary that they do not speak Castilian Spanish. This comment does not refer to the many Mexican American students who do not speak, read, or write good Spanish; rather, the comment refers to those who have acquired high linguistic skills of translation and comprehension of English and Spanish and who, in elementary school and high school, instead of being considered "gifted" children were labelled "problem" children. Such misjudgments of human resources and talents have cost the United States programs in Latin America many thousands of linguists and workers with language abilities, despite federal aid for higher education, and have deprived the Mexican American of the best educational system which money can buy.

Admission requirements of our state colleges and universities continue to speak of "standards" in terms of the past, not the future. These standards do not reflect changing criteria and the changing times. For example, they do not take into account quotas and proportions of the ethnic community.

In the midst of unbalanced quotas and proportions, administrators have felt no responsibility when there were only seventy Mexican Americans at the University of California at Los Angeles in a community in which over eight hundred thousand Mexican Americans reside.[8] Proportions and quotas, it is argued, have nothing to do with standards; yet what kind of academic ideals and commitment can deny the Mexican American student and community from participation in the vitally important learning process? Have not these same standards effectively excluded the minority student from learning and at the same time rewarded the Anglo-Saxon, middle-class student not only with admission — a prognosis of academic success — but also with scholarship benefits and financial aids that often he does not need?

Has it occurred to the general public, as it has to educators, that we have in higher education the same gerrymandering tactics which we have in our political structure? For example, in *barrios* and ghettos with block votes, we divide the districts in order to insure a predetermined political outcome. This weakens the black and brown communities in the realities of power acquisition in our two-party system. Likewise, in higher education we have raised the grade-point average to an arbitrary figure which excludes the vast majority of minority students. Is there any valid diagnostic test or a valid prognosis of future academic success of any American student from Beverly Hills or East Los Angeles when their respective grades of 3.0 and 2.5 admit one to UCLA and keep the other out? And how many times does the student with high grades from Beverly Hills and Sherman Oaks receive the cash awards for tuition, fees, and books when the family is financially affluent, while the student with a C-plus average from East Los Angeles, who really needs the money, is neither admitted nor financially assisted?

I am reminded by this irony that the selective service also rewarded the middle-class Anglo who attended college and penalized the lower-class Chicano who could not afford college, through the medium of service deferment. Admission to college throughout the United States meant the difference between life and death for many of our young people, and the heaviest burden has been carried by our black and brown citizens who could not afford college, who could not meet admission standards, and who were not granted financial aids. For example, Mexican American casualties in Vietnam represent 30 percent of the men from Texas compared with a Mexican American population of 14 percent of that state's total; or for California, the casualty rate is 33 percent for 10 percent of the population.[9]

My recommendation is that admission standards be reevaluated in the new light of minority problems and community needs and that new criteria of admissions be found that will bring more and more disadvantaged Americans to the learning process. This is imperative if our cities and societies are to survive the crisis of the future. I can think of at least three suggestions in this regard. First, I would appoint minority professors of the faculty, minority students of the student body, and professional advisers of the minority community to sit with the administrators, alumni, Anglo students, and professors of the admissions committees. Second, I would draft guidelines that incorporate and define some of the new and future needs of our institutions of higher learning. Third, to protect the traditional standards of scholarship and excellence, I would have each candidate for admission recommended by principals and teachers, civic leaders and pastors, and I would give the candidate a personal interview before a committee which represents both the academic and minority groups of the community.

In the case of the Mexican American, if the student is truly bilingual and bicultural, I would indeed accredit his talents where at the moment there is no accreditation for bilingualism and biculturalism on the intellectual, social, or educational scale. Not even grades in English and Spanish attest to the talent and understanding of the bilingual student. Do you suppose this linguistic and cultural talent, this psychological ability to function in two worlds, is worth one-half of one grade point, say, 2.5 to 3.0? If so, and you concur with me, then you would agree that we have been excluding many young men and women on the basis of an arbitrary grade point average and "standards" which are *meaningless* rather than *meaningful*.

Private and sectarian colleges and universities have differing views of minority students. Roman Catholic institutions have provided encouragement and opportunities where no other hope existed. This is partly because of the catholicity of their point of view, and partly because most Mexican Americans are Roman Catholic. But it should be stated briefly that the paradox lies in the fact that the Roman Catholic Church seems to have done the least in the area of social progress and welfare compared to other churches, and in the Southwest it has contributed to the exploitation of the Mexican American in the paternalistic perpetuation of his caste and status.

Private colleges and universities, like the professional schools of our state universities, have not admitted Mexican American students nor hired Mexican American scholars and professors in any number indicative of a serious intellectual challenge.

Schools of law, engineering, and medicine are the greatest offenders, and here, as elsewhere, society in general has sustained the greatest loss of resources and talents, not simply the individuals involved. In fact, private schools have been the private fraternity of the Anglo-Saxon middle class and have never entertained a serious philosophy of democratic education geared to the needs of all Americans. Admission standards and academic standards have been very useful instruments to exclude those undesirable elements — blacks and Mexicans — particularly if the latter do not run the one-hundred-yard dash in less than ten seconds, or break all touchdown records.

And now that blacks and Mexicans are raising their voices, knocking on the ivy walls of admission, and filling out application forms, I still do not find a single student body of a private college or university that has 20 to 25 percent minority students. I do observe, however, hundreds of such schools in cities where there are thousands of black and brown citizens. Neither recruitment nor religion has reached this horizon of thought. Lack of money is the usual excuse.

Lest I be accused of trying to destroy our valid academic standards, I would like to say that I acknowledge the existence of ignorance, prejudice, and inability on the part of student applicants, both Mexican American and others. I recognize the shortcomings of many of our students of minority background in reading, speaking, thinking, understanding, studying, and knowledge. I make no excuses for substandard scholarship or ability. But I do claim that the college or university is the proper place to correct deficiencies and that our first responsibility is to get our students to come to the college or the university where knowledge and understanding may be imparted. I do subscribe to the belief that academic standards are the sacred cow of many institutions when in reality they are the fossils and myths of the departed past. They serve no contemporary purpose or usefulness except to perpetuate the myth of superior scholarship and academic excellence, of high standards in empty classrooms, of sophism and pedantry in the society of pretense and hypocrisy.

I do not recommend scuttling Plato and Aristotle, Dante and Cervantes, Goethe and Dostoevski. What I would like to see is the application of the virtues and intellect of those great men to our crisis of human relations of the twentieth century. Thus, if Plato spoke of democracy and ethics and kept his slaves, and Cervantes spoke of liberty and freedom and adhered to the concept of noble blood, and Dostoevski championed the underdog but could not repudiate Siberia; I would hope that the wisdom and prudence of these great men and the advancement of science and the humanities would combine in a rich humanistic reform of intellectual, spiritual, and artistic character. We need not fewer standards, but better standards — standards that represent reality, not fantasy; sincerity, not hypocrisy; faith in the future, not nostalgia for the past.

Two problems jeopardize the retention of Mexican American

students in higher education: financial capability and academic scholarship. Concerning the former, the idea of raising tuition costs and fees seriously threatens the Mexican American student's ability to enter and stay in college. In fact, financial problems are acute and fatal to the Mexican American student who must work outside of class to support himself or his family. The poor and underprivileged Mexican American student not only cannot earn high wages while in college, but he deprives his family of financial support, a family which may already be on relief.

Mexican American girls are often persuaded to stay home, find a job, and supplement family income, because there is no money or financial aid to send them to college. Mexican American parents of the lower classes do not embrace the idea of sending their daughters to college, particularly living in the dorms, because these parents do not adhere to the same Anglo concepts and customs of Anglo society but retain their own traditions of familial practices and authority. Many Chicano parents send their daughters to college only after much persuasion, because they fear that their children will imitate the worst Anglo manners and habits and there will be no parental supervision. The idea of spending family money for the college education of the daughter is not intrinsically part of the Mexican heritage, and the liberty and opportunity given to the son is seldom extended to the daughter. Indeed, our Chicano students often come to college in spite of their parents rather than because of them, and their presence in college is evidence of their rebellion rather than familial conformity.

It is to be hoped that some day the poor in America will be guaranteed a college and university education, which in every respect is good business and good government. Millions spent on the education of ghetto children will some day bear fruit in higher income taxes and consumer purchasing power, but most importantly in the health and welfare of the community and the enrichment of the individual.

Until such a day arrives, the concept of scholarship awards should be the first priority for those who do not have money to go to college, and those less needy could be rewarded for their scholarship with certificates, diplomas, and trophies. For the retention of Mexican American students we must grapple with this problem and find new sources of financial aid.

But the academic problem remains. Mexican American students bring to college their own primary and secondary school deficiencies. If they were not taught to read and write, speak and study, their problems are compounded in college. They are placed in a competitive situation with Anglos who have acquired basic language skills. Conversely, the Mexican American student who is a true bilingual, that is, who understands and speaks English and Spanish equally well, is usually capable of competing successfully and even does better than his Anglo classmates.

But the problem arises in the fact that most Mexican American students have serious deficiences in both English and Spanish. What is more, psychological problems stem from conflicts of loyalty between the cultural worlds of the school and home and the maladjustments of the Anglo world of materialism and technology and the Hispanic world of humanism and emotional temperament.[10]

Chicanos in the primary grades were never taught to understand and speak English first, but they were expected to read English with all Anglo children from the first day in school. They did not receive special reading texts geared to the Spanish-speaking home and the adjustment to Englsh, nor did they have the compassion of an empathetic teacher. These students came to college with many scars and handicaps.

The dropout rate in junior high and high school because of inability to read and lack of motivation is very high, and it claims many students in college, too. In fact, language "hangups" are the basic causes of most Chicano failures in college. Therefore, those who are concerned with the problem of retention of Mexican American students must consider language and culture as the most important areas of education for the entering Mexican American student. The college language instructional program should be, for this reason, the best planned, coordinated, and organized of all programs.

All Chicano students who enter college or the university under an EOP (Educational Opportunity Program) should take a diagnostic English and Spanish test. All Chicano students could profit from such tests, and they should be encouraged to take them. Such tests, given in the language laboratory and auditorium, test understanding, speaking, reading, and writing, in that order. Also, some translation questions would be given. The objective of such tests should be to determine the level of achievement of the Chicano student in both English and Spanish. The student's level of language achievement would then suggest to counselors the level of English and Spanish which he should undertake.

English instruction for the Chicano student should be geared to his unique needs. New language tapes should be cut; new materials, pictures, and kinesics should be developed; and an intensive course in both English and Spanish, with language laboratory and classroom contact, should be prescribed. This should not be for only a one-hour lesson per day, but for a minimum of two or three hours of language per day. Comprehension and speaking should be primary goals, followed by reading, writing, and translation. Phonemic analysis and study of structure and vocabulary development should be taught in a new key. Verb conjugations in sentence contexts should expand language control. Dictation and composition may be used to study structure and thought development, as well as spelling and accentuation. In fact, Chicano students should not be required to take traditional elementary and intermediate Spanish courses which do not relate to their needs. But every effort should be made to return the Chicano student to the integrated language classes of higher ability as soon as possible, and not to continue the artificial and expedient homogeneous grouping any longer than necessary. Segregation for any valid reason contains its own drawback and weakness. Both ethnocentricity and monolithic psychology and sentiments isolate the Mexican American from society and deprive both him and his Anglo classmates of the benefit of classroom intellectual and social exchange.

Thus, Chicano language classes should be intensive English and Spanish courses designed for his needs. But bicultural studies should be the outgrowth of such language instruction, too. Much of the material in history, art, and political science addressed to the Chicano will be written in English. But folklore, art customs, and traditions could be learned in Spanish instruction, and some civilization of Mexico, the southwestern United States, and California history could also be learned in Spanish.

Bicultural studies available run the gamut from the sophisticated writings of sociology and philosophy of Jose Vasoncelos,

La Raza Cosmica and *Indiologia;* of literature and fiction of Mariano Azuela, *Los de Abajo,* or Martin Luis Guzman, *El Aguila y la Serpiente;* of Mexican mural art and art history of Diego Rivera's paintings of the Palacio Nacional or Jose Clemente Orozco's paintings in Escuela Preparatoria or the University of Guadalajara, to the earthy and grassroots discussion of the grape boycott in Delano, *Sal si puedes,* and the Chicano *barrio* of East Los Angeles. Study can include the political structure and leadership of such Chicano organizations as MAPA (Mexican American Political Association), G.I. Forum, LULACS (League of United Latin American Citizens and Societies), LACA (Latin American Civic Association), Council of Mexican American Affairs, AMAE (Association of Mexican American Educators), and Mexican American student groups.

The whole area of Mexican American studies will include almost every discipline, as well as specialization in individual disciplines like language and sociology and interdisciplinary research, such as psychology and anthropology. Music, both classical and popular, will be studied as never before, and we may expect to see plays and dramas that feature *teatro universitario* in a theatre of social ideas. The *Teatro Campesino* of Fresno has already pointed the way in this direction. Poetry and painting will make their appearance in this renaissance of artistic self-expression once the Chicano has resolved his personal identity crisis and has made peace with the two cultures he carries in his soul. We may expect to hear new rhythms and ballads and new jazz and melodies, once the Latin beat and the Anglo concept join hands. We may expect to see new dances and arrangements when the Chicano puts into motion what he senses and feels. We may expect to read new poems, stories, and novels once the Chicano can express his thoughts in the sophisticated language of his professors.

Chicano studies and curriculum, featuring future teachers of American projects in the *barrios* and public schools where recruitment has never been conducted before, where counseling has never succeeded before, where students have never been invited to college campuses before, will bring new motivation and retention force to the Chicano college student and a new and valuable role for him to play as an activist for *La Raza.*

In conclusion, I have explored the educational system of

higher education insofar as the Mexican American student and community are concerned, and I have observed several areas where I believe any effort to improve retention of our students must begin. Admission standards and academic standards must be reviewed in the light of their own pronouncements and whether or not they are achieving the deeper and more meaningful purposes of higher education. Realistic reforms must be initiated in both admissions and academics if higher education is to accept the intellectual and social challenge of the times. Not fewer standards, but better standards are desired in a fusion of humanistic tradition and contemporary values. Ivy walls may be desirable, but they are crumbling in the large cities where the ogre of ignorance and poverty rears its ugly head. Scholarships for the affluent student who is a high achiever should be reviewed in the light of far-reaching educational objectives, whereas medals, diplomas, and trophies may recognize and reward achievement and leave the money for those students of good scholarship and character, but poor economic means, who need it the most.

Bilingual and bicultural problems are by far the most serious jeopardy of the Mexican American student from the *barrio* and EOP programs. College retention and motivation of this student are involved. The Chicano student, with numerous psychological problems stemming from insecurities of poor academic achievement, poverty, and inability to read and study, needs special courses in intensive English and Spanish, beginning with diagnostic tests and then language courses geared to his level and needs. Language laboratory and contact for at least two to three hours per day are recommended for every Chicano student who enters college from the *barrio*.

Instruction in bicultural studies reinforces language studies and gives the Chicano an· opportunity to resolve his identity crisis, to find the discipline of his interests and talents, and to make the scholastic and social adjustments that college life demands.

New tapes and textbooks must be made and bought, and new techniques must be developed to give the Chicano a valuable college education which supplements rather than substitutes the standards of traditional curricula.

Just as bilingual and bicultural problems of the Chicano pose the greatest dangers, so do bilingual and bicultural talents pass unperceived and unappreciated by tradition-minded educators. I recommend that high scores on language prognostic and diagnostic tests give the Chicano student at least one-half to one grade point in admissions consideration, and that his true linguistic and cultural talents be correctly evaluated toward the bachelor of arts and sciences degrees in the humanities. It seems ironic that our requirements for a Ph.D. degree include reading ability in two languages for the extension of more universal scholarship, while our bilingual Chicano who masters English and Spanish is not accredited at the admissions office for the merits and talent of his cultural achievement. Like the foreign language program in the elementary schools, we chastise Juanito for speaking Spanish on the playground only to reward the Anglo child for speaking Spanish in the classroom, as if the propriety of language and the environment of the child were both factors in the teacher's attitudes. Higher education must set the pace for the public schools to follow. In this regard, if bilingualism and biculturalism are academically rewarded by way of admissions, academic disciplines, and financial aids, the opinion of the public schools toward Juanito's talents will change accordingly, and a better understanding of his language assets will follow.

NOTES

[1] *Bilingual Education Programs,* Hearings before the General Subcommittee on Education, House of Representatives, 90th Congress, H.R. 9840 and H.R. 10224, U.S. Government Printing Office, 1967. Statement of Dr. Miguel Montes, California State Board of Education, p. 235.

[2] *Ibid.,* pp. 236-245.

[3] *Los Angeles Times,* April 12, 1967.

[4] Much evidence was brought to the attention of the California Fair Employment Practices Commission, 1964–1968, to corroborate this statement.

[5] Dr. Miguel Montes, California State Board of Education, brought evidence before the board of labeling Mexican American children in Orange County, California, as "mentally retarded" following intelligence testing in 1967–1968.

[6] Cf. *Bulletin,* San Jose City College, p. 16.

[7] Consult the UCLA Mexican American Study Project (Dr. Ralph Guzman) for statistics: 850,000 in Los Angeles County; 2,000,000 in California; 5.5 to 6 million in the United States; and 11 million Spanish-speaking citizens altogether in the U.S.

[8] Miguel Montes, *op. cit.,* p. 236.

[9] Consult Congressman Henry B. Gonzalez, *Congressional Record,* 1968, for additional statistics.

[10] Consult Manuel H. Guerra, "Why Juanito Doesn't Read," pp. 103-107 of this book.

BIBLIOGRAPHY

Berney, Tomi D., and Eisenberg, Anne, *Doble Research Supplement.* New York: Yeshiva University, December, 1968, "Selected Bibliography."

Bibliographies: UCLA Mexican American Studies Project, Dr. Ralph Guzman; Bibliography of Paul Sheldon, Occidental College; Y. Arturo Cabrera, San Jose State College; Dr. Robert G. Hayden, Assistant Executive Director, Research Interagency Committee on Mexican American Affairs, Washington, D.C.

Brooks, Nelson, *Language and Language Learning.* 2nd ed. New York: Harcourt, Brace & World, Inc., 1964.

Ervin, Susan M., and Osgood, C. E., "Second Language Learning and Bilingualism," *Journal of Abnormal and Social Psychology,* no. 49, Supplement (1954), pp. 139-146.

FEPC, *Negroes and Mexican Americans in South and East Los Angeles.* Publication of the state of California, July, 1966.

Guerra, Manuel H., "Why Juanito Doesn't Read," California Teachers' Association *Journal,* October, 1965.

Guerra, Manuel H., and Cabrera, Y. Arturo, "An Evaluation and Critique of the Mexican American Studies Project; A Ford Foundation Grant Extended to the University of California at Los Angeles," Los Angeles, 1966.

The Invisible Minority, publication of the National Education Association, Washington, D.C., 1966.

Lado, Robert, *Linguistics Across Cultures: Applied Linguistics for Language Teachers.* Ann Arbor: University of Michigan Press, 1957.

Lado, Robert, "Report on a Conference on the Meaning and Role of Culture in Foreign Language Teaching," March 10-11, 1961. Washington, D.C.: Georgetown University.

The Mexican American, testimony presented at the Cabinet Committee Hearings on Mexican American Affairs, El Paso, Texas, 1967. Inter-Agency Committee on Mexican American Affairs, Washington, D.C.

Revolt in the Barrios, a series of articles on the Mexican American reprinted from the *Los Angeles Times,* by Jack Jones,

May 8–13, 1966. See "Bilingual Approach May Provide Answer to Educational Problem."

U.S. Government Printing Office, *Bilingual Education*, S. 428, Hearings, Parts 1 and 2, Washington, D.C., 1967.

U.S. Government Printing Office, *Bilingual Education Programs*, Hearings before the General Subcommittee on Education, H.R. 9840 and H.R. 10224, June 28–29, 1967.

Wonder, J. P., "Bilingual Mexican American as a Potential Teacher of Spanish," *Hispania*, March, 1965.

Concerns Relating to the Testing and Special Education of Minority Children*

CALVIN D. CATTERALL

THE CALIFORNIA ASSOCIATION OF School Psychologists and Psychometrists (CASPP) is pleased to be asked to make a presentation to the California State Board of Education about its position on the current concerns of the parents of minority group children over testing and placement of their children in various special education programs in California. CASPP shares with the Board of Education its concern that all children be given the best possible education, that each child be treated fairly, that all be encouraged to grow to the fullest extent of their potential, that each person coming in contact with these students provide competent professional service which is in the best interests of the child, and that our limited educational finances be expended wisely and judiciously. We, with you, want to honor the request of these minority parents to look carefully at our current practices in special education. If changes are

* This paper was presented before the California State Board of Education on May 8, 1969. Reprinted by permission of the author. Although members of the California Association of School Psychologists and Psychometrists Supplementary Education Committee helped to prepare this paper and it reflects CASPP'S basic position, time has not permitted clearance of the entire paper with other parts of the organization.

necessary as a result of improved knowledge and technologies, we want to make them in such a way as to reflect possible societal changes. After these changes are made, we feel we should stand firmly behind what we believe to be good educational practice.

We have been working on this problem with the staffs in the Division of Compensatory Education and the Department of Special Education for almost a year. We have urged all existing committees, and appointed a special group, to investigate these concerns and to suggest possible solutions. We have met with the Association of Mexican-American Educators and have found a great many areas of agreement with them, and we have established a joint committee to work with them toward a more common understanding.

CONCERNS

The minority parents are concerned that their children are overrepresented in programs of special education. Observation of prevailing conditions and statewide statistics both support the fact that a greater percentage of minority children need and receive the special help of various programs of special education. It is equally true, however, that Anglo-American children from the lower socioeconomic groups are also represented to a greater degree than their percentage of the population would indicate. It has long been known that there is a high correlation between socioeconomic status and the ability to achieve in school.

The parents of minority children are concerned that education has tended to become a means of keeping their children from participating and profiting more freely in the rewards of this society. They feel that the present avenue of education as a means of upward social mobility has become, in many instances, a "dead-end" street. Certainly observant, sensitive people would agree that our minority members do not share equally in the social and material rewards of our country. School psychologists, along with all other educators, should help to identify the factors which interact between the society and the school to cause this to happen, and should attempt to help alleviate it.

The parents of minority children, especially from the Mexican-American groups, are concerned that group testing tends to discriminate against their children because of their inability to understand, to work with, and to think in English. It is obviously true that tests designed to measure progress in an English-oriented curriculum will place those who do not handle this language at a disadvantage. Without appropriate facilities for teaching in Spanish, the assessment of progress toward a curriculum based on another language does not seem indicated.

The parents of these same minority children are concerned more specifically that the use of group ability tests discriminates against their children. They feel that these cause teachers to diminish their expectations for minority children, with the result that a self-fulfilling hypothesis is established and the child's level of functioning tends to be allowed to lower to meet the teacher's expectations. Recent experimental evidence does seem to support the idea that the expectations of teachers are affected by I.Q. scores. In the past it has been widely held and taught that the I.Q. remains relatively constant and that, once a valid score was obtained, subsequent retesting would not produce scores that significantly varied from the so-called "real" I.Q. Modern psychologists, however, tend to feel that the I.Q. is not constant, that it can be changed, and that much of the previous research which indicated constancy of I.Q. merely reflected the fact that the factors which keep the culture stable also tend to keep the I.Q. from changing.

Minority group parents are concerned that once their children are placed in EMR (Educable Mentally Retarded) classes, they are indelibly marked and can never get out. Once again, we would agree that altogether too often adequate follow-through has not been made. The EMR classes were initiated at a time when the I.Q. was still believed to be constant, and the assumption was made that the children, if properly placed, would remain in the program for the rest of their school lives. Furthermore, the law was written to keep these children full time under specially credentialed teachers, in order to protect them. The result has been that an EMR placement has indeed been a "one-way street," and its curriculum has been reduced to a slower pace. Because of this the student gets further behind, thereby making it subsequently difficult to transfer him out of the special class. We are in accord with the changes currently proposed by the State Department which give the program more flexibility, but we feel that the proposals are inadequate to give the amount of maneuverability that is so urgently needed. CASPP is currently studying a concept of supplementary education which would eliminate the necessity for labeling students as mentally retarded and would increase our ability to keep moving children back into the mainstream of education.

Minority parents feel that once their children are placed in EMR classes they tend to be forgotten. Although both the CASPP position paper and the guidelines set up by the State Department strongly recommend systematic reevaluation of students after they have been placed, we would agree that frequently this has not, in fact, taken place. Too often we have not demanded that adequate psychological staff be provided to protect the rights of all of the children, and the pressure of new referrals has taken precedence over the needs of the child who is already getting help in a special program.

The minority parents are concerned that districts, in order to increase their revenue, apply pressure to put children in special education. Admittedly there is a great deal of pressure to get children who are not achieving out of the regular program (especially if they are also behavior problems). However, the pressure is not sparked by a financial motive; it is to provide special placement and to get children who are not achieving out of the regular program so the teacher can better help those children who are progressing normally. Funding for special education is not so plentifully available as to motivate districts to place children just to make money. During the early years of the program there was some difficulty in trying to keep the classes at maximum size in order to make them pay for themselves. Under current funding, procedures which pay for total classes rather than for ADA (average daily attendance) have largely eliminated this problem. What continues to be an increasingly complex problem, however, is for business departments to straighten out the maze of regulations and restrictions governing the funding of all types of special education and to maintain a balance between overcharging the state and getting all that is properly allocated in order to continue to maintain and expand special programs. Wide variations in accounting procedures exist; there is a definite need for further clarification in this important area.

Minority-group parents are concerned that their children are overrepresented in all special education programs, but most specifically in the educable mentally retarded (EMR) classes, and have inferred that some psychologists have accepted money to screen and erroneously place children in such programs. That minority children are to be found in special education — especially the EMR program — at a higher rate than nonminority children is an established fact. For a psychologist to receive money for evaluating children, either minority or otherwise, and to help legitimate cases to receive the special help they need is definitely an ethical and professional service. To screen such children into programs when they do not need them, for either personal gain or for district-imposed financial considerations, is clearly unethical as defined in CASPP's Code of Ethics. We would welcome information about any of our members who are engaged in unethical practices in this or any other area.

The minority-group parents imply that altogether too often their children have been placed in EMR classes punitively and without careful thought. Although it is quite normal for any parent to have some concerns about having his child placed in a program for the mentally retarded, the choice usually left open to the school personnel has been either to leave him to "sink" in the regular program or allow him to "swim" in the special program. The advent of the educationally handicapped (EH) program has helped, and in many districts the percentage of children in the EMR program is decreasing as the EH classes become more available. The EH program has also made it possible to leave a child primarily in a regular class and place him under a Learning Disabilities teacher for part of the day, thereby reducing the possible effects of segregating the child from his normal friends. CASPP has been working hard to help its members make the difficult differential diagnosis between the requirements for EMR and EH as they are currently described in the Education Code. The suggestion has been made that another program change which would be helpful would be to encourage English as a second language class. Although this probably has some advantages in presenting factual material for that percentage (presumably about 20 percent) who think and speak almost entirely in Spanish, it would probably only tend to confuse the larger number of Mexican-American children who predominantly operate with English. There is some reason to believe that continued exposure to television programs in English has increased the ability of those who come from primarily Spanish-speaking homes to handle receptive English, but it probably has not encouraged a related development in their ability to express themselves in that language. Although special funds, primarily federal money, have encouraged a great variety of programs to try to help minority children, especially those in the lower socioeconomic groups, the truth remains that we do not have a clear perspective as to which specific programs will be most helpful for these children.

The minority groups are concerned that their children are being placed in special education programs without parental consent. Once again, although this is against the recommended procedures established by both CASPP and the State Department, some districts have not adopted the policy of requiring written parental approval, especially from parents who do not speak English. CASPP feels that it is the responsibility of all school personnel to help parents to understand the need for and value in a special class placement. Community volunteers and bilingual teaching aides have recently made this process easier with the parent who does not speak English.

Although minority parents agree that individually administered I.Q. tests are better utilized because of the higher level of training of the psychologist administering them, the Mexican-American parents feel that the results obtained are generally invalid because the psychologists do not speak or understand Spanish. It is very true that, with the shortage of Spanish-speaking psychologists, the great majority of such testing must be done by professionals who are not conversant in the child's primary tongue. We have gone on record as strongly supporting the need for more minority members entering our profession and are happy to see some progress in this area. Although the problem of assessing children who speak Spanish exists in greater magnitude due to the larger number of such children in California schools, it is not basically different from testing children who speak other foreign languages or children who have defects such as severe hearing problems and markedly delayed speech. Even though it is obviously not possible always to assess children correctly, a large part of the psychologist's training and expertise is devoted to estimating ability or potential which has not been directly displayed. Furthermore, rather than pre-judging that all children with Spanish surnames have language problems, or any other single problem, we feel that we are in a stronger professional position to focus in on *individual* strengths and weaknesses, and not assume generalized problems related to minority-group membership.

Although the instruction for group intelligence tests has to be given in English, when such instruments are given early in the school experience, they must rely primarily on nonverbal skills to measure ability. Many of the tests that have been tra-ditionally used at all age levels have also measured both verbal and nonverbal ability. We encourage teachers to rely primarily on the nonverbal score as an estimate of the child's ability if he has difficulty with English. The testing program mandated by the state does not require I.Q. tests be given until the sixth grade and, although many districts do give such tests earlier, the trend in recent years has been to delay intelligence testing until later in the primary block and to encourage teachers not to rely too heavily on the scores because of the difficulties of obtaining a good measure of ability of the younger children.

Minority parents feel that their children should be distributed normally on an intelligence curve if the tests are not discrimi-natory. Although we do not have evidence which would lead us to believe that the people who live in Mexico, for example, would not be distributed normally over a curve on a test if it adequately reflects an exposure to their own culture, it seems evident that there are many social/cultural factors which would cause these same people to do poorly on a test reflecting their exposure to the American culture.

The minority parents feel that the I.Q. scores their children obtain prevent them from getting help from other programs such as Remedial Reading and the Educationally Handicapped program. Once again, although there has been some truth to this charge, in that some districts have required an "above 90" I.Q. for inclusion in such programs, the tendency more and more has been to interpret "normal ability" more broadly and to allow students into these programs with any level of ability, providing they were not eligible for an EMR class. Once again, the supplementary education concept would help children with the most need, regardless of their scores on tests which cover a broad area and do not focus on specific needs.

Representatives of minority parents are concerned that group intelligence test scores are not clearly distinguished from achievement tests. We would certainly agree with the position that in reality there is an overlap in the measurement of intelligence and achievement. However, the attempt to separate the acquisition of facts — achievement — from the ability to think and learn — intelligence — still seems to be a valid goal, especially for the large majority of pupils. There have been many cases where minority children have moved so frequently that they score poorly on achievement tests, but they have been kept out of special classes because individual ability tests have indicated a higher level of ability to think and to learn than one would expect with their lowered achievement. We would agree that teachers need more help with the way in which intelligence tests should be competently interpreted and used. CASPP is willing to attempt to assume statewide leadership in this area.

The parents of minority children feel quite strongly that lowered I.Q. scores and special class placement affect their children's feeling of self-worth, which in turn affects the child's ability to achieve. We would strongly agree that any cooperative effort that the school and community could make which would help these children to maintain a better feeling about their ability to function in school would be advantageous. Attempts to encourage greater knowledge about Afro-American and Mexican-American cultures are steps in this direction. It would seem that in the American culture, however, ultimate pride in self will come more with achievement and production than it will through pointing to cultural accomplishments in the past. We need to find more powerful techniques to help these children to attain and to become reinforced by continued success in the school setting.

RECOMMENDATIONS

It is respectfully recommended that the following steps be taken:

1. We recommend a plan of supplemental education [1] be envisioned and studied which would:

   a) Reduce the need to label children according to provisions in the Education Code and help us to group them according to their social and learning needs.

b) Increase the flexibility of the ways in which we can help children and can keep them as close as possible to their normal classroom setting.

c) Serve to support the Basic Educational Program and help to increase its effectiveness in meeting the needs of an increasingly large number of students.

d) Help all students with the greatest need, even though they would not have fitted into previous categories of special education.

e) Require frequent reevaluations to make certain that only those children who really need it are taken out of the mainstream of education, even for a short period of time.

2. We recognize that we cannot, nor should we, attempt to dismiss deeply held concerns with an intellectual argument. Many of the claims of the minority groups are either wholly or partially justified. We commend the board of education for opening up communication with these parents and pledge CASPP's willingness to work closely with the Association of Mexican-American Educators and other interested groups representing the minority community, to try to arrive at acceptable, meaningful solutions.

3. We do not feel that intelligence testing should be eliminated. We do feel that a great deal of further work needs to be done to insure that the results are used and interpreted wisely, and that:

a) The research evidence about the effect of teacher expectations should be widely disseminated.

b) The concept of the nonconstancy of the I.Q. be further advanced and the idea that the child can be increasingly helped to learn and to profit from his environment be explained.

c) The State Department, Bureau of Compensatory Education, and CASPP work jointly to insure that the highest standards of testing and test interpretation be used with all students, but especially with those who are bilingual.

4. We recommend that an Advisory Committee, which has been proposed recently by the State Board to study the

problems of testing and special class placement as it affects members of minority groups, be selected as soon as possible and that it use the resources of people who are highly competent in testing as well as those who intimately know the needs and ways of the minority groups.

5. We further recommend that the State Board encourage extended communication between representatives from the following groups in order to clarify any questions with regard to budgetary and accounting procedures in special education:

   a) California Association of Public School Business Officials
   b) State Department of Education, Division of Public School Administration
   c) State Department of Education, Division of Special Schools and Services
   d) California Association of School Psychologists and Psychometrists

6. Because we feel strongly that no child should be placed in a special education program on the basis of group tests, we support the current Education Code provisions which require an individual evaluation.

7. We recommend that a school psychologist who is well-versed in both group and individual testing, as they are used with both the majority and minority groups, be appointed immediately to the existent State Board Advisory Committee on Testing to help to insure that the recommendations of that group take into consideration the concerns to which this paper is addressed.

8. Finally, we recommend that the board continue to spend its energy and resources on assisting promising new programs to be developed and evaluated. If I.Q. tests were suddenly discontinued, we would still be faced with the same problem. How can we best help all children; but even more specifically, how can we assist that large group of minority students who need special help to learn, to know success, and to take their productive places in our society?

NOTE

[1] For further information see the CASPP *Newsletter*, vol. 16, no. 3, Spring, 1968–1969.

Performance of Mexican-American Children on Selected Nonverbal Tests of Intelligence*

UVALDO H. PALOMARES

TEACHING ENGLISH TO IMMIGRANTS has always been a problem in the United States. Since many schools enroll children of Mexican immigrants who speak little or no English, the problem is particularly acute in the southwestern part of the United States. At present, California is providing funds to help such children to overcome their language problem. Schools which are starting programs designed to help these children are faced with identification of their intellectual ability.

Essentially, two problems are apparent in identifying the intellectual ability of lingually deprived students. First and most obvious is the need for I.Q. tests which do not penalize the student for his inability to speak English. The second and less obvious problem is peculiar to the Mexican-American child in the southwestern area of the United States. Particularly in southern California, these children are, to a great extent, born of immigrants who have come to the United States to do manual labor. Such children are handicapped not only by their inability to speak English, but they are also deprived of some of the cultural advantages available to other children whose parents belong to

* An original paper printed by permission of the author.

the middle-class culture. Most I.Q. tests, therefore, tend to penalize Mexican-American children, not only for their inability to speak the English language, but also for their cultural unawareness.

Developing tests for measuring the intellectual ability of Spanish-speaking, Mexican-American children by simply translating our present tests into Spanish is inadequate. Such a test, even if given in Spanish, still penalizes the individual for his cultural handicap because of the cultural bias inherent in the test items. Some effort has been made to develop cross-cultural tests which would not penalize the individual taking them because of his inability to speak the English language or because of his cultural handicap. Anastasi [1] included the *Leiter International Scale, Goodenough-Harris Intelligence Test, IPAT (Institute for Personality and Ability Testing) Culture-Free Intelligence Test, Semantic Test of Intelligence,* and the *Ravens Progressive Matrices* as those which have been developed for cross-cultural testing. The *Leiter International Scale,* the *IPAT Culture-Free Intelligence Test,* and the *Semantic Test of Intelligence* must be administered individually by a trained psychometrist or psychologist. The large numbers of lingually deprived children in some schools and the absence of trained examiners would make a testing program with these instruments expensive and time-consuming, if possible at all. Thus, the need in this area seems to be for a valid and reliable I.Q. test which, as closely as possible, would meet the following criteria:

1. A test which would not penalize children for their inability to speak English.

2. A test which would not penalize children for their cultural handicaps.

3. A test which could be administered and scored inexpensively.

PROCEDURE

To select tests for evaluation which would meet the needs outlined above, a review was conducted of the cross-cultural tests now in use. Of those reviewed, the male portion of the recently published *Goodenough-Harris Intelligence Test* (G-H) [2] was selected for evaluation. The G-H was published as an extension and revision of the older *Goodenough Draw-A-Man Test*

(Goodenough) [3] which is also included in this evaluation. For comparison of the Goodenough scores, the *Leiter International Scale* (Leiter) was chosen as a control test because of its apparent success with bilingual and culturally handicapped children.[4] The G-H and the Goodenough were administered on a group basis while the Leiter was administered individually.

The group that was studied consisted of twenty girls and seventeen boys, ranging in chronological age from five years, four months, to twelve years, nine months, with a mean age of eight years, three months. At the time of the testing, these thirty-seven students were enrolled in a class in which they studied English as a second language, in Jefferson Elementary School, Carlsbad, California. The greater number of this group were from a low socioeconomic level. All had been born in Mexico and had recently come to the United States.

RESULTS

The first step was to determine the examiner's reliability in scoring the G-H and Goodenough, since the scoring of these tests is less objective than that of the Leiter. To determine this, each figure was scored by an independent second scorer, using the Goodenough and G-H scoring standards. The score-rescore correlation between the examiner's and that of the second scorer was .83 for the G-H and .74 for the Goodenough. These figures indicate acceptable reliability for these tests and also the relative ease with which the Goodenough and G-H scoring criteria can be mastered.

The correlations of the G-H and the Goodenough with the Leiter are summarized in Table No. 1. The correlation of the G-H and Leiter was .55; G-H and Goodenough, .68; and Good-

TABLE 1

CORRELATIONS OF G-H, GOODENOUGH, AND LEITER TESTS

	G-H	LEITER
GOODENOUGH	.68	.65
G-H		.55

enough and Leiter, .65. To rule out any possibility that the correlation between the Goodenough and the Leiter could be spurious, the effect of chronological age was parceled out.

It should be noted that the $+5$ I.Q. correction suggested in the Leiter *Manual* was added to all Leiter I.Q.'s. Because the mean of the Leiter is 95, this addition of 5 points is required when comparing the Leiter with I.Q. tests which use 100 as the mean. The mean I.Q.'s, standard deviations, and t-test for correlated means of the three tests used are summarized in Table No. 2. The difference among correlated means was not significant enough to reject the null hypothesis at the .05 level of confidence.

DISCUSSION

For the present sample of Mexican-American children, a significant positive correlation was found between both the G-H and the Goodenough, and the Leiter. The correlation of the G-H and the Leiter indicates that both cross-cultural tests appear to be tapping similar intellectual factors in this language-handicapped group. The possibility of being able to use the G-H in place of the Leiter is of practical significance. Whereas many districts will not be able to buy the Leiter or to hire a trained psychometrist or psychologist to administer the test, most districts will be able to single out a specially gifted and interested teacher to become proficient with the G-H. Using the simple, group-administered G-H, this teacher would be able to show data which would give some estimate of language-handicapped children's intellectual ability.

TABLE 2

MEAN I.Q.'S, STANDARD DEVIATIONS, T-TEST FOR CORRELATED MEANS FOR G-H, GOODENOUGH, AND LEITER TESTS

	G-H	GOODENOUGH	LEITER
X	92.9	96.9	93.6
0	10.9	10.7	10.8
t	1.90		1.65
p	NS($>$.05)		NS($>$.05)

SUMMARY

Mexican-American children (N=37) were tested at Carlsbad, California, with the male portion of the G-H, the Goodenough, and the Leiter. Correlations between the three tests were significant at the .01 level of confidence, as follows:

$$\text{Goodenough} - \text{Leiter} = .65$$
$$\text{G-H} - \text{Leiter} = .55$$
$$\text{Goodenough} - \text{G-H} = .68$$

No significant difference was found in mean I.Q.'s of the three tests. The score-rescore correlations of the Goodenough and the G-H were .74 and .83, in that order. Therefore, nonverbal tests of intelligence can be used effectively and economically in schools where Mexican-American children are enrolled.

NOTES

[1] Anne Anastasi, *Psychological Testing*, 2nd. ed. (New York: The Macmillan Company, 1962).

[2] Dale B. Harris, *Children's Drawings as Measures of Intellectual Maturity* (New York: Harcourt, Brace, & World, Inc., 1963).

[3] Florence L. Goodenough, *Measurement of Intelligence by Drawings* (Tarrytown-on-Hudson, New York: World Book Company, 1926).

[4] R. G. Leiter, *Leiter International Performance Scale* (Los Angeles: Western Psychological Services, 1947).

The Relationship of Acculturation, Achievement, and Alienation Among Spanish-American Sixth Grade Students*

IGNACIO R. CORDOVA

THE PHILOSOPHY OF THE AMERICAN EDUCATIONAL SYSTEM is based on the assumption that education is not the sole responsibility of parents, but that at a certain point society, or rather its agencies, must step in and take over the task of formally educating its members. Consequently, public education in the United States has become an important socialization instrument of society, a society which has developed a dominant culture as a result of years of sharing common experiences. While there are local variations of this culture pattern, basic commitments commonly are to particular patterns of behavior in the dominant culture.[1] This common culture not only is transmitted by the public schools, but is the basis for its philosophical assumptions. The American public school functions best when middle-class administrators and teachers address themselves to middle-class students who possess the value orientations and experiences which are part of the dominant culture.

The ability to read and write has become the basic require-

* Prepared for the Conference on Teacher Education for Mexican Americans, February, 1969. Sponsored by ERIC Clearinghouse on Rural Education and Small Schools.

ment for success both in school and out. This is so because it is taken for granted all over the country that reading and writing skills are the keys that open the doors to opportunity. Children socialized in the dominant culture take this for granted even before they are ready for school. However, when the child's environment is not book-centered, is lacking in conversations about the happenings of the world, and is lacking in models that substantiate this belief, and when subcultural beliefs and experiences do not embrace this orientation, then, most likely, the child will enter school unmotivated, diffident, "inwardizing," unaware, and uninterested.

Many of the children of Spanish cultural background enter school without a functional knowledge of the English language and the dominant culture. Cultural differences and the resulting handicaps pose a greater learning task for Spanish-American students than for English-speaking students in terms of both language and culture. Many Spanish-American students enter school without the kinds of experiences which develop readiness for school or which are stressed in the school environment. The schools, on the other hand, do not generally make the first exposure to American values and educational skills the exciting experience it could be.

Spanish Americans have lived in this country since before the founding of Plymouth Colony. Yet, Heller, writing in 1966, claims that Spanish Americans are among the least "Americanized" of all ethnic groups in the United States.[2] Bogue, in 1959, found that of all ethnic groups in the United States, the Spanish Americans constitute "the only ethnic group for which a comparison of the characteristics of the first and second generations fails to show a substantial intergenerational rise in socioeconomic status."[3] For Spanish Americans the school is perhaps the most important acculturating force and the most available source of socialization into the dominant society. However, to find success in the American public school the Spanish-American students need the skills of assimilation and support in the notion of acculturation. This is a paradox because Spanish-American children are rejected from full participation in school because they are unable to acquire the skills necessary for acculturation.[4] The child who enters school with a language deficiency and cultural deprivation (from the dominant society's standpoint) due to cultural differentiation, is made unbearably aware of his disadvantages. Ironically, school is supposed to help him solve these problems, but instead it convinces him that they are beyond solution.

Upon entering school the Spanish-American student moves into a social system whose normative culture has been derived from a culture pattern which varies considerably from the cultural elements which he has internalized. Therefore, the probability of a discrepancy arising from the student's perception of his role and the expectations of teachers and administrators who have accepted the dominant culture's normative system as binding is greatly increased. Symbols which were once meaningful to him are either absent or have been assigned different meanings. Confronted with a normative pattern which is at variance with his internalized values and experiences, the student will, initially at least, become alienated from that system.

The student is presented with a problem of adjustment necessitating either a restructuring of his system of orientations or of the educational system in which he is a student. Since the latter is out of his realm of possibilities, he has the following alternatives:

1. The student may restructure his system of need dispositions which are not gratified in the educational system's social relational context.

2. The student may change his need disposition system, displacing his previously internalized value orientations with a system of value orientations which coincide with those of the school's.

3. The student may terminate the relationship and transfer his cathexis to a new object which shares the same value orientation pattern as he, and therefore promises to be of greater significance.

The ideal situation is one in which a student selects alternatives one and two. However, evidence strongly suggests that lack of acculturation results in Spanish-American students who find rejection from full participation in school and who seek support in *La Raza*, the language, and the traditional cultural values, and have withdrawn from the school.

The language barrier, the experience barrier, and the cultural barrier are formidable problems in the education of Spanish-

American students. As several studies have shown, Spanish-American children tend to start school at much the same level as children from the dominant society in terms of both I.Q. and achievement. However, the longer they remain in school the less they resemble the other children in these endeavors.[5] The Spanish-American students are conditioned to failure in the early years of their schooling, and each passing year serves only to reinforce this conditioning. As soon as they are sixteen, or can pass for sixteen, they begin to drop out of school. The tragedy is that the unresponsiveness of the school forces these children out of school without an adequate knowledge of English and without the foundations of education in health, work skills, social practices, and personal duties.

The educational disparity between the Spanish American and his fellow citizens is quite evident. A study of the educational level of the population bearing Spanish surnames in California, as of 1960, revealed: "More than half of the males and nearly half of the females 14 years old and over had not gone beyond the eighth grade." This study further revealed that "only 48.5 percent of the males and 52 percent of the females of Spanish surnames" had completed one or more years of high school. "No more than 8.8 percent of the Spanish surnamed males and 6.2 percent of the females" had completed one or more years of college.[6] An analysis of the 1960 census reveals that in the Southwest there exists a four-year schooling gap between the Mexican Americans fourteen years of age and over and the rest of the population.[7]

The high dropout rate among Spanish-American students, the high degree of overageness in grade placement, the low academic achievement, the unmotivated and disinterested students, and the low educational attainment among the Spanish-surnamed population suggests that some degree of educational alienation exists among members of this subculture. Lack of acculturation, lack of achievement, poverty, and teacher-pupil relationships have been ventured as explanations for the educational failures of Spanish-American students. The paucity of empirical studies designed to test these assumptions has prompted this study.

STATEMENT OF THE PROBLEM

The problem of this study is to determine what relationships exist between acculturation, achievement, teacher expectations, and the alienation of Spanish-American students.

Conceptual Hypotheses

1. Inadequate assimilation of Spanish-American students into the dominant society, and specifically into the dominant society's middle-class-oriented school, contributes to their educational alienation.

2. The low educational achievement of Spanish-American students leads to a lack of gratification and acquisition of a low self-concept which contribute to a feeling of alienation from school.

3. The internalization of different value orientations and disparate expectations by Spanish-American students and the dominant society's middle-class-oriented teachers leads to teacher-pupil relationships which contribute to the alienation of students from the school.

Specific Null Hypotheses

1. There is no significant relationship between the level of acculturation of Spanish-American students and alienation from school.

2. There is no significant relationship between the level of achievement of Spanish-American students and alienation from school.

3. There is no significant relationship between the level of acculturation and the level of achievement of Spanish-American students.

4. There is no significant relationship between the type of teacher expectation of Spanish-American students and alienation from school.

5. There is no significant relationship between the level of acculturation of Spanish-American students and the type of teacher expectations.

Sample

The sample selected for investigation consisted of two groups of subjects: a student sample and a teacher sample. The student sample consisted of 477 Spanish-American sixth grade students from 32 classrooms in 16 schools from Albuquerque and northern New Mexico. This sample was divided into three groups on the basis of socioeconomic level and geographic location. The urban middle-class group consisted of 90 Spanish-American students. The urban lower-class group included 198 Spanish-American students. The teacher sample consisted of the 32 teachers of the students investigated. Self-contained classrooms were selected because it was felt that this situation provided for more pupil-teacher relationships than a departmentalized situation.

MEASUREMENT OF VARIABLES

Acculturation

As used in this study, acculturation refers to the transmission of attitudes, concepts, and points of view from one people to another with the accompanying processes by which the minority culture adopts the elements of the dominant culture. Factor analysis was used to develop the instrument used to measure this variable. The factor analysis yielded the factors of education, recreation, religion, economics, politics, family, and health. A composite score and seven factor scores were used in the analysis. Scoring was by a Likert Type response technique.

Achievement

Achievement, as used in this study, refers to academic achievement as measured by standardized achievement tests. A composite achievement score was used to analyze this variable.

Teacher Expectation

As used in this study, teacher expectation refers to the behaviors or attitudes that teachers stress, expect, or demand in their teaching. The instrument used to measure this variable was developed from items yielded by a factor analysis. The factors yielded were those of study habits, interaction, achievement, independence, courtesy, responsibility, work habits, and participation. Scoring of items was by a Likert Type response technique.

Alienation

Alienation, as used in this study, is defined as a feeling of estrangement from some social system of collectivity (the school)

and a feeling of self-estrangement in that situation. This definition incorporates the following factors:

1. *Powerlessness* — a low expectancy on the part of an individual that he can, through his own behavior, achieve the rewards he seeks.

2. *Normlessness* — a high expectancy on the part of an individual that socially unapproved behaviors are required to
achieve the given goals stressed by a system or collectivity (the
school).

3. *Self-estrangement* — a high degree of dependence of a given
behavior upon anticipated future rewards that lie outside the
activity itself, that aspect of self-alienation characterized by a
loss of intrinsic meaning or pride in work.

4. *Isolation* — the tendency to assign low reward values to beliefs or goals that are highly valued in a social system (the
school).

TREATMENT OF THE DATA

The data collected for investigation was analyzed by means of
a Pearson Product Moment Correlation. Differences between
groups were analyzed by means of a Fisher t-test. Correlation
analyses were computed for the total sample and for each group.

In securing responses concerning teachers' expectations, the
teachers were asked to give their expectations of their pupils' behavior for their classes as a whole and not for each individual
pupil. In essence their responses represent a mean score of their
expectations. For this reason it was felt that to use each pupil's
individual scores in conjunction with his teacher's expectation
score would be to introduce a bias. To prevent a biased analysis,
the mean score of the pupils' responses for each variable was
used. It was recognized that this procedure had major limitations. First, it was recognized that the number of subjects was
reduced drastically. Second, it was recognized that this procedure
reduced the variance among subjects. However, it was felt that
results obtained were still valuable in providing insights into
the relationships between these variables.

Analysis and Interpretation of the Data

Differences between the urban middle-class group, the lower-
class group, and the rural groups in terms the variables of

acculturation, achievement, and alienation were not statistically significant.

Relationship Between Acculturation and Alienation

Analysis of the total sample and the three separate groups indicated no significant relationships between the composite acculturation measure and the composite alienation measure. Correlation coefficients obtained for these groups failed to show relationships that were significant at the .05 level of probability.

Analysis of the relationships between the factors of acculturation and the factors of alienation for the total student sample yielded the correlation coefficients presented in Table No. 1. According to this analysis, low acculturation in the areas of education and politics was significantly related to a general feeling of educational alienation. Conversely, an increase in acculturation in these areas decreased this usual feeling of general alienation. Acculturation in the area of family was found to be positively related to a feeling of powerlessness. This indicated that as Spanish-American students became acculturated in this area, there was an increase in the feeling that they could not, through their own behaviors, attain the rewards or goals that they sought in the educational setting.

Analysis of the total sample further indicated a positive correlation between the acculturation factor of recreation and the

Table 1

Analysis of the Subtest Measures of Acculturation and Alienation for the Total Sample

Acculturation	Alienation				
	Composite	Powerlessness	Normlessness	Self-estrangement	Isolation
Composite					-.146
Education	-.136			-.107	-.224
Family		.140			
Politics	-.147			-.159	-.167
Economics					
Recreation			.104		
Religion					-.153
Health					-.134

Significance at .05 level = .088
Significance at .01 level = .115

normlessness factor of alienation. This relationship seemed to indicate that as Spanish-American students are acculturated in the area of recreation, there is an increase in the feeling that socially unapproved behaviors are required to attain the goals stressed in the school setting. Correlation coefficients also indicated a negative relationship between the acculturation factors of education and politics, and the alienation factor of self-estrangement. This relationship indicated that low acculturation in the areas of education and the family increased the feeling that school activities are not intrinsically meaningful and reduced the pride in the students' work. Conversely, as acculturation in these areas increased, there was a decrease in the feeling of self-estrangement.

The analysis for the total sample indicated negative relationships between the acculturation factors of composite acculturation, education, politics, religion, and health, and the alienation factor of isolation. This indicated that low acculturation in these areas increased the feeling that the beliefs, values, and goals stressed as important in school are not valuable. This relationship further indicated that acculturation in the areas mentioned decreased the feeling of isolation.

Correlation coefficients obtained for the urban middle-class group indicated no statistically significant relationships between the acculturation factors and the alienation factors. The correlation coefficients obtained for the urban lower-class group revealed the significant relationships presented in Table No. 2. These findings revealed that for subjects in the urban lower-class group, acculturation in the area of the family increased a feeling of general educational alienation. The findings also revealed that low acculturation in the area of politics was significantly related to a feeling of general alienation. As acculturation proceeded in this area, there was a decrease in the feeling of general educational alienation. It was further observed that as acculturation occurred in the area of the family, there was an increase in the feeling that the students' behavior could not obtain for them the rewards they sought in the school setting and an increase in the feeling that the values and beliefs stressed as important were not valuable.

Correlation coefficients for the urban lower-class group also indicated that a low acculturation in the area of politics increased the feeling that school activities were not intrinsically meaningful. It was also found that for the subjects in this group, low acculturation in the areas of family, politics, and religion increased the feeling that the beliefs and values taught in school were not valuable. As acculturation proceeded in these areas, this feeling decreased.

Analysis of the relationships between acculturation and alienation among the subjects in the rural group are presented in Table No. 3. This analysis indicated that low acculturation in the areas of education and politics increased the general educational alienation among the subjects in this group. As acculturation in this area increased, the feeling of general alienation from school decreased. The findings also revealed a positive relationship between the family and religion factors of acculturation and the powerlessness factor of alienation. This indicated that as there was an acceptance of the beliefs and values presented by the dominant society concerning politics and religion, there was an increase in the feeling that the students' behaviors could not obtain for them the rewards they sought in the school setting.

The findings also indicated a negative relationship between the politics factor of acculturation and the self-estrangement factor of alienation. This indicated that low acculturation in the area of politics increased the feeling that school activities were not intrinsically meaningful. As the subjects accepted the be-

Table 2

Analysis of the Subtest Measures of Acculturation and Alienation for the Urban Lower-Class Sample

Acculturation			Alienation		
	Composite	Powerlessness	Normlessness	Self-estrangement	Isolation
Composite					
Education					-.193
Family	.187	.200			.150
Politics	-.184			-.228	-.175
Economics					
Recreation					
Religion					-.171
Health					

Significance at .05 level = .138
Significance at .01 level = .181

liefs and values they came into contact with in school, this feeling decreased. This analysis also revealed that low composite acculturation and low acculturation in the areas of education, politics, recreation, and health increased the feeling among this group of subjects that the beliefs, values, and goals stressed in school were not valuable. Conversely, as there was an increase in acculturation in these areas, there was a decrease in the feeling of isolation.

Relationship Between Achievement and Alienation

Analysis of the relationships between composite achievement and composite alienation failed to show any statistically significant relationship for the total sample. Further analysis found no statistically significant relationships between these variables for any of the three separate groups. An analysis of the correlation between the composite achievement and the factors of alienation indicated no statistically significant relationships for the total sample, the urban middle-class sample, nor the urban lower-class sample. However, a statistically significant correlation was found between composite achievement and self-estrangement in the rural group of subjects. This correlation was positive and significant at the .05 level of probability (Table No. 4). This relationship indicates that as achievement increased there was an increase in the feeling that school activities were not in-

Table 3

Analysis of the Subtest Measures of Acculturation and Alienation for the Rural Sample

Acculturation		Alienation			
	Composite	Powerlessness	Normlessness	Self-estrangement	Isolation
Composite					-.216
Education	-.160				-.270
Family		.165			
Politics	-.179			-.141	-.238
Economics					
Recreation					-.172
Religion		.145			
Health					-.197

Significance at .05 level = .138
Significance at .01 level = .181

Table 4

Analysis of Achievement and Alienation Measures

Alienation		Achievement		
	Total Group	Urban Middle Class	Urban Lower Class	Rural
Composite	-.063	-.036	-.084	.078
Powerlessness	-.053	.034	-.080	.054
Normlessness	-.033	-.013	-.133	.046
Self-estrangement	-.001	-.051	-.026	.151
Isolation	-.102	-.019	-.001	-.042

Levels of Significance

Total Group	.05 level = .088
Total Group	.01 level = .115
Urban Middle Class	.05 level = .205
Urban Middle Class	.01 level = .267
Urban Lower Class	.05 level = .138
Urban Lower Class	.01 level = .181
Rural Group	.05 level = .138
Rural Group	.01 level = .181

Table 5

Analysis of Achievement and Acculturation

Acculturation		Achievement		
	Total Group	Urban Middle Class	Urban Lower Class	Rural
Composite	-.006	-.315	-.039	.028
Education	.009	-.287	-.018	-.005
Family	-.045	-.131	-.058	-.061
Politics	.019	-.286	.050	.008
Economics	-.015	-.179	-.018	-.009
Recreation	-.044	-.241	-.121	.045
Religion	-.035	-.228	.022	.056
Health	.033	-.280	.026	.081

Levels of Significance

Total Group	.05 level = .088
Total Group	.01 level = .115
Urban Middle Class	.05 level = .205
Urban Middle Class	.01 level = .267
Urban Lower Class	.05 level = .
Urban Lower Class	.01 level = .
Rural Group	.05 level = .138
Rural Group	.01 level = .181

trinsically meaningful. There was also a decrease in the student's pride in his work.

Analysis of the correlation between composite achievement and the factors of alienation, using mean scores, for the total sample of students, revealed that achievement was negatively correlated with powerlessness at the .05 level, with self-estrangement at the .05 level, and with isolation at the .01 level (Table No. 4). This indicated that low achievement increased the feeling of powerlessness, the feeling of self-estrangement, and the feeling of isolation.

Relationship Between Acculturation and Achievement

An analysis of the relationship between composite achievement and composite acculturation failed to show any statistically significant relationship between these two variables for the total sample, for the urban lower-class group, and for the rural group. A significant negative relationship between these two variables was found for the urban middle-class group (Table No. 5). This relationship, significant at the .01 level, indicates that as general acculturation increases, achievement decreases.

An analysis of the relationship between composite achievement and the factors of acculturation revealed no statistically significant relationships for the total sample, the urban lower-class group, and the rural group. However, significant relationships were found to exist for the urban middle-class group. For this group, composite achievement correlated negatively with politics, education, and health at the .01 level of significance, and with recreation and religion at the .05 level of significance (Table No. 5). This indicated that as acculturation increased in the areas of politics, education, health, recreation, and religion, there was a decrease in composite achievement.

Relationship Between Teacher Expectation and Alienation

A correlation analysis of the relationship between teacher expectations and composite alienation for the total sample revealed a positive relationship that was significant at the .01 level. This indicated that as teachers of Spanish-American students increased their expectations for middle-class behaviors, there was an increase in the students' feeling of general alienation from school. No significant relationship was found between these two variables for the urban middle-class and rural groups. However, a negative relationship, significant at the .05 level, was found for the urban lower-class group (Table No. 6). This indicated that as teachers of the urban lower-class Spanish-American students increased their expectations for middle-class behaviors, there was a decrease in the general feelings of alienation among the students. Conversely, low expectations increased the students' feelings of general alienation.

Analysis of the relationships between teacher expectations and the factors of alienation for the total sample revealed that as teachers increased their expectations for middle-class behaviors, there was an increase in the students' feelings that their behaviors could not attain for them the rewards they sought, an increase in the feelings that school activities were not intrinsically meaningful, and an increase in the feelings that the beliefs and values considered unimportant in school were of no value (Table No. 6).

Relationship Between Teacher Expectation and Acculturation

Correlation analysis of the relationships between teacher expectations and composite acculturation did not reveal any signifi-

Table 6

Analysis of Teacher Expectations and Alienation

Alienation		Teacher Expectations		
	Total Group	Urban Middle Class	Urban Lower Class	Rural
Composite	.522	.333	.609	-.348
Powerlessness	.393	-.379	-.295	-.781
Normlessness	.169	.172	.204	-.136
Self-estrangement	.435	-.163	.041	-.494
Isolation	.615	-.604	.135	.228

Levels of Significance

Total Group	.05 level	= .349
Total Group	.01 level	= .449
Urban Middle Class	.05 level	= .707
Urban Middle Class	.01 level	= .834
Urban Lower Class	.05 level	= .553
Urban Lower Class	.01 level	= .684
Rural Group	.05 level	= .602
Rural Group	.01 level	= .735

Table 7

Analysis of Teacher Expectations and Acculturation

Acculturation		Teacher Expectations		
	Total Group	Urban Middle Class	Urban Lower Class	Rural
Composite	-.064	-.220	.009	-.061
Education	-.191	-.230	.226	.182
Family	-.110	-.290	-.283	-.397
Politics	-.004	-.508	.197	.161
Economics	-.005	-.174	-.159	.089
Recreation	-.047	.317	-.113	-.374
Religion	-.063	-.470	.017	.051
Health	-.180	-.242	.179	-.162

Levels of Significance

Total Group	.05 level = .349
Total Group	.01 level = .449
Urban Middle Class	.05 level = .707
Urban Middle Class	.01 level = .834
Urban Lower Class	.05 level = .553
Urban Lower Class	.01 level = .684
Rural Group	.05 level = .602
Rural Group	.01 level = .735

Table 8

Analysis of Teacher Expectations and Achievement

Achievement		Teacher Expectations		
	Total	Urban Middle Class	Urban Lower Class	Rural
	.331	-.151	.479	.369

Levels of Significance

Total Group	.05 level = .349
Total Group	.01 level = .449
Urban Middle Class	.05 level = .707
Urban Middle Class	.01 level = .834
Urban Lower Class	.05 level = .553
Urban Lower Class	.01 level = .684
Rural Group	.05 level = .602
Rural Group	.01 level = .735

cant relationship between these variables either for the total group or for any of the three separate groups (Table No. 7). No significant relationships were found between teacher expectations and the factors of acculturation for any of the groups (Table No. 7). These findings suggest that teacher expectations are made without regard to the beliefs, values, and cultural experiences of the Spanish-American students.

While conducting the study, the question arose whether teachers made different types of expectations based on the achievement levels of Spanish-American students. This question was prompted by the fact that no significant relationships were found between teacher expectations and acculturation. The idea arose that perhaps teachers base their expectations on achievement rather than on acculturation. Analyses of the relationship between these two variables yielded no significant relationships for any of the groups (Table No. 8). These findings suggest that teachers make expectations without regard to the achievement level of students, as well as without regard to their cultural differences.

Since the sample used in the study was categorized in terms of their socioeconomic status (SES), the decision was made to analyze the relationships between the SES and the other variables. An analysis of the relationship between SES of the subjects and alienation yielded various significant relationships. The findings revealed positive relationships, significant at the .01 level, between the SES of the subjects and composite alienation, powerlessness, self-estrangement, and isolation (Table No. 9). These findings suggest that as the socioeconomic status of the subjects increased, so did their alienation from school.

An analysis of the relationships between SES and achievement and between SES and teacher expectations failed to show relationships that were statistically significant.

IMPLICATIONS

The findings of this study indicate that significant relationships exist between acculturation, achievement, teacher expectations, and alienation which have important implications for the education of Spanish-American children. The situation of the Spanish American presents special problems for educators. It is educators who must rectify the shortcomings of a system of edu-

Table 9

Analysis of Socioeconomic Status and Alienation

Alienation		Socioeconomic Status
	Total	
Composite	.182	
Powerlessness	.169	
Normlessness	.078	
Self-estrangement	.140	
Isolation	.198	

Level of Significance .05 level = .088
Level of Significance .01 level = .115

cation that thus far has failed to maximize the full potential of the Spanish-American students.

Heretofore, it has been the belief that eradication of language problems and an increase in general acculturation would solve the educational problems of the Spanish-American students. The results of this study indicate that this is a faulty assumption, or to say the least, a very limited one. This study indicates that there exists a great need for further study and research on holding and retaining these students perhaps through more intense participation by the Spanish American in the educational endeavor, restructuring of the curriculum, reorganization of school activities, and a differential approach to the training of school personnel.

This study revealed enough significant relationships between acculturation and alienation to have deep implications for the education of Spanish-American students. The overall results of this study indicate that it is not very profitable to consider the acculturation and alienation of Spanish-American students in general terms. It was not until these variables were divided into their component factors that they became meaningful in their educational implications. The fact that a composite measure of alienation is not very meaningful implies that until educators are able to see acculturation and alienation meaningfully in their various factors, they will not be able to comprehend and get to the basic educational problems of Spanish-American students. Consideration of these variables in general terms presupposes educators to neglect the interrelationships between the factors of acculturation and alienation and thus pass over many problems as being insignificant.

It was observed from the findings that the values and beliefs in the area of politics (importance attributed to taxes, policemen, judges, courts, governors, senators, and the like) and education (importance attributed to school attendance, school activities, finishing school, and the like) were negatively related to a general feeling of alienation and feelings that school activities were not rewarding or valuable. This implies that as there is an increase in the acceptance by the Spanish-American student of the dominant values and beliefs concerning education and politics, there is a decrease in the feeling of alienation. The greatest exposure to these values and beliefs comes from contact with them in school. This implies that educators must place more emphasis in these areas in preparing programs, curricula, and experiences in the school setting. Spanish-American children must become more involved in programs in which they can achieve. They must have experiences that will expose them to, and will confirm their faith in, these values and beliefs.

Relationships observed between the family and recreation factors of acculturation and alienation were felt to have important implications for education. It was observed that acculturation in the area of beliefs concerning the family leads to an increase in feelings that their behaviors cannot obtain the goals and reinforcements they seek. This indicates that detachment from his family's beliefs and values concerning familial relationships leaves the student confused and insecure.

It was also found that as students acculturate to the beliefs about recreation in the dominant society, there is an increase in the feeling that socially unapproved means are justifiable and necessary to attain the all-important goals and values in the school situation. This factor, together with the relationship between beliefs about the family and a feeling of powerlessness, indicates the insecurity that Spanish-American students feel when they detach themselves from their traditional values, beliefs, and ideals. Thus, feeling powerless in the face of competition in the school situation, many students may rely on socially unapproved means to lessen the threat and to save face.

One thing that may prove fruitful in solving this problem is to provide more involvement of parents and students in planning educational programs and extracurricular activities. Involvement could do much to reorient the parents' values and beliefs and to provide support for the student's new beliefs. This could serve to create a merger of the two generations' beliefs concerning familial relationships and recreation. This could also help to give students more respect for their culture and beliefs and to afford them more security as they continue to acculturate. As the situation now stands, accepting the dominant society's values in these areas often implicates them in the role of traitor to their culture, their family, and their friends. This, in part, can explain the general guilty feelings experienced by people found in the process of acculturation.

Educators could also involve students and their parents in new organizations, extracurricular activities, and educational experiences that could serve as mechanisms of displacement. This would serve as a means to bring the family together on their educational beliefs and also as objects to which they can transfer their cathexes.

This study also revealed that the low composite acculturation of Spanish-American students and their traditional beliefs about education, politics, religion, and health serve to arouse feelings that the goals and values considered important in school are not important or desirable. As these students accept the dominant culture's values and beliefs in these areas, their feelings of isolation decrease; then they begin to see school as full of rewarding and valuable experiences and activities. However, the problem still exists of how to close the gap between the cultures' ideas to achieve a rapid and effective relationship.

To achieve a synthesis, educators do not have to condemn the pupils' values and beliefs nor must they feel that the values and goals typically valued in school are indispensable. A synthesis in the personality and the educational endeavors of Spanish-American students can best be arrived at through biculturalism. This implies that educators must find a way not to treat Spanish-American students as if they were children of the dominant society. Educators must realize the students' special talents and their special attributes and learn to capitalize on these. Instead of being made to feel foreign, different, or inferior, educators must realize that to function adequately in an Anglo society, Spanish-American students do not have to be turned into "little

Anglos." Educators must realize and act on the assumption that there are good aspects in the Spanish-American culture and that these students can function adequately, if not better, if they can retain these as part of their heritage. Biculturalism would mean a merger of the traditional aspects with the compatible aspects of the dominant society. Biculturalism would mean an increase in self-respect, self-confidence, and the feeling of self-worth. However, the achievement of biculturalism demands the development of new approaches to teaching, reorganization of the existing curriculum, and the training and retraining of personnel with a new orientation. This new orientation would imply a background and exposure to psychological, sociological, and anthropological theory and understanding of the relationship between culture and behavior.

The findings of this study indicate that not many relationships exist between achievement and alienation. The fact that only one significant relationship was found between these two variables indicates that the large dropout rate, the insecurity, confusion, and frustration suffered by Spanish-American students is not due to a lack of achievement as many educators have heretofore assumed. However, a significant relationship between these two variables indicates that as achievement goes up, there is an increase in the feeling that the school activities are not intrinsically rewarding or meaningful. Heretofore, the assumption has been that Spanish Americans are low achievers because they lack the capacity, the skills, or the motivation. It was felt that by means of acculturation and eradication of language problems, educational achievement could be increased and the high rate of dropouts could be reduced. However, this study indicates that this has been a faulty and overstretched assumption. This study found no significant differences in achievement between the three groups. However, it was found that for middle-class Spanish-American students there existed a negative relationship between acculturation and achievement. Consequently, one must conclude that the alienation of these students is due to the inflexible curricula, programs, and activities which are not geared to the needs and experiences of these children.

Up to now the emphasis in Spanish-American education has been on the technical skills and technical readiness. This study indicates that the focus has been misplaced. The findings of this study indicate that psychological readiness is as important as technical readiness, if not more important. Spanish-American students have learned to memorize and recite the facts and figures but have still failed to attain an education. Psychological defiance, psychological unreadiness, and psychological blocks to learning have been detrimental to the learning of values, beliefs, and feelings. Educators must thus realize that effective learning and evaluative learning cannot and will not proceed in the most effective manner until these students are psychologically ready.

Another significant finding of this study is that acculturation alone is not sufficient to insure achievement. This study revealed a significant negative relationship between acculturation and achievement. It was found that as acculturation in the areas of the family and politics increased, the achievement of urban middle-class Spanish-American students decreased. This seems to indicate that beliefs about education and politics held by the dominant society are not reflected in the schools. These findings further imply that previous assumptions that acculturation is a cure-all for educational problems of Spanish-American students need a new orientation. These findings again point to the need for educators to reassess their assumptions and the programs devised to assist the Spanish American.

Relationships between teacher expectations and the alienation of Spanish-American students revealed by the findings of this study also indicate grave implications for educators. A positive relationship was found between teacher expectations and feelings of powerlessness, self-estrangement, and isolation for the total sample. A negative relationship was found between teacher expectations and powerlessness for the rural group. This would seem to indicate that Spanish-American students feel powerless in school and that the lower the acculturation the more intense the feeling. This feeling of powerlessness can be attributed to their lack of familiarity with the system and lack of commitment to the values and goals stressed in the situation. Upon entering the system, these students need a definition of the situation and a structuring of activities. Therefore, the students who are less familiar and less committed need more guidance to calm their fears and insecurities.

Regardless of the need for a definition of the situation discussed above and the need for guidance felt by these students, this study revealed that teachers make expectations and demands without reference to the acculturation level and the achievement level of the students. It seems that teachers have set expectations of their pupils regardless of their students' values, beliefs, needs, and capabilities. It was further observed that the less acculturated and the less predisposed students are of fulfilling these expectations, the stronger these expectations are. This serves to create more insecurity, conflict, and indignation in these students. This again points to the need for teachers to be trained in the psychological, sociological, and anthropological relationships between culture and behavior. Furthermore, it points to the grave need to have teachers that have the technical skills to develop and adapt materials and curriculum programs to fit the needs and capabilities of these students. While many teachers fail to recognize the differences and special problems of these students, there are many who do but lack the technical skills to solve them.

The findings of this study revealed that the higher the socioeconomic status and acculturation of these students, the higher the alienation. It was found that these students found the school activities, values, and goals less rewarding, intrinsically less meaningful, and less valuable. These findings serve to negate the belief that Spanish-American children dislike and distrust school because of their lack of acculturation. These findings serve further to point out that it is not that these students lack acculturation and lack technical skills, but that there exists a grave need to develop and study the effects of new programs, new materials, new methods of teaching, and new methods of training personnel that can psychologically get these students ready and involved in the activities of the school.

Alienation per se has not received much attention in the education of Spanish Americans. The high dropout rate, the lack of achievement, the lack of interest, and the lack of motivation among this segment of our student population suggest that this phenomena warrants more attention. This phenomena further suggests the need for new approaches to the education of Spanish-American students.

The traditional middle-class-oriented system of education has to a high degree failed to motivate, challenge, hold, and adequately prepare these students. Some programs and techniques have been developed which have helped to eliminate many language problems and to increase cognitive learning. However, by and large, these programs have been of a remedial nature. They have focused on relieving the symptom rather than curing the cause. Alienation is not bred by a lack of achievement, but rather by cultural conflicts, confusion, insecurity, and meaninglessness. Low achievement is only a symptom of alienation. Programs to combat alienation need to involve the Spanish-American students both cognitively and effectively; they need to involve them physically as well as psychologically. Educational programs for these children should not seek to eradicate their beliefs, values, experiences, and customs. These programs and curricula should seek instead to help them fuse their beliefs, values, and experiences with the orientations, attitudes, and skills they need in order to function effectively in the mainstream of American society.

NOTES

[1] Nathaniel Hickerson, *Education for Alienation* (Englewood Cliffs, N. J.: Prentice-Hall, Inc., 1966), p. 9.

[2] Celia S. Heller, *Mexican American Youth: Forgotten Youth at the Crossroads* (New York: Random House, Inc., 1967), p. 4.

[3] Donald J. Bogue, *The Population of the United States* (Glencoe, Ill.: The Free Press, 1959), p. 372.

[4] Herbert B. Wilson, "Evaluation of the Influence of Education Programs on Mexican Americans." Paper presented at the National Conference on Educational Opportunities for Mexican Americans, Austin, Texas, April, 1968, pp. 3–5.

[5] Heller, *op. cit.*, p. 46.

[6] The NEA-Tucson Survey on the Teaching of Spanish to the Spanish-Speaking, *The Invisible Minority* (Washington: National Education Association, Department of Rural Education, 1966).

[7] Leo Grebler, *The Schooling Gap* (Los Angeles: University of California Graduate School of Business Administration, March, 1967).

Recruiting and Training Teachers for Spanish-Speaking Children in the Southwest*

HERSCHEL T. MANUEL

THE RECRUITMENT AND TRAINING of teachers for Spanish-speaking children is part of the general problem of providing an adequate and competent staff for public and private schools. Year after year new teachers must be found to fill positions left vacant or to expand the teaching staff. Year after year new personnel must be trained. Year after year retraining must be provided for teachers in service and for former teachers who reenter the profession.

The continuing problem of providing qualified teachers is now aggravated by the imbalance of supply and demand. The number of qualified teachers is far short of present needs. For example, a recent issue of the Texas State Teachers Association's *Texas Schools* carried a statement that the state is faced with the worst teacher shortage in twenty-five years. The shortage over the nation appears to be greatest in the elementary school. The October 9, 1966, issue of the *NEA Reporter* reports an estimated shortage between 37,700 and 66,500 beginning teachers in elementary schools. This shortage may be expected to increase

* From *School and Society*, March 30, 1968, pp. 211–214. Reprinted with permission.

as education is extended downward unless heroic efforts are made to improve the situation. There is evidence that the education of five-year-olds will soon be accepted generally as the responsibility of public education, and that in increasing numbers four-year-olds (at least the disadvantaged) will be included. Persons of goodwill may well pray, "God speed the day."

Although the profession of teaching attracts many able men and women toward a career in teaching, the supply of fully qualified and experienced teachers is likely to remain for some years below the number needed. For many, teaching is only a temporary occupation preliminary to the rearing of children (in the case of women) or to other employment.

The shortage of qualified personnel suggests two remedial measures: (1) the provision of help in the schoolroom for routine jobs and for such instructional activities as can be carried on by untrained and partially trained assistants under supervision (in order to allow the fully qualified personnel to render their best service); (2) the making of teaching a more attractive profession.

One can easily think of four ways to make teaching more attractive: (1) by providing improved working conditions, with standard physical plant, equipment, teaching materials, and the like; (2) by assuring a reasonable working load (for example, in the number of pupils to be taught), and by providing assistants both at the clerical level and the professional level (counselors, for example); (3) by improving the public concept of the profession of teaching, and in some cases the teacher's own self-concept as a teacher; (4) by adjusting salaries to make them more nearly competitive with salaries in other areas which require an equivalent period of preparation.

Turning now to the problem of providing qualified teachers for Spanish-speaking children, one may observe first that the supply of these teachers is influenced by the same factors as those which influence the supply of teachers in general. The basic qualifications of the good teacher of Spanish-speaking children are precisely those of other good teachers — superior native ability, mastery of subject matter, understanding of human nature, broad general education, satisfactory teaching skills, well-adjusted personality, dedication to the work, and the like. In other words, the problem is part of the general problem of staffing schools, and it differs only because of the special needs which the teacher of Spanish-speaking children must meet.

What are these special needs? How does the learning of Spanish-speaking children differ from that of other children?

In discussing Spanish-speaking children, one must ever be mindful that one is dealing with an extremely varied population and with schools which differ widely. Like other children, these children vary in native ability from feebleminded to genius, in living standards from very low to superior culture, in economic status from extreme poverty to wealth. In language, many are comfortably bilingual when they enter school, many know Spanish only, many have a limited knowledge of English, and some (strange as it may seem) speak English only. The schools in which they are enrolled vary in financial resources, in the proportion of Spanish-speaking and other children enrolled, in the background and preparation of the children who attend, and in the level at which instruction is offered. "The Spanish-speaking child" turns out to be a number of very different children and the school which he attends turns out to be a number of very different schools.

The stimulating report of the NEA Tucson survey, *The Invisible Minority,* contains a statement which one may lift from its setting and generalize: ". . . different schools present different problems . . . and thus tend to require somewhat different solutions." [1]

Not all is discouraging. Large numbers of Spanish-speaking children have understanding and capable teachers, make normal or superior progress, and are happy in their school work. Through the years great progress has been made.

However, we still see too many children retarded in their school work, too many with low academic achievement, too many dropped out of school, and too many with serious personality problems. We must improve the educational process and recruit and train teachers to carry it forward effectively.

The problem of providing qualified teachers for Spanish-speaking children — aside from the problem of schools in general — appears to be more a matter of training than of recruitment. Even the provision of teachers for the disadvantaged appears less difficult than one might expect. Additional remuneration is probably unnecessary; as an assistant superintendent points out, a monetary bonus might attract "persons interested more in money than in children." This administrator finds that geographical location is a factor in placing qualified teachers. Teachers prefer assignments close to their residence, which may be far from the schools in which most of the disadvantaged children are enrolled. Another administrator, a director of personnel, takes a similar view of additional remuneration as an incentive: "We have no additional remuneration for the teachers of the disadvantaged, but . . . I find no more problem in staffing in this area than I do in the area where the children are not disadvantaged — incentives are certainly not material."

Although teachers in general have retarded children in their classes, teachers of Spanish-speaking children need special help in this area because of the large proportion of the children who are retarded and because of the special difficulties which contribute to their slow progress.

Retardation in any group is in part a result of native endowment. In part, however, the retardation of Spanish-speaking children is a result of the disadvantage which many suffer. The level of achievement reached by any child at any year of age is determined by his inherited capacity and the conditions under which he develops. The cultural poverty of the disadvantaged home lacks the stimulus to normal intellectual growth, and quite naturally the reduced rate of growth increases the gap between his achievement and that of others of equal potential who develop under more favorable conditions.

There are two ways to reduce the retardation which results from the disadvantages of the home: (1) to remove the disadvantages, and (2) to compensate for them outside the home. Removing the disadvantages of the home is a socioeconomic problem of the community as a whole. In this process the school can play an important part through adult education, but for the foreseeable future large numbers of children will continue to enter the school from disadvantaged homes. The task of the school is to compensate as far as possible for the cultural deficiences of the home. At best the school can compensate only in part, and what it can do is limited by the time in the child's life when the school is given the opportunity.

Children whose home language is Spanish, advantaged and disadvantaged alike, are handicapped by having to learn a second language and to do most of their school work in that language. They have other difficulties also, which for the moment one may group together as cultural conflicts.

These special difficulties of Spanish-speaking children are compelling reasons why formal education should be extended downward. Earlier entrance into school will enable a large number to make normal progress with English-speaking children beginning in first grade, and for this blessed event we should prepare. Earlier school enrollment will change the situation radically for many children. It will require the development of materials and methods adapted to children of the lower ages. It will require also extensive revisions of the materials and methods which have been developed for Spanish-speaking children who have entered school without these earlier learning experiences. Its impact will be felt throughout the elementary school.

One of the important specifics in the training of teachers of Spanish-speaking children is the problem of policy and philosophy. Trained teachers should have a clear concept of the goals toward which Mexican Americans are striving. Perhaps everyone can agree that one objective is the development to the maximum of the capacities of every child; but some may be ill-prepared to follow this objective through. To do so requires the transfer of attention from groups to individual children. It means teachers must be prepared for an individualization of teaching which schools in general have never mastered.

A second objective depends upon the concept of the position which Spanish-speaking people should have in the larger group. One point of view stresses strong group ties and places emphasis on group relations. Another advocates the weakening of divisions on ancestral lines and the preparation of all children for full membership in the larger community. This view holds that every child should be prepared to participate freely and effectively in the business, industry, commerce, government, and community life in general, with equal rights and responsibilities working for the common good.

In this point of view, the central problem is not one of subgroup identity and power and of the relation of minority and majority; it is the problem of building a united community. It is not to make all children Anglos; it is to make children of every origin members of the new community which we are building in the Southwest.

To be sure, every child may well be proud of the great achievements of his ancestors, but the major goal of education is to help him find his identity in the community as a whole. Exaggeration of group differences and of past conflicts can only be divisive. A child may properly say, "I am of Mexican [English, German, or other] ancestry" — or he may be blissfully ignorant of the national origin of his ancestors — but he should be able to say with a feeling of reality, "I am an American. This is *my* community. This is *my* state. This is *my* country." Then in cooperation with others, "This is our country."

This point of view has an immediate application to the teaching of language, making efficiency in the use of English the primary language problem in the education of Spanish-speaking children. But this does not mean that Spanish should be neglected. On the contrary, the Spanish-speaking child has a built-in language resource which is valuable both in advancing his own education and in contributing to the public welfare. The teaching of Spanish should begin with the first enrollment and continue through the grades. It should be a functional kind of Spanish, not devoted exclusively to mechanics of the language or to literature, but directed toward the mastery which can be acquired only by teaching "content" in various subject-matter areas. If teaching Spanish means a longer day and additional personnel, schools must be prepared to pay that price.

If it were possible, all teachers in schools of the Southwest in which both Spanish-speaking and English-speaking pupils are enrolled should be bilingual. If children of other home languages are enrolled, they should know those languages also.

But this degree of language competence for all teachers is obviously impossible if other requirements of a teacher's preparation are to be met. In many cases a compromise may have to be made by providing teachers of Spanish who are expert in that language and acquainted in some degree with English, and teachers of English who are expert in that language and acquainted in some degree with Spanish. Naturally, most experts will be native speakers of the language in question, but not exclusively. The provision of competent teaching in both languages will often require a form of team teaching in which one teacher is primarily responsible for Spanish and another for English.

Although a great deal is known about the teaching of language, there is still uncertainty as to the best way of teaching both languages together. As a matter of fact, there is probably no single best way for all situations. Additional experimentation, such as that carried on by Theodore Andersson and Thomas D. Horn, and a number of others elsewhere, is needed. But experimentation as contrasted with mere experience in this area is difficult, expensive, and time-consuming. It requires careful supervision with scientific controls and painstaking measurement of results. One must be patient and not seek quick answers, or rush to embrace the new simply because it is new.

A major unsolved problem in dealing with young children whose home language is Spanish is that of providing sufficient contact with and participation in spoken English. In 1938 the Office of Education published a bulletin by J. L. Meriam entitled *Learning English Incidentally: A Study of Bilingual Children*. That intriguing title expresses precisely how young children should learn much of their language — incidentally as a by-product of the activities in which they engage and of their communication in these activities. But ways must be developed to increase such activities and turn them toward language acquisition. Assistants who can work with children other than those being instructed at the moment by the teacher offer a partial solution. Tapes, television, and other mechanical assistance may provide a partial answer. But in all of these there must be careful systematic work toward some goal. Just having children play or look at pictures and listen to tapes can be only a kind of merry-go-round rather than something that carries a child forward.

Somewhere in the training of teachers for schools in the Southwest, attention must be given to the characteristics of disadvantaged people in general and to the cultural traits of the Spanish-speaking population. Again, however, individual differences must be emphasized. It would be a grave error to substitute for the study of the child himself a study of his group, but a knowledge of the conditions that are frequently found helps the teacher and counselor to discover the traits and the difficulties of individual children.

What can one say about the conflict of cultures? Of course, knowledge and appreciation of the culture of our neighbors and the contributions which they have made to our common life is of value. At the same time, there is no need to be greatly concerned with preserving any aspect of a culture on the basis that it is hereditary. One should see himself as inheritor of the culture of many peoples and of all the ages. It is a privilege to choose freely from the past and to develop a way of life that best fits the present and future needs in a world that is constantly changing.

Not only understanding of the situation, but ways of moving forward must be sought. The problems are obviously difficult and complex, requiring action by many different people in different areas. Partly by way of summary and partly for emphasis, the following seven recommendations for action are listed:

1. Work toward a reduction of the teacher shortage in general —

    a) by raising salaries to make them competitive with the salaries of other occupations;

    b) by providing good working conditions in school plant, equipment, educational materials, and the like;

    c) by assigning teachers a reasonable working load with clerical and professional help to enable them to do a thorough professional job;

    d) by improving the concept of the teacher as a member of a learned profession.

(The primary responsibility for these general measures rests upon legislators, executives, and the public in general, for they alone can give the schools the support which they need.)

2. Promote programs in which school systems cooperate with colleges and universities in the training and retraining of teachers who will have both the general qualifications of good teachers and the special qualifications required for effective teaching of Spanish-speaking children.

3. Continue and extend experimentation, with careful scientific controls and measurement of results, to improve policies, materials, and methods of teaching disadvantaged children, children whose home language is Spanish, children of different cultural background, children who enter school at varying ages, children of different native endowment, children of different

levels of achievement in Spanish and English, and children who are taught in groups with varying proportions of children whose home language is Spanish or English.

4. Continue emphasis on English in preparation for full participation in the community at large, giving earlier and more extensive experiences with English in interesting activities — experimenting to find more effective ways of using tapes and other mechanical aids, experimenting also to extend experiences in the use of English through paid and volunteer English-speaking assistants, working under careful supervision.

5. Develop the home language of the Spanish-speaking child, beginning with the child's first enrollment in school. The schools have been right in assuming that the major language problem of the Spanish-speaking child is the mastery of English, but they have not been right in neglecting his native language. Spanish should be taught in all grades of the elementary school. Whether the six-year-old who knows no English should read first in Spanish is a question on which we need careful experimentation.

6. Extend education downward to include the five-year-old and, at least for disadvantaged children, the four-year-old — possibly even the three-year-old. Appropriate early experience with English will increase the possibility of normal progress with English-speaking children. Early enrollment will compensate in part — but only in part — for the deficiencies of the home. Until one can break the chains of poverty which enslave children, the achievement of many will continue to lag behind the possibilities which were theirs when they were newborn.

7. Finally, cultivate in the school and in the community the concept of a united community in which every person participates freely and effectively for the common good, with equal rights and responsibilities for all.

The building of a united community dedicated to the welfare of all should be a major goal of civic and religious organizations, of parent-teacher associations, of educators, and of all people of goodwill. Here is the key to the solution of group tensions and cultural conflicts. Here is the motivation for dealing effectively with the special problems which we face. The building of such a community is part of the most difficult and most urgent problem of the human race — that of learning to live together — a problem still only partially solved nearly two thousand years since the command, "Thou shalt love thy neighbor as thyself."

NOTE

[1] The NEA-Tucson Survey on the Teaching of Spanish to the Spanish-Speaking, *The Invisible Minority* (Washington, D.C.: National Education Association, Department of Rural Education, 1966) , p. 26.

EDITOR'S NOTE

Since this article was first published, a reversal in the relationship of the supply of teachers and the demand for them seems to have taken place so that in many areas there was an apparent surplus of teachers by 1970. However, this development in no way invalidates the author's main thesis that more fully trained and qualified teachers are needed for Mexican American children as well as children of other culturally different groups.

Preparing Teachers
for Mexican-American Children*

THOMAS P. CARTER

Nations may put on blustering shows of strength to conceal political weakness, erect grand facades to conceal shabby backyards, and profess peace while secretly arming for conquest, but how they take care of their children tells unerringly who they are.[1]

The most personally disturbing part of this introductory quotation by George Bereday is the last phrase. The serious undereducation of Mexican Americans implies numerous unpleasant things about present and past Anglo society. We have not taken very good care of some of our children. In spite of our "professtations" and grandiose statements concerning the goals of democratic education, the facts glare in our collective face. Innumerable social forces have belatedly brought the grievous conditions of this major sector of our population to society's serious attention. Governing elements of that society are slowly but surely directing the agencies and institutions under their control to take steps to improve the minority's status. The school is the only primary social institution directly under the authority of

* Prepared for the Conference on Teacher Education for Mexican Americans, February, 1969. Sponsored by ERIC Clearinghouse on Rural Education and Small Schools.

193

the community and as such is being directed to assume a major role in these efforts. Specifically, educational institutions must radically improve the academic achievement and school attainment of children of Mexican descent, thus providing them with the skills and credentials essential to climb the social ladder. Educators willingly accept this role. However, problems do exist. Schoolmen often do not know how best to accomplish this goal; they do not comprehend the complexity of the problem; and they often assume too great a share of the responsibility for creating it. Educators tend to give too much credence to the exaggerated statements of both vocal minority-group spokesmen and members of the "establishment." The school may be becoming the scapegoat of southwestern society. Too many see the school as principally or solely responsible for the disadvantaged status of the minority. Unfortunately, very few educators or laymen recognize that the school reflects and is a microcosm of the society it serves. Indeed, the backyards of southwestern communities are shabby, to paraphrase Professor Bereday. However, the total society, including formal educational institutions, created and perpetuated the shabbiness — the subordinate Mexican American "caste." Whereas the school has accepted its role in remedying the situation, one must not assume that it can accomplish the task alone. As the total community created the problem, it must cooperate to resolve it; the school unsupported by other agencies and institutions can accomplish little.

School board members and administrators faced with community pressure to accept the "guilt" for the minority's socio-economic plight often "pass the buck." They merely transfer the responsibility for the Mexican Americans' "school failure" to a single institutional ingredient — the teacher. It is regularly argued that the qualities and capabilities of southwestern teachers are at fault. The villain within the institution is the teacher; reeducate the teacher, and the Mexican American will succeed. Although all agree that teachers must be better equipped in the skill area and must better understand minority children, it is not true that this alone will radically improve the school performance of the ethnic group. As is the case in general society, numerous forces are at play within the school. To improve the teacher without modifying other institutional elements is of little avail. Quality teachers plus other institutional changes can create the quality of schooling essential to contribute to other forces leading to raised Mexican American group status. A multitude of socioeconomic and cultural conditions hold the minority subordinate; these same forces must help raise the group to parity with other ethnic groups. Regardless of the complexity of the situation, programs to improve the capabilities of the teacher are at least steps in the right direction.

APPROACHES TO SOLVE THE PROBLEM

The type of approach or orientation taken by schools is crucial in determining the kind of teachers required and the nature of programs to prepare them. Educators have three major alternative approaches theoretically open to accomplish the goal of a better-educated Mexican American. The three avenues for action correspond to an equal number of "causes" of low school and societal achievement. The first orientation perceives the Mexican American culture and the socialization it provides its children as being principally responsible. This is the very prevalent "cultural deprivation" or "disadvantaged" position. The logical action by the school in this case would seem to be "change the child" — make him as much like average middle-class children as possible. A second position argues that conditions existing within the school itself produce the undereducated population. The remedy becomes "change the institution." Finally, there are those who see the nature of the rather distinctive southwestern social systems as being responsible, the contention being that the agricultural economy and caste-like communities provide only limited opportunity for the minority. If this is the case, the school conceivably could encourage changes in the community. This threefold division of "causes" of Mexican American low achievement in school and society is oversimplified, as are the three "solutions." In actuality we are not dealing with distinct causes or cures. Suffice it to say, for the purpose of this paper, that causal relationships exist among: (1) diverse Mexican American subcultures and subsocieties, (2) school systems and the social climates they foster, and (3) community socioeconomic systems. All are interrelated and mutually supportive. The qualities and capabilities required of teachers for minority children are dependent on which orientation is taken by the public schools. It may well require one kind of teacher to "change the child," another to "change the institution," and still another to lead in changing the local society.

To those schoolmen who subscribe to the interpretation that the Mexican American home provides little of the experience deemed essential for school success, the solution appears clear. The "culturally deficient" Mexican American child must be artificially provided with those experiences that the middle class enjoys naturally. This is the very common, almost omnipresent, approach of compensatory education. These programs imply as objectives the reorientation and remodeling of the culturally different child in order to adjust him to the regular school — into standard school programs and curricula. Indeed, the measure of success of these efforts is the degree the "disadvantaged" become like the middle class. These objectives are to be accomplished by exposing the children to middle-class experiences and by providing remedial services when they fail to live up to the school (middle-class) norms. If this is possible, the Mexican American can be expected to be as successful (or unsuccessful) in school as are present majority-group children. Such programs entail few major institutional changes and only slight modifications in the quality or quantity of teachers. There is no clear evidence that the school can remake the ethnically distinct child into a facsimile of the "standard American child." Nor is there objective data that clearly establish that any specific compensatory or remedial program reaches its long-term objectives of sustained higher academic achievement or higher rates of participation in secondary or higher levels of schooling. Perhaps only time is lacking, and future longitudinal studies will clearly demonstrate that ESL (English as a Second Language), Head Start, remedial reading, or "cultural enrichment" will produce the kind of Mexican American who will succeed in school and society.

The *training* of teachers for compensatory and remedial programs presents far fewer problems and necessitates much less curricular reorganization at the college level than would the *education* of individuals for other and more comprehensive approaches. Many of the skills necessary for a capable compensatory or remedial teacher are essentially technical. In-depth understanding of the total teacher-learner and school-community situation would be ideal; however, it is not absolutely essential for such tasks as being an acceptable remedial teacher, using a language lab, conducting a "culturally enriching" field trip, or using the most modern overhead projector. While the distinction between *training* (how to do something — perform some skill) and the broader concept of *educating* is much oversimplified, it is here made to stress a crucial consideration. The minimal preparation of teachers to mesh with the overwhelming majority of existing school programs entails little more than technique acquisition; colleges and universities could with relative ease provide this training. In spite of this, observations in the field support the notion that very few teachers of Mexican Americans in regular, compensatory, or remedial classes have acquired even minimal quantities of the essential skills. Either the colleges have not provided the training; the teachers have not attended the programs; or if they did, the teachers have not learned what was taught. Something is amiss.

The second orientation or approach implies that conditions within schools inhibit academic achievement and encourage early dropout by Mexican Americans. Steps to remedy this situation require teaching personnel possessing comprehensive understandings not required in schools operating under the simpler compensatory education approach. It is extremely difficult to find programs that involve a conscious desire to modify substantially the school. This "adjust the school to fit the culturally different population" position finds even fewer practitioners than adherents. Quite a few educators agree that standard middle-class schools have failed many Mexican Americans. Regardless, few are able to institute programs to modify substantially curricula, teacher attitudes, school social climates, home-school relationships, or other crucial areas. Unfortunately, most present school practices and programs are approaching the stage of self-justification and self-perpetuation. Very few schools are flexible enough to adjust realistically to local situations. Only a very limited number have objectively investigated negative school social climates [2] sustained by such common conditions as cultural exclusion, fostering too-rapid Americanization, rigid tracking, curricular rigidity, rote teaching, overly rigid behavioral standards, ethnic cleavage, de facto segregation, and biased and pessimistic staffs. The limited number of educators who recognize the causative relationship between such conditions, low achievement, and early mental and physical dropout are hard pressed to improve the situation substantially. It is far simpler and much less threatening to concentrate school efforts on "phasing in" the "out of phase" Mexican Americans than it is seriously to study and change institutional factors.

However, if a school system takes this more radical avenue, it requires teachers educated to a rather sophisticated level. These teachers must be able to comprehend and grapple with the often intangible, but multitudinous, aspects of their own and others' society, culture, language, learning styles, personality, and behavior. Additionally, such teachers must understand the role and function of the school as a social institution, especially as it relates to ethnic minorities. The problems created by cross-cultural schooling and the possible remedies must be understood. In the course of the last five years, I have conducted hundreds of interviews with teachers of Mexican Americans and have observed countless classrooms. Very few teachers with the comprehensive insights necessary to cope with culturally diverse students were encountered. Most of them manifested extremely shallow and biased appraisals of the situation. Few recognized the importance of institutional factors. Of the exceptions, the majority were impotent, powerless to change institutional practices and conditions.

The education of teachers as described in the previous paragraph is a big order. Their preparation would demand substantial modifications in institutions of higher learning, a task perhaps even more difficult than that of changing lower-level schools. Regardless, if educational leadership is essentially satisfied with present school conditions, practices, and curricula, as well as with the compensatory education orientation, there is little need to educate such individuals. They would have few places to go — few school districts would employ such teachers. The teacher who is prepared to contribute to institutional self-analysis and change, if hired by districts with little desire to do either, would probably be seen as a troublemaker and a disruptive influence. He would not last long.

A third possible avenue to improve Mexican American school and societal achievement is that of using the school as an agent of directed or nondirected social change. Here the school would attempt by numerous means to change conditions in society.

The present socioeconomic systems in much of the Southwest provide only limited numbers of social slots and roles for their subordinate Mexican American populations. The very common caste-like social structures inhibit upward mobility and the high aspirations of most minority members. School and community leaders profess that job, residential, social, and political discriminations do not exist and that the ideals of America are practiced locally. Regardless, Mexican Americans learn early that the inverse is often the case. With this recognition, many correctly perceive that "Mexicans" have little chance in local society and that school perseverance and high school graduation do not guarantee them the higher social and economic status they desire. Local school boards and educators might lead the way to change these community conditions and belief patterns; however, it is very doubtful that they will, as educational leaders are too intermeshed with conservative community power elements. Further, it is doubtful that the school could accomplish much by acting independently of other institutions or counter to the mores of local society. If the teacher prepared to contribute to institutional change would find few schools desirous of his services, what of the teacher who actively attempts to change society? Very few districts would knowingly employ teachers who actively campaign for or promote the elimination of job discrimination, de facto school or residential segregation, or "five o'clock social segregation."

NEEDED: A NEW BREED OF TEACHERS

Without a clear understanding of the interrelated causes and the possible solutions of Mexican American low achievement and attainment by both educators in the field and in the college, there is little hope of establishing realistic programs to prepare teachers. Both understanding of the problem by the two groups and cooperation between them are essential. Heedless of these two necessities, teacher-preparation institutions blithely continue to certify teachers who will have lifelong contact with the minority, but do little or nothing specially to prepare them. I know of few special courses, sequences, or tracks intended to provide future elementary or secondary teachers with either essential skills or understandings. Though there are specific courses in some colleges that concern the disadvantaged, the poor, and the urban school crisis, few of such courses are required in the regular credential sequence; very few specifically treat the problem of the Mexican American. Little is done by the institutions legally charged with the preservice preparation of teachers; nevertheless, many of these same institutions sponsor in-service programs. Most are in the form of federally assisted summer institutes. Programs on the teaching of Mexican Americans are among these; the majority stress specialized, almost technical aspects of teaching the minority. Understandably, the bulk are based on the compensatory approach so prevalent in public schools.

Teacher-preparation institutions have done, and continue to do, little to aid their students in coping with the problems associated with cross-cultural schooling and the teaching of the ethnically different Mexican American. Public schools are attempting much more. Colleges and universities are not only failing to lead the way toward improved school opportunity for the minority, but they also are failing to follow the lead of lower-level institutions. The preparation program for teachers of Mexican Americans in the lower Rio Grande Valley of Texas in the seventies is on about the same level as that for teachers in upstate New York thirty years ago. This condition prevails in spite of the fact that most southwestern education faculties are well aware that: (1) the vast majority of their students will teach some Mexican Americans; (2) a large percentage will teach in classes or schools with a majority of Mexican Americans; (3) most future teachers of Mexican descent will teach in schools where their own group predominates; (4) both minority-group spokesmen and public school educators advocate special programs for teachers; and (5) the federal government promotes and could in numerous ways support such programs. Yet little or nothing is done. The University of Texas at El Paso graduates about 450 students a year who are granted elementary, secondary, or "all-levels" credentials. Of these about 75 percent will teach in the immediate geographic area — an area composed of over 50 percent Mexican Americans. If the graduate is of Mexican descent (and about 35 percent are), he is almost inevitably assigned to de facto segregated minority schools by local school districts. In spite of this, there is no required course or course sequence within education to acquaint our students with any aspect of

the so-called "Mexican problem." However, as a stopgap measure, student teachers are exposed to from three to six lectures
on the subject — the only time in their entire college education
sequence that such content is introduced. What makes the situation even worse is that the required teacher preparation omits
those courses in which content might logically apply to minorities, culture, or values. No sociology, history, or philosophy of
education is required. The dean and the faculty know that
something should be done, but little is. The situation is bad;
however, a token gesture toward teacher understanding has been
made. How different are other southwestern teacher-preparation
institutions?

CHANGES IN TEACHER PREPARATION

The state of the art of teaching the culturally different Mexican American is at a low ebb. Improvements in the quality of
teachers, as well as in all segments of the institution and general society, will hopefully enhance the minority's socioeconomic
chances. Improvements in the teacher must be recognized as
only an easy place to begin the needed chain of changes. However, the teacher is the one element in this chain over which
control can be easily asserted. The present or future teacher can
be helped to do a better job with minority children. Before
any program to accomplish this is proposed, some further exposition of present teacher weaknesses is necessary. Regardless
of the orientation taken by a school, two aggregates of teacher
inadequacies are evident. One is the lack of technical skill in
the "science of teaching" area; the other is a severe personal limi-
tation in understanding culture, personality, and behavior.

Teacher inadequacies in the skill area should be obvious to
any well-informed and careful observer. Administrators are usually quite vocal in describing teacher shortcomings of a more
or less technical nature. Too many teachers are ill-prepared to
use effectively the more modern approaches to teaching English
as a second language. Although most "direct methods," including
the audio-lingual, are simple to use, few know how to use them.
The technical equipment connected with these foreign-language
teaching techniques is rarely utilized to its full potential or
even close to it. I have observed the most traditional sort of
formal grammar being "taught" with a most sophisticated and

expensive electronic language laboratory. Numbers of audio-visual aids likewise are not utilized maximally. This failure to best use such expensive equipment, and therefore to waste the taxpayers' money, is legend. Teachers of remedial subjects usually are ill-prepared to measure, to diagnose, or to "treat" learning problems. The crucial need for well-trained remedial teachers was mentioned by almost every administrator I interviewed. The more modern techniques for the teaching of reading seemed to have missed most teachers; "projective techniques" are rarely employed in many schools. The inability to interpret validly the measurements of achievement and I.Q. of ethnically different children is widespread. However, perhaps the biggest skill failure among teachers of Mexican Americans is their almost universal inability to communicate in Spanish. All factions seem to concur that this skill is essential for teachers of the minority. There is no valid reason, except institutional ineptitude and rigidity, why teachers cannot become relatively proficient in the language spoken by so many of their pupils. I could go on; however, I'm sure that, at least in regard to skill deficiency among teachers, many would concur.

The most severe weakness of teachers is their failure to understand a number of concepts concerning culture, society, personality, and behavior. Teachers almost universally have little understanding of the effects of the first two on the latter two, or of interrelationships among the four concepts. Specifically, three areas of teacher deficiency are evident: The great majority (1) fail to recognize the overwhelming influence of culture on personality and behavior; (2) have extremely limited knowledge of, or contact with, Mexican Americans; and (3) do not grasp the role and function of the American school in general society or recognize its influence on the ethnically different child. Very briefly, the following common teacher behaviors, and many others, encourage the belief that most fail to comprehend fully the concepts mentioned above or their importance to learning. Teachers regularly are pessimistic concerning the minority's ability to learn; they equate race (national origin) and intelligence, prohibit the speaking of Spanish, act negatively toward ethnic peer groups, misinterpret Mexican American behavior in school, stereotype the group, maintain extreme social distance with minority members, and take absolute ethical and moral stances. They obviously fail to recognize how all these affect the child who is growing up in two cultures.

The two preceding paragraphs have touched upon teacher inadequacies. Any program to prepare teachers specially for Mexican Americans must have as its prime objective the overcoming of the inadequacies described. Teachers must acquire both skill and knowledge. As no one can really know what someone else knows, changed teacher behavior must be the principal criterion of success or failure of programs. The existence of concepts and theories in the mind of the teacher can only be demonstrated by action. The appropriateness of this action is *the* important test. The teacher well-prepared to teach minority children must be able constructively to synthesize skills and knowledge into appropriate school practices and curricula.

In order better to prepare teachers of Mexican American children, I suggest that some rather radical surgery be done upon present programs. What is proposed is a clean removal of existing formats of teacher preparation. From the static which colleges of education receive from their various constituencies, one would suppose radical reorganizations were an everyday occurrence. They are not. Regardless, for teachers of the minority, three major changes are suggested. First, the content taught must be reorganized and presently slighted areas strengthened. Second, vastly increased student involvement with the minority must be arranged. Students must be forced to interact with the real world within the school, with the minority community, and in activities such as P.T.A. that bridge the two. The field experiences should, as much as possible, be coordinated with the content presented in the classroom. Third, small group seminars, modeled after "T-group" or "sensitivity sessions," must become an integral part of the program. These seminars are catalysts; without adding any new ingredient, they should hasten the process of interaction between what is presented in class as reality (and the theories to explain it) and what is observed and coped with in the field. These seminars must force a reconciliation, or at least a constructive encounter, between content taught by more formal methods and content "taught" through experience. Content, seminars, and field experience are all essential to the preparation of quality teachers. One of the components without the others strikes me as little improvement over present emphasis on content. It is impossible to propose specific arrangements of these proposed program components. Whether they are utilized in a special track for teachers of Mexican Americans, a special course or two, an institute, or an in-service program depends on innumerable conditions. The three components can be modified to fit specific requirements as to time, money, faculty, and the nature of students. Even a one-day "pre-first-day-of-school" teacher institute could be organized along the recommended lines.

Much of the present content of teacher-certification programs is applicable for our specially prepared teachers and should be retained. However, all material should be carefully scrutinized and reorganized to eliminate repetition. It seems to me that the "knowledge," theory, and skills might be better arranged into three cores: (1) the sociocultural, (2) the psycho-personal, and (3) the professional-technical. However, other descriptive terms might be applied. What matters is that content be somehow interrelated. The psycho-personal core should stress psycholinguistics, the effect of cultural marginality and value conflict on personality, and areas related to adolescent ethnic behavior. The professional-technical core includes those skills usually taught in methods courses: the how to teach, how to organize, and how to test areas of instruction. Teachers of the minority need additional skills. Four major aggregates of skills must be stressed. These include the skills associated with remedial teaching, the ability to use psychometric instruments and to interpret them correctly vis-à-vis the culturally different, the crucial ability to communicate in Spanish, and the techniques of modern foreign-language teaching. Perhaps an ideal way to accomplish the last two would be to use the audio-lingual technique in teaching Spanish to the future teacher. Thus the English speaker would gain the essential new language while learning techniques usable in teaching English. The student's ongoing experience in the school and community must provide ample opportunity to practice and demonstrate competence in these skills.

The so-called sociocultural content core is the most crucial for teachers of Mexican Americans and is also the area that is most slighted in regular teacher-preparation sequences. Indeed, it is appalling how few teachers are objective in their views of society and culture or have any real grasp of culture's influence on themselves or their students. This core must bear the burden of providing an objective understanding of: (1) the concept of culture and society; (2) cultural evolution, social change, and the individual problems in coping with them; (3) the profound and perhaps all-pervading influence of culture in determining human personality and behavior; (4) the concepts of caste and subculture as they exist in the modern world, especially in the southwest; (5) the nature and history of the diverse Mexican American groups and their cultures; (6) the role played by the school in transmitting the "general national culture"; and (7) the theoretical and practical aspects of problems related to cross-cultural schooling, especially vis-à-vis language difference and normative conflict. The objective presentation of theories and concepts relative to the preceding may well induce a sense of shock in many, especially since the concurrent field experience forces the student to confront social reality. This real world so different from, yet so similar to, the one in which he lives may produce "culture shock"; it is intended to. No teacher can succeed with the culturally different and/or poverty community unless some rather personal things occur. The student's basic assumptions about himself, the world he lives in, and his explanations of both must be subjected to reappraisal. The "folk myth" explanations of such items as race, achievement, or poverty must be destroyed. Too often such unsound explanations deter an individual's ability to cope with the very real problems associated with such ideas. The sensitivity session experiences in the seminars must provide the emotional support essential to the individual as he reconstructs himself and his beliefs. This core hopes to demonstrate that culture, society, and human behavior are understandable, and that to understand them fully, one's own values, beliefs, and attitudes must be examined objectively.

Specific attention should be focused on the influence of culture on personality and behavior. Man's views of himself, others, and the world are all influenced by the social environment in which he is nurtured. Inherent in this is the idea that truth, beauty, and morality are socioculturally determined. Claremont Graduate School conducted a teacher "reeducation" project with content and objectives similar to those proposed here. In this project participants were encouraged or "forced" to understand culture's influence on their own individual perceptions, attitudes, and behavior — to see culture as manifest within themselves. Teachers were aided in this process by participating in small group seminars not unlike those suggested here which provide some real insight about the extent of cultural influence.

Teachers must become aware of the Mexican American culture characteristics. The world view, value orientations, family relationships, and roles of the group must be well known. However, major problems exist that must discourage the teaching of any set list of distinctive characteristics. One problem is that we have very little objective information concerning Mexican American culture in general. Inversely, we have too much subjective information. Let me illustrate. No contemporary widespread empirical study indicates that a monolithic or static Mexican American culture exists. Every indication is that minority culture varies by geographic area, that even within the same geographic area differing kinds and rates of acculturation are evident, as well as that distinct adaptations to the dominant Anglo societies have been and are being made. Only two cultural items appear even close to universal — Mexican Americans *tend* to speak Spanish and to be Roman Catholics. The cultural diversity of the group is extreme; however, most of the literature describes one uniform and rather static culture.[3] Mexican Americans are usually pictured as being, among other things: fatalistic, present-time oriented, patriarchal, superstitious, personalistic, and generally carriers of a "folk culture." Although such may describe certain isolated groups or be valid appraisals of older conditions, there is no reason to believe it characterizes present Mexican American culture in general. What we are constantly told about the culture does not appear to correspond with reality.

There are other reasons for not teaching the specifics of Mexican American culture. The characteristics ascribed to minority culture in most descriptions mesh all too perfectly with the almost universal Anglo stereotype of "Mexicans" in general.[4] To teach these might lend a certain measure of scientific validation to presently held but unsound overgeneralizations. It is also doubtful that descriptive statements foster the in-depth awareness of cultural differences teachers must acquire. Dr. Fred Romero's recent research on teacher knowledge of the influence of culture on school behavior points up the dangers of the casual treatment of culture. He found a

> general teacher sensitivity to, and awareness of, socio-cultural differences of the . . . Spanish-American and Anglo. This teacher awareness . . . could very well be superficial and not based on real knowledge of what constitutes a culture value system. In addition, cultural sensitivity may result from attitudes formed from operating stereotypes. Under these conditions a lack of real sensitivity could, in fact, exist.[5]

Too detailed, but superficial, descriptions of cultural characteristics or Anglo-Mexican cultural differences probably discourage in-depth understanding. For example, if teachers are taught that minority families teach their sons to be *macho,* this one characteristic (whether valid or not) may be used to describe or interpret wildly diverse male behavior. Such treatment of culture is entirely too simplistic. The objective of this core is not to describe Mexican American culture in general, but to provide teachers with the skills and insights necessary to determine the cultural characteristics of the group with which they are in contact. The teacher's knowledge of local cultural variations is essential to the ability to incorporate cultural items into the curriculum, and to the teacher's skill in coping with children's difficulties in "learning" two sets of norms. The combination of theory of culture and society, and the continual field experience plus the seminars, should help the student to describe and interpret objectively any culture he encounters. No teacher should be told about Mexican American culture; instead, programs must be established to force him to "see and feel it."

I recently came across a statement in an education text that is the very antithesis of the kind of knowledge teachers must acquire. To illustrate the general lack of information rampant, let me quote the only paragraph in the book concerning America's second largest minority:

> In the Southwest, the Mexican-Americans continue to live in the slum atmospheres they have known for so long. The work they undertake is seasonal and they are finding that greater mobility is necessary.[6]

This sort of misinformation must be countered. Teachers must understand the present socioeconomic status of this group as well as recognize the forces that led to the present situation. An objective history of this minority in the Southwest and the group's Hispanic roots must be presented. But glorification and idealization of this tradition must be avoided.

In summation, let me stress a number of points. Two major considerations are evident in planning teacher-preparation programs or projects. What kind of teachers do the public schools want? This must be determined by a careful analysis of the orientation of a school and the nature of programs it undertakes to enhance Mexican American school performance. After arriving at the answers to these riddles, it is essential to cooperate with teacher-preparation institutions to establish the kinds of programs necessary. Schools of education, it must be remembered, may be just as inflexible and rigid as the public schools. Thus, it may be necessary to prod them a little or to aid the "young turks" inside to do so. Both schools and teacher-preparation institutions must change before any real benefit will trickle down to our ultimate clients — children. Perhaps steps to prepare teachers specially for minority children will encourage the needed changes.

Hopefully, some of the items suggested to equip teachers specially for minority children will be useful. The specific items in any program must be determined "on the spot." However, every program should include the crucial components — content and field experience and some arena where students can reconcile the two. What has been suggested is far from a perfect outline — it was not intended to be. I have omitted many considerations and slighted others. Regardless, let me emphasize in conclusion that teachers must be prepared to cope with the problems associated with cross-cultural schooling. To do so involves teacher awareness and understanding of social reality. Any program must force teachers to comprehend and deal with the real world of children, minorities, and poverty. As the function of all teachers is some sort of action, it behooves any program to destroy "folk myths," stereotypes, and idealized pictures of reality. If programs fail in this regard, we can expect teacher behavior to be less than adequate, since it would be based on false premises. The school is charged with helping to solve grievous social problems. To do so requires a new breed of educator — one equipped to make objective appraisals of problems, and to take rational and appropriate steps to encourage their elimination. It's a big order. WE must get on with it.

NOTES

[1] George Z. F. Bereday, *Comparative Method in Education* (New York: Holt, Rinehart & Winston, Inc., 1964), p. 5.

[2] For additional information on conditions and practices in schools that promote negative social climates see:

Thomas P. Carter, *The Mexican American in School* (tentative title). Published in 1969 by the College Entrance Examination Board, New York.

C. Wayne Gordon, *et al.*, *Educational Achievement and Aspirations of Mexican American Youth in a Metropolitan Context*. Mexican American Study Project Educational Sub-Study, Center for the Evaluation of Instructional Programs, Graduate School of Education, University of California at Los Angeles, March, 1968. (Mimeographed.)

Theodore W. Parsons, Jr., "Ethnic Cleavage in a California School." Unpublished Ph.D. dissertation, Stanford University, 1965.

James S. Coleman *et al.*, *Equality of Educational Opportunity*, U.S. Department of Health, Education and Welfare, Office of Education (Washington, D.C.: U.S. Government Printing Office, 1966). See also the unofficial analysis of the Coleman document by George W. Mayeske, "Educational Achievement Among Mexican-Americans: A Special Report from the Educational Opportunity Survey," National Center for Educational Statistics, U.S. Office of Education. Technical Note 22, Washington, D.C., January 9, 1967.

John A. Michael, "High School Climates and Plans for Entering College," *The Public Opinion Quarterly*, vol. 25, no. 4 (Winter, 1961), pp. 585–595.

Alan B. Wilson, "Residential Segregation of Social Classes and Aspirations of High School Boys," *American Sociological Review*, vol. 24 (December, 1959), pp. 836–845.

[3] For detailed contemporary description of these assumed characteristics see: Kenneth R. Johnson, *Teaching the Culturally Disadvantaged*, Unit I (Chicago: Science Research Associates, Inc., 1966).

Miles V. Zintz, *Education Across Cultures* (Dubuque, Iowa: William C. Brown Company, Publishers, 1963).

Robert G. Hayden, "Spanish-Americans of the Southwest," *Welfare in Review*, vol. 14, no. 4 (April, 1966), p. 14.

[4] See:

Ozzie G. Simmons, "The Mutual Images and Expectations of Anglo-Americans and Mexican-Americans," *Daedalus*, vol. 90, no. 2, Spring, 1961.

Theodore W. Parsons, Jr., "Ethnic Cleavage in a California School," unpublished Ph.D. dissertation, Stanford University, August, 1965.

[5] Fred E. Romero, "A Study of Anglo-American and Spanish-American Culture Value Concepts and Their Significance in Secondary Education," *A Research Contribution for Education in Colorado* (Denver: Colorado State Department of Education, September, 1966), vol. 3, no. 2, p. 7.

[6] Helen E. Rees, *Deprivation and Compensatory Education: A Consideration* (Boston: Houghton Mifflin Company, 1968), p. 13.

Potential Contributions by the Behavioral Sciences to Effective Preparation Programs for Teachers of Mexican-American Children*

MANUEL RAMIREZ III

THE THESIS OF THIS PAPER is that the most valuable contributions which the behavioral sciences can make to the development of effective preparation programs are research findings which have identified the value orientation of the Mexican-American culture. More specifically, the most important data is that which relates elements of the value orientation to perceptions, needs, behaviors, and beliefs of Mexican-American students which clash with the value system of the schools. A familiarity with this information will make it possible for teachers and school administrators to identify and remove those barriers which are presently hindering the performance of these students. This approach is by no means new. Several investigators (Deutsch, Landes, and Madsen [1]) have observed that underprivileged children are not prepared to cope with the intellectual and social demands of the school as it is presently constituted. Furthermore, they have noted that what these children learn in school frequently comes into conflict with that which they have learned

* Prepared for the Conference on Teacher Education for Mexican Americans, February, 1969. Sponsored by ERIC Clearinghouse on Rural Education and Small Schools.

210

from their parents, thus creating severe personality problems and inadequate intellectual performance.

Regarding the effect of culture conflict on academic performance, Landes states:

> The anthropologist believes that adults teach and pupils learn in keeping with habits absorbed from their cultural backgrounds. Hence, apparently stupid behavior may actually reflect irreconcilable culture *differences* felt by the "stupid" person, whereas success may testify to cultural *harmony* between a person and his environment.[2]

The results of a study by Demos seemed to provide some support for the hypothesis that membership in the Mexican-American culture is related to certain unfavorable attitudes toward education expressed by Mexican-American students. The investigator selected 105 Mexican-American (M-A) and 105 Anglo-American (A-A) junior high and high school students who were matched as to age, grade, sex, social class, and intelligence. These students were given an "attitudes toward education" scale which contained twenty-nine different issues dealing with school and school personnel. The results indicated that the M-A students had expressed attitudes which were more unfavorable than those of the A-A's. Furthermore, there were several issues on which students of the two cultural groups expressed divergent opinions. These attitudinal differences appeared to be related to the different value orientations of the two cultures. Specifically, M-A students expressed attitudes which were significantly more unfavorable than those of A-A students on the following issues: (1) importance of an elementary education, (2) staff concern about students, (3) desirability of dropping out of school, (4) desirability of belonging to a gang, and (5) importance of regular attendance.[3]

Although the foregoing study provides a link between cultural membership and perception of the school, it leaves a number of questions to be considered here. Which values differentiate between M-A and A-A students? Which of these are related to needs, perceptions, and behaviors which affect performance in school? Finally, which of these characteristics of the M-A culture clash with the value orientation of the schools?

MEXICAN-AMERICAN VALUES

The initial study in the series to be reviewed here was that of Manuel Ramirez III, "Identification with Mexican Family Values and Authoritarianism in Mexican-Americans." [4] It was concerned with three aspects: (1) the extent to which M-A's are identified with family values which had been isolated in Mexican and Mexican-American anthropological research, (2) the extent to which M-A's agreed with an authoritarian ideology, and (3) the relation between identification with Mexican and M-A family values and agreement with an authoritarian ideology. It was predicted that M-A's would express more agreement than A-A's with an attitude scale reflecting Mexican and M-A values. In addition, it was also predicted that since the M-A family structure resembled that of the high authoritarian family described by Adorno and his colleagues,[5] M-A's would score higher on the F (authoritarianism) Scale than A-A's. Finally, a significant positive correlation between the two scales was expected in the data of the M-A's.

The Ss [subjects] were 70 Mexican Americans (third generation) and 70 Anglo-Americans (not belonging to any identifiable cultural or racial minority group), ranging in age from 18 to 24. All the Ss were middle class, Catholic, college students. There were equal numbers of males and females within each of the cultural groups.[6]

The items of the Family Attitude Scale employed were selected to represent the Mexican and Mexican-American family values which had been identified by Diaz Guerrero, Gillin, Lewis, Madsen, and Saunders.[7] Some of the items were selected from a scale which had been employed by Diaz Guerrero in a previous study. Others were taken from the Traditional Family Ideology Scale (Levinson & Huffman) [8] and the Parent Attitude Research Instrument (Schafer & Bell).[9] The remainder of the items were constructed by the author. Subjects were asked to respond to each item on a seven-point scale, from "agree very much" to "disagree very much."

The results showed that M-A's had made significantly higher scores on both the Family Attitude Scale and the F Scale ($tFAS = 5.13$ $p < .005$, $tFS = 6.35$ $p < .005$). In addition, the data of the M-A's showed a significant positive correlation between the scores of both scales.

Means and discriminatory powers (D.P.) of some of the items which succeeded in differentiating between M-A's and A-A's are listed on the following page.

Family Attitude Scale

Item	Means		
	M-A	A-A	D.P.
The stricter the parents the better the child.	6.8	3.5	3.3
For a child the mother should be the dearest person in existence.	5.5	3.0	2.5
It helps a child in the long run if he is made to conform to his parents' ideas.	5.4	3.0	2.4
More parents should teach their children to have unquestioning loyalty to them.	5.2	3.2	2.0
Some equality in marriage is a good thing, but by and large the husband ought to have the main say-so in family matters.	5.8	4.2	1.6
It doesn't do any good to try and change the future because the future is in the hands of God.	5.7	3.9	1.8

F Scale

Item	Means		
	M-A	A-A	D.P.
There is hardly anything lower than a person who does not feel a great love, gratitude, and respect for his parents.	5.8	3.4	2.4
Obedience and respect for authority are the most important virtues children should learn.	6.0	3.8	2.2

The higher scores obtained by M-A students in the Family Attitude Scale indicated that they were identified with the Mexican and M-A values isolated through anthropological research. Their higher scores on the F Scale indicated that rearing in a family atmosphere emphasizing father domination, strict child-rearing practices, submission and obedience to the will and dictates of authority figures, strict separation of the sex roles, and interpersonal relationships based on dominance and submission had resulted in agreement with an authoritarian ideology.

Comparison of Family Attitude Scale item means of M-A's with those of Mexicans reported by Diaz Guerrero [10] indicated that M-A's had rejected the concepts of male superiority and separation of the sex roles. The results of acculturation were thus evidenced in a lessening of the father's traditional authority in the family and of the authority of the male in general. It was also noted, however, that M-A women had obtained the highest scores on both the F and Family Attitude Scales. It appeared, then, that although the M-A female was achieving increasingly more freedom and equality, she still showed signs of strong adherence to conformity and submission to authority.

The second study to be reviewed was done in California. The sample consisted of 100 M-A's (third generation) and 100 A-A's of the middle class in a junior college and a state college in Sacramento. Since the previous study had been conducted in Texas and since the subjects had been of the same age and socio-economic class as those of the present study, this provided an excellent opportunity for comparison of value orientations of M-A's in the two states. In the California study the subjects were administered an attitude scale of M-A values which had been revised somewhat but which still contained many items which had been used in the previous study in Texas (see pp. 230-231). The results showed that M-A's scored higher than A-A's. The differences between the means of the cultural groups obtained were, however, considerably lower than those which had been obtained in Texas. M-A males also scored higher than females, indicating that, in contrast to the Texas results, females in this sample were less identified with the M-A values and were considerably more emancipated. This is not surprising, since most of the Texas subjects had been reared in the Rio Grande Valley where there is close proximity to the Mexican border and M-A's make up a large percentage of the total population. In this area there is more support and reinforcement given for identification with the culture. M-A's in Sacramento, on the other hand, make up less than 10 percent of the total population and are distant from the Mexican border.

Items which discriminated best between M-A's and A-A's are listed below. It was noted that M-A females disagreed with those items reflecting the authority and superiority of males; thus, these items did not discriminate well between the M-A and A-A groups as they had in the Texas sample.

	Means		
Item	M-A	A-A	D.P.
All adults should be respected.	5.5	4.1	1.4
More parents should teach children to be loyal to the family.	5.1	4.0	1.3
For a child the mother should be the dearest person in existence.	4.8	3.5	1.3
Fathers should always be respected.	5.5	4.2	1.3
Some equality in marriage is a good thing, but by and large the husband ought to have the main say-so in family matters.	4.52	3.52	1.0
Old people are wiser than young people.	4.7	3.8	0.9

The third study in this series compared the degree of identification with the M-A culture exhibited by M-A students of three different age groups. It was predicted that junior high students would be more identified with the M-A culture than high school students and that high school students, in turn, would exhibit more identification with the culture than college students. It was expected that two phenomena would account for increasing acculturation with age: (1) more acceptance of Anglo middle-class values as the students progressed in school and (2) a greater tendency for those who were more identified with the M-A culture to drop out before completion of junior high.

There were 400 subjects in the sample. Two hundred of these were M-A's and two hundred were A-A's. Half of the subjects in each of the cultural groups were junior high and half were high school students. In addition, there were equal numbers of males and females in each of the cultural groups. As predicted, the mean of the junior high group was significantly higher than that of the high school group (t=3.32 p<.01). The mean of the high school sample was also significantly higher than that of the college sample (t=1.89 p<.05).

Listed below, along with means for each of the age groups, are those items which differentiated well between M-A's and A-A's in all three age groups.

Item	J.H.	H.S.	C.
All adults should be respected.	5.94	6.10	5.50
More parents should teach their children to be loyal to the family.	5.35	5.00	5.10
Some equality in marriage is a good thing but by and large, the husband should have the main say-so in family matters.	5.20	5.05	4.52
Women think less clearly than men and are more emotional.	5.19	4.50	4.40
The father should be the final authority in the family.	5.00	4.4	4.60

In general, M-A junior high subjects agreed with most of the items of the attitude scale, thus indicating their strong identity with the following characteristics of the culture: family loyalty, strictness of child rearing, submissiveness to parents, respect for age, male superiority, traditionalistic view of parental roles, inability to manipulate the future, present-time orientation, and separation of the sex roles. Subjects of high school age demon-

strated evidence of acculturation in the following areas: submissiveness to parents (items 20, 24; see end of chapter, Family
Attitude Scale), strictness of child rearing (1, 21), separation of
sex roles (16, 22), and inability to manipulate the future (14).
Responses of college students showed evidence of acculturation
in submissiveness to parents (20, 21, 24, 29), separation of the
sex roles (15, 16, 22), present-time orientation (2, 11), and
rebelliousness as a passing phase of youth (28). The data of
college students indicated that acculturation had not affected
the following areas: respect for age (3, 17) and traditional con-
ception of parental roles (9, 13, 26). The greatest effects of
Americanization were evidenced in the value orientation of college females. They overwhelmingly rejected items reflecting a
present-time orientation, male superiority, and the belief that
rebelliousness is merely a passing phase of youth.

The fourth study in the M-A values series compared value
orientations of M-A students of the middle and lower socioeconomic classes. The subjects were 200 M-A junior high and
high school students in Sacramento, California. Half the subjects were of the middle socioeconomic class and half were of
the lower socioeconomic class. Two criteria — education and employment of father — were used to classify students as to SES
(socioeconomic status). Most of the fathers of the low SES subjects were agricultural or railroad laborers with a mean of 7
years of education; most of the fathers of the mid SES subjects
were state employees with an average of 13 years of education.
It was predicted that subjects of the low SES would obtain higher
scores on the M-A value scale, i.e., would express more agreement with the M-A values than mid SES students. Specifically,
it was expected that low SES students would show more agreement with items in the submissiveness to parents, separation of
sex roles, and present-time orientation categories. Contrary to
expectations, however, differences between the two groups on
total scale scores were not significant ($t=1.04$ $p>.05$). The following are items which differentiated best between the two
groups.

It is apparent, then, that expected differences between the
two socioeconomic groups were obtained on the categories of
submissiveness to parents and separation of the sex roles, but
not on present-time orientation.

Item	Means LSES	MSES	D.P.
Girls should not be allowed to play with boys' toys, such as soldiers and footballs.	5.2	4.2	1.0
It is not good for a married woman to work outside the home.	5.1	4.2	0.9
More parents should teach their children to be loyal to the family.	6.0	4.7	1.3
It helps a child in the long run if he is made to conform to his parents' ideas.	5.6	5.0	0.6
The word of an adult should never be questioned.	5.8	4.9	0.9

MEXICAN-AMERICAN VALUES AND ATTITUDES TOWARD EDUCATION

The research reviewed above showed that there are differences in the value orientations of M-A and A-A students. How do these relate to differences in attitudes toward education in these two groups of students? Demos,[11] in a study reviewed above, had attributed the differences to M-A ethnic group membership, but did not specify details. A study by the author and a colleague (Ramirez and Taylor [12]), sought to throw some light on this subject.

It was predicted that M-A junior high and high school students would express attitudes toward education which were more undesirable than those expressed by A-A's. It was also predicted that the specific attitudinal differences between subjects of the two ethnic groups could be explained in terms of the differences in value orientations between their two cultures.

The subjects were 600 (300 M-A, 300 A-A) junior high and high school students of the lower socioeconomic class (as determined by residence patterns in the community). The study was conducted in two schools in Sacramento, California. All 600 subjects were administered an attitude scale comprised of 62 items. The scale assessed attitudes toward school and school personnel. Some of the items were drawn from the Demos D Scale (1965) whereas others were composed by the authors.

The results showed that, as predicted, M-A's had expressed attitudes toward education which were significantly more unfavorable than those of A-A's. A summary of the results of an item analysis performed on the data is given on page 218.

Table 1

Attitude Scale Items Which Differentiated Significantly Between M-A and A-A Students

Item	M-A % Agree	A-A % Agree	X^2
17 It is far more important for a man to get a good education; a woman can always raise a family and do housework.	58.8	45.0	9.8**
20 Teachers do not understand the problems of students.	75.4	59.8	13.8**
21 Even though a student speaks another language at home, he should not do it at school.	46.4	61.0	10.9**
26 One should not question the word of a teacher.	32.1	21.3	7.0**
27 Sometimes talking is not enough and you must use your fists to convince someone.	51.4	34.2	15.1**
29 It is good to mix only with people of your own kind.	22.6	13.3	6.8**
42 If anyone insults me because I am different, I fight.	42.9	23.3	21.0**
45 It is hard to take orders from a woman.	41.4	33.3	2.9*
49 It is good for parents to put pressure on their children to get as much education as possible.	76.9	52.3	34.0**
61 It is more important to get a job as soon as it is available, even though you may not have a high school education.	25.0	15.4	6.7**

* P .10
** P .01

Greater agreement by M-A's with items 17 and 45 is reflective of the belief in masculine superiority and separation of the sex roles evident in their culture. Agreement with items 26 and 49 is probably a consequence of the authoritarian nature of the M-A culture. Items 21 and 29 represent the loyalty of an M-A to his ethnic group and item 61 reflects an acceptance of the present-time orientation of the culture.

Agreement with item 20 coupled with agreement with item 29 indicates that interpersonal relationships between M-A students and teachers have been unsatisfactory and fraught with misunderstanding. Item 49, however, seems to offer some hope, since it would appear that M-A students are asking parents to give them permission to accept the educational system. This will become more evident in the results of the next study to be reviewed.

MEXICAN-AMERICAN CULTURAL MEMBERSHIP
AND NEEDS, PERCEPTIONS, AND INTERPERSONAL
RELATIONSHIPS OF MEXICAN-AMERICAN STUDENTS

The research discussed thus far does not give any insight into the psychological dynamics of the M-A student. For this reason a new analysis, which was actually the second study of the attitudes-toward-education work (see p. 213), was designed to isolate motives, expectations, and unique perceptions of M-A students which were related to their culture and which in turn affected their performance in school.

The predictions made in this study were based on the following information which had been obtained by prior research (Clark, Madsen, Ramirez [1967 and 1969], and Rubel).[13] Child-rearing practices in the M-A culture do not emphasize independence training; this approach, along with the passivistic, collectivistic, and present-time orientation of the culture, inhibits the development of competitiveness and achievement motivation in M-A children. Fear of envy, as well as fear of being accused of discarding the values of the folk culture for those of Anglo society, also discourages the M-A child's motivation to excel in school. The culture's emphasis on close ties to the family and suspiciousness of strangers results in a reluctance to establish close interpersonal relationships with school personnel and with peers who are not of M-A descent. Furthermore, the authoritarianism of the culture leads M-A's to perceive interpersonal relationships as the attempt of one of the participants to control the others, thus causing them to misperceive the motives of others.

Certain characteristics of the sex roles in this culture were also considered likely to figure rather prominently in interpersonal relationships between students and school personnel. The M-A male, like the Mexican male, does not assume the full responsibilities of his role until adolescence. Throughout childhood he receives considerable succorance and support from his mother and other females in the family. Once he reaches adolescence, however, he is urged to make a complete break with the female set of values and to identify with the male set. At this time in his life he views any attempts on the part of females to control him as a threat to his *machismo*. He develops a fear of being dominated by females and responds with aggression whenever he feels threatened by them. The M-A females, on the other hand, are expected to live up to very demanding and restrictive role requirements and are given complete responsibility for rearing children. As a result of the great demands which are made on them, they are likely to develop a fear of failure which may generalize to their school work. Some changes have occurred in the female role as a result of acculturation and are affecting the M-A female's behavior at school and at home. They are becoming increasingly more rebellious and competitive, rejecting the submissiveness and abnegation which were characteristic of their traditional roles. These changes have also affected the role of the male, lessening his authority in the family, and permitting females to compete for those areas of influence which are being abandoned by males.

The following predictions were made by the authors:

1. M-A students would score lower on need (n) Achievement and need Affiliation and higher on n Rejection (escape or avoid) and n Power (Dominance) than A-A students.

2. M-A males would express more n Succorance from females, more n Aggression toward females who were domineering (e.g., who attempted to control males), and would relate more stories with themes of female control than A-A males.

3. M-A females would express more n Autonomy (rebelliousness) and more n "Infavoidance" (fear of failure), and would relate more stories with themes of power struggles than A-A females.

4. Those students in both ethnic groups whose attitudes toward education (as expressed on the attitude scale administered in the first phase of the study) were more unfavorable would score higher on n Power and n Rejection and lower on n Achievement and n Affiliation than those who had expressed the more favorable attitudes.

The subjects were selected from the original sample of 600 who had already participated in the studies. They were selected on the basis of their performance on the Attitudes Toward Education Scale as follows: 60 were selected from each ethnic group — of this number 20 had scored high on the attitude scale (e.g., had expressed unfavorable attitudes); 20 had achieved scores which were similar to the mean of their respective ethnic group; and 20 had obtained low scores (e.g., had expressed favorable attitudes toward education). There were equal numbers of males and females and junior high and high school students within each of the ethnic groups. A set of ten picture cards was administered to the subjects individually. The instructions given to the students were as follows: "I have a number of cards with pictures on them. I will show you the cards, one by one, and I would like you to tell me a story to fit each one. Tell me what is happening in each picture. What led up to it? What is wanted? By whom? What will happen in the end?"

Four sets of pictures were constructed, one for each of the sexes within the ethnic groups. The content of the pictures in each set was as follows: (1) student sitting at a desk; (2) two students, one M-A, one A-A, either playing basketball (in the male set) or standing outside a classroom (in the female set); (3) young female teacher and student; (4) young male teacher and student; (5) older female teacher and student; (6) older male teacher and student; (7) student at home with books in hand and older male in background (father card); (8) student sitting at a desk at home with older female in background (mother card); (9) male and female students; and (10) young male with rake, and college campus in background.

The stories were scored for n Power, n Achievement, n Affiliation, and n Rejection by employing a scoring system suggested by Ricciuti and Clark.[14] In addition, stories given by male subjects were scored for n Succorance from females, for expressions of aggression against females who attempted to control males, and for female domination of males. Stories given by females were also scored for n "Infavoidance," for n Autonomy, and for competition for positions of influence.

Results of analyses of variance performed on the n Power, n Achievement, n Rejection, and n Affiliation data are summarized in Table No. 2.

The F's for the ethnic group main effect were significant for the Power, Rejection, and Achievement data. Thus, in line with the predictions of the investigators, M-A's scored higher on n Power and n Rejection and lower on n Achievement. They did not, however, score lower on n Affiliation. When another analysis was made comparing n Affiliation scores of M-A and A-A subjects on cards depicting teachers and peers versus those containing parental figures, significant differences were found ($t =$

2.54 p<.05) with M-A's expressing less n Affiliation to the former type of card and more to the latter.

As predicted, M-A males scored higher than A-A males on n Succorance from females ($\overline{X}$ M-A=1.8, $\overline{X}$ A-A=.3, t=4.75 p<.001) and on aggression toward females who were domineering ($\overline{X}$ M-A=1.03, $\overline{X}$ A-A=.17, t=4.30 p<.001). M-A males also had scored higher on the tendency to perceive females as domineering ($\overline{X}$ M-A=2.53, $\overline{X}$ A-A=1.86, t=.86>.05), but the difference between the two groups was not significant. M-A females expressed more n Autonomy ($\overline{X}$ M-A=2.93, $\overline{X}$ A-A=1.53, t=3.9, p<.01) than A-A females, but the two groups did not differ significantly on n "Infavoidance" or on the power struggle variable.

Ramirez and Taylor [15] concluded that the differences obtained between M-A and A-A students on the projective technique data reflected the differences in the value orientations and other characteristics of their respective ethnic groups. The higher scores obtained by M-A's on n Power were interpreted as reflecting the authoritarianism of the culture and revealing that they tend to perceive interpersonal relationships as the attempt of one person to control the other. It was considered that this

Table 2

Summary of Analysis of Variance of Need Affiliation, Need Power, Need Rejection, and Need Achievement Scores of Mexican-Americans and Anglo-Americans

SOURCE	df	Need Achievement MS	F	P
Ethnic (E)	1	53.4	4.00	<.05
Within (Error)	96	13.2		

SOURCE	df	Need Rejection MS	F	P
Ethnic (E)	1	172.8	16.8	<.005
Within (Error)	96	10.2		

SOURCE	df	Need Affiliation MS	F	P
Ethnic (E)	1	.2	<1.0	
Within (Error)	96	15.5		

SOURCE	df	Need Power MS	F	P
Ethnic (E)	1	119.9	4.02	<.05
Within (Error)	96	29.5		

view of interpersonal relationships, along with the fact that M-A adolescents are sensitive to domination by others, is potentially conducive to maladjustment in the schools. The aggression toward domineering females expressed by M-A males and the rebelliousness against authority evidenced in the data of the M-A females, then, seemed to indicate that M-A students react negatively against control. M-A males were considered likely to come into conflict with school authorities for behaving aggressively toward females whom they perceived as attempting to dominate them, while M-A females would most likely get into trouble for rebelling against authority in general and refusing to obey the rules and regulations of the school. The content of the stories which were given by M-A students supported these conclusions.

The researchers were also of the opinion that the adjustment of M-A's to school is being hindered further by their avoidance reaction to school tasks and school personnel as was evidenced by their high scores on n Rejection (e.g., content of the stories revealed a tendency on the part of M-A's to reject teachers and Anglo peers who approached them). This tendency toward "ethnic isolationism" was further supported by agreement with certain items on the attitude scale of the previous study (e.g., "mix only with people of your own kind"), as well as lower n Affiliation scores to picture cards depicting teachers and students. This isolationism was believed to be a result of two features of the culture: (1) suspiciousness of strangers and (2) a belief that relationships with strangers pose a threat to the loyalty which the individual owes to his family and ethnic group. It was hypothesized that this fear is further reinforced by the actions of some school personnel who encourage the M-A to abandon his identification with the folk culture (Rubel).[16] This perceived threat to family and cultural ties might also have accounted for the low scores obtained by M-A's on n Achievement. Other features of the culture which may have interfered with the development of n Achievement are the culture's authoritarian child-rearing practices, its emphasis on mother dependency, and its passivistic, collectivistic, and present-time orientation. Previous research by Rosen [17] had shown that children from cultures with the aforementioned characteristics had obtained lower n Achievement scores than children from cultures characterized by activistic, individualistic, and future-time orientations.

Listed below are samples of stories given by M-A students. They have been categorized as to the particular aspect of the culture which they seemed to reflect.

1. Loyalty to the family

This boy and his father are very unhappy. The father just lost his job, and he is worrying about what will happen to his family. The boy is sad also. He wants to continue in school because he is doing so well, but he knows he cannot abandon his family now that they need him most. He will drop out of school and get a job. He cannot turn his back on his family when they are in need.

2. Loyalty to the ethnic group

This boy is being scolded by the teacher for speaking a language that wasn't English on the school grounds. The boy doesn't know what to do. He doesn't want to make the teacher angry, but he also knows his friends are watching him. If he doesn't stand up for his rights and for his people, they will call him a traitor. The teacher tells him not to do it again or she will send him to the principal. He continues to do it and is suspended for three days.

3. Effects of acculturation on heterosexual relationships

This is her boyfriend, and they just left the coffee shop. It looks like they had a quarrel. Well, he wants her to marry him now, and she wants to go to college and be a doctor. He got mad because he wants her to be his wife and mother of his children. She looks like she will continue with school and just break off with him.

4. Criticism for acceptance of school goals

Her name is Mary and that is her brother Gordon. Her brother is always playing around and calling her names. He is always bothering her because she doesn't like to go out; she is a bookworm. Her brother and his friends tease her. Nobody, no boys will look at her.

5. Anglo values threaten father's influence with family and lead to interpersonal conflicts between parents and students as well as between parents

a) This is the father, and the girl is coming home from school. This is Martha and her dad is angry because when he comes home he wants to find his family at home, and Martha always comes late from school and everytime her father asks her what happened she just goes and hides in her room. They never get a chance to be together. After a little while Martha comes out and says she knows she has been annoying her father lately and she will want to communicate more with her father and family. She wants her family to be happy. Her father says, "I've been trying to do this for years, but you have been forgetting I'm the boss of the house."

b) It's a girl. She's sad because her father is real strict with her. He won't let her be modern like the other girls and won't let her wear her hair high like the other girls. She talks to her counselor about this, and the counselor writes her father a note to come to the school. Her father won't go talk to the counselor. The girl runs away from home.

c) These are husband and wife who just got into a fight over their child who is in high school. The girl's father doesn't like her going out on dates because he thinks she is too young, and her mother thinks that it wouldn't hurt to let her go out for a few hours.

6. Difficulty with the English language and interpersonal conflicts with teachers

This is about a girl who is from a different country, and she is in the class in English. The teacher is very mean to her. She tries her best to reply in English but she just can't. He keeps on scolding her and telling her to repeat. So she went to her girl friend and told her, and they both went to the principal and told him what was happening. The principal had a talk with the teacher and told him to take it easy and don't rush her.

7. Unwillingness to seek help when in trouble

This looks like a girl who is having trouble in school. So the teacher is trying to tell her that she should get an education because that is one of the important things that you should have in order to have a good future, but the girl said, "I don't understand. I have trouble with the language." So the teacher said, "You should have told me and I would have helped you a long time ago."

8. M-A's need for structure and control by authority figures

Looks like a principal and a girl that doesn't cooperate right in the classroom. The principal is not happy she has been sent to her because she has been a good student in the other classes. The principal says she wants it stopped and for the student to try and make better grades in that class so she can pass that class just like the rest of the classes. The principal says she doesn't want this to happen again otherwise she will talk to her parents. The girl is scared now and will try to do better. She was goofing off because the teacher in that class let the class do anything they want to do, so she got out of hand.

9. M-A female's rebelliousness and power struggles with authority figures

Looks like a nagging school teacher yelling at a pupil. She is yelling at her because of her grades, because they are not as high as the rest of her classmates. The girl does try and study but she just hates the teacher. She eventually does knuckle down and study. She makes a fool out of the teacher by studying hard and embarrassing the teacher in class to show her classmates she can study.

(This latter story and the previous one point out a major contradiction in the Mexican-American's psychological makeup. That is an approach-avoidance conflict with respect to authoritarian control. Their experience in an authoritarian culture leads them to expect strict control by authority figures, but the peculiarities of their sex roles mentioned above leads them to view control as a threat to their well-being. The male considers it a threat to his masculinity, the female a threat to her new-found freedom.)

10. Culture conflict as the student views it

He is a student. He probably has problems in his studies and he is trying to figure out a problem. He has problems in something else, too, that he is trying to figure out. Seems as if he is caged in, trying to find a way to escape. He feels as if he is on trial, as though two different worlds are pushing him. In one sense, society is trying to push him, in another, it is trying to pull him back. It seems like society is too far advanced for him to figure it out.

EFFECTIVE PREPARATION PROGRAMS
FOR SCHOOL PERSONNEL

The research reviewed above shows that there are differences in the value orientations of M-A and A-A students of comparable ages and socioeconomic classes. Furthermore, the unique value orientations of the M-A seem to have influenced their attitudes toward education, as well as their motives, perceptions, behaviors, and, indeed, their entire personality structures and dynamics. These results also show that these characteristics of the M-A students clash with the cultural values represented by school personnel, resulting in tension and unhappiness for the students. These research results, then, should be employed in preparation programs. Unfortunately, a review of the literature revealed only one report of a program which was based on the culture-clash hypothesis. The Claremont Project in Anthropology and Education (Landes) [18] was designed to train teachers in culture concepts and methods affecting public education. Dr. Ruth Landes, an anthropologist, directed the project at the Claremont Graduate School. For two years Dr. Landes presented data, theories, and skills of cultural anthropology to graduate classes of public school teachers, counselors, and administrators who were employed in schools having large enrollments of disadvantaged students.

The most unique, and in the author's opinion the most beneficial, aspect of the training program was the assignment of work projects designed to introduce teachers to practical uses of anthropological methods. These projects carried teachers into the homes and streets where pupils lived. Research procedures employed by students were direct observations of individuals and groups as well as interviews of the open-ended type. The first project dealt with aspects of the fact that man "carries" the culture taught him and functions according to its directions. Through this work, teachers became aware of the varied cultural forces acting in them and the effect these had on their pupils. They were also able to see these same forces operating in their pupils. This made them more sensitive to conflicts which occur as a result of different expectations reinforced by culture. Another one of the projects concerned itself with the topic that man's behavior was learned from older generations and contemporaries. Still another assignment asked participants in the program to reconstruct the cultural ways of their own families in the three immediate generations of parents, children, and grandparents on both sides. The student was required to specify details about such things as the family's home, education, work, marriages, obligations, and crises. At the same time, students were trained to chart lines or channels of authority and responsibility in the family, and the direction of flow, as mirrored in pupils' opinions. This was done to find out who in each pupil's family made decisions, about what, when, where, how, and why; who punished, who rewarded, and in what forms, and under what circumstances; how the punished individual responded; to whom authority was delegated, and under what conditions. These findings were contrasted with the features of middle-class life. At the conclusion of their projects, students were asked to answer certain questions based on their findings in the field projects. Some of these were: How can a minority assimilate and advance in American life and retain its traditions? Must all cultural groups in America assimilate? Should we impose middle-class standards on children of all backgrounds?

The Claremont Project is undoubtedly a step in the right direction with respect to development of good preparation programs. The idea of involving the participants by having them research problems arising from ethnic differences is in particular a significant contribution.

There is, however, need for more research by behavioral scientists which can provide material for preparation programs. It is the author's belief that future research efforts should be concentrated on person perception. It is the unique perceptions of both pupils and teachers, as conditioned by their respective cultural backgrounds, which in the end will determine how they will relate to each other. The importance of these variables is reflected by stories given by M-A students to the picture cards in the Ramirez and Taylor study.[19] These indicated that whenever M-A students experienced interpersonal relationships with teachers and school administrators who were concerned about them, their performance in school improved. Thus, when these students perceived their teachers as being interested in their welfare, they performed much better.

The results of a study by Rosenthal and Jacobsen support this finding. The investigators, at the beginning of the school year, selected students at random from the student body of a school district in San Francisco and "labeled" them as being likely to improve. In reality, there was no basis in fact for their predictions. The names of the students identified as "spurters" were given to the teachers, and some months later they were evaluated. The results showed that the "spurters" had made more gains than students of a control group. One explanation which can be offered for these results is that when the "picture" which teachers had of their students became more favorable, this was in one way or another communicated to the student who then proceeded to respond more favorably to the demands of the school. For example, when the experimenters compared I.Q. scores of M-A children with teacher attitudes towards the "Mexican-ness" of their appearance, the results indicated that boys who looked "more Mexican" showed greater increases from their teachers' positive evaluations. Thus, this shows that the teachers' preexperimental expectations for these boys' intellectual performance were lowest of all.[20] It appears, then, that information on person perception as it relates to interpersonal relationships between students and school personnel, and school personnel and parents of students, is a necessary ingredient to any effective preparation program.

NOTES

[1] See Martin P. Deutsch, "The Disadvantaged Child and the Learning Process," in Frank Riessman et al., eds, *Mental Health of the Poor* (New York: The Free Press, 1964) ; Ruth Landes, *Culture in American Education* (New York: John Wiley & Sons, Inc., 1965) ; William Madsen, *The Mexican Americans of South Texas* (New York: Holt, Rinehart & Winston, Inc., 1965) .

[2] Landes, *op. cit.*, p. 18.

[3] George D. Demos, "Attitudes of Mexican-American and Anglo-American Groups Toward Education," *Journal of Social Psychology*, vol. 57 (1962), pp. 249–256. See also George D. Demos, *The Demos D Scale* (Beverly Hills, Calif.: Western Psychological Services, 1965) .

[4] Manuel Ramirez III, "Identification with Mexican Family Values and Authoritarianism in Mexican-Americans," *Journal of Social Psychology*, vol. 73 (1967), pp. 3-11.

[5] T. W. Adorno et al., *The Authoritarian Personality* (New York: Harper & Row, Publishers, 1950) .

[6] Ramirez, *op. cit.*, p. 4.

[7] See R. Diaz Guerrero, "Neurosis and the Mexican Family Structure," *American Journal of Psychiatry*, vol. 112 (1955), pp. 411-417; John Gillin, "Modern Latin American Culture," *Social Forces*, vol. 25 (March, 1947), pp. 243-248; O. Lewis, "Family Dynamics in a Mexican Village," *Marriage and Family Living*, vol. 21 (1959), pp. 218-226. See also O. Lewis, *Life in a Mexican Village—Tepoztlan Restudied* (Urbana: The University of Illinois Press, 1951) ; L. Saunders, *Cultural Difference and Medical Care: The Case of the Spanish-Speaking People of the Southwest* (New York: Russell Sage Foundation, 1954) .

[8] Daniel J. Levinson and Phyllis E. Huffman, "Traditional Family Ideology and Its Relation to Personality," *Journal of Personality*, vol. 23 (1955), pp. 251-273.

[9] Earl S. Schaefer and Richard O. Bell, "Development of a Parental Attitude Research Instrument," *Child Development*, vol. 29 (Sept., 1958), pp. 339-361.

[10] Diaz Guerrero, *op. cit.*

[11] Demos, *op. cit.*

[12] M. Ramirez and C. Taylor, "Sex Role Determinants in Attitudes Toward Education Among Mexican-American Adolescents." Report submitted to the Office of Education, Bureau of Research, U.S. Department of Health, Education and Welfare, 1967.

[13] See Margaret Clark, *Health in the Mexican-American Culture* (Berkeley and Los Angeles: University of California Press, 1959); Madsen, *op. cit.;* M. Ramirez, *op. cit.;* Manuel Ramirez III, "Identification with Mexican-American Values and Psychological Adjustment in Mexican-American Adolescents," *The International Journal of Social Psychiatry*, vol. 15 (Spring, 1969), pp. 151-156; A. J. Rubel, *Across the Tracks: Mexican-Americans in a Texas City* (Austin: University of Texas Press, 1966).

[14] H. N. Ricciuti and R. A. Clark, "A Comparison of Need-Achievement Stories Written by 'Relaxed' and 'Achievement-oriented' Subjects: Effects Obtained with New Pictures and Revised Scoring Categories" (Princeton, N. J.: Educational Testing Services, September, 1957).

[15] Ramirez and Taylor, *op. cit.*

[16] Rubel, *op. cit.*

[17] Bernard C. Rosen and Roy D'Andrade, "The Psychosocial Origins of Achievement Motivation," *Sociometry*, vol. 22 (1959), pp. 185-218.

[18] Landes, *op. cit.*

[19] Ramirez and Taylor, *op. cit.*

[20] Robert Rosenthal and Lenore F. Jacobsen, *Pygmalion in the Classroom: Teacher Expectation and Pupils' Intellectual Ability* (New York: Holt, Rinehart & Winston, Inc., 1967).

FAMILY ATTITUDE SCALE

1. The stricter the parents the better the child.
2. It is all right to have a good time even when there is work to be done.
3. All adults should be respected.
4. More parents should teach their children to be loyal to the family.
5. Girls should not be allowed to play with boy's toys, such as soldiers and footballs.
6. If a boy's family does not approve of his girl friend, he should not marry her.
7. Relatives are more important than friends.
* 8. Women are just as intelligent as men.
9. For a child the mother should be the dearest person in existence.

10. Fathers should always be respected.

*11. It is more important to work and plan for the future than it is to enjoy life now.

12. Some equality in marriage is a good thing but, by and large, the husband ought to have the main say-so in family matters.

13. It is more important to respect the father than to love him.

14. It doesn't do any good to try to change the future, because the future is in the hands of God.

*15. It is more important for a woman to obtain a college education than it is for her to learn how to take care of the house and raise a family.

16. Boys should not be allowed to play with girls' toys, such as dolls and tea sets.

17. Old people are wiser than young people.

18. We must live for the present. Who knows what tomorrow may bring?

19. If a girl's family does not approve of her boyfriend, she should not marry him.

*20. A child should follow his conscience. If he believes his parents are wrong, he need not obey them.

21. Children should never disappoint their parents.

22. It is not good for a married woman to work outside the home.

23. Women think less clearly than men and are more emotional.

24. It helps a child in the long run if he is made to conform to his parents' ideas.

25. The father should be the final authority in the family.

26. For a child the mother should be the most loved person in existence.

27. The word of an adult should never be questioned.

28. Young people get rebellious ideas, but as they grow older and wiser they give them up.

29. A girl should not date a boy unless her parents approve of him.

*Reversed items.

Part 4
THE STATUS OF
BILINGUAL EDUCATION

A New Focus on the Bilingual Child*

THEODORE ANDERSSON

EVERY PROFESSIONAL GROUP NEEDS PERIODICALLY TO PAUSE to take stock, to focus anew, and to make a fresh start. I believe that this is an opportune moment for modern foreign-language teachers to do precisely these things.

To many it will appear that with the passage of the National Defense Education Act in 1958 the teaching of modern languages has just taken such a new direction. This is true. We have plotted a new course to follow, but we are still far from having persuaded all — or perhaps even a majority — of our colleagues that the new objectives are better than the old. There are still many language teachers who believe that in stressing understanding and speaking in the early stages of a second-language learning we will inevitably neglect reading and writing and especially the study of literature. Nothing could be farther from the truth. On the contrary, we further believe that a sound basis in hearing, understanding, and speaking will assure better achievement in reading and writing and will permit

* First published in the *Modern Language Journal*, vol. 49, no. 3 (March, 1965), and reprinted by permission.

a more intimate understanding of literature and indeed of other aspects of a foreign culture.

But while our profession still needs to work hard to consolidate the theoretical gains envisaged by the Foreign Language Program of the Modern Language Association of America and by the Congress of the United States in its National Defense Education Act and succeeding legislation, we need to foresee and plan our next advance.

The language laboratory, television, and teaching-machine enthusiasts will perhaps envision our next step as a harnessing of these technological devices for the greater efficiency of teaching. I am completely in favor of continuing to study and experiment with these and other devices, which should be made to serve language teachers and learners more efficiently. Programmed instruction appeals to me, particularly, for two reasons. First, in order to program material successfully, a teacher needs to observe and test the learner's reaction to the materials, a process which will have the inevitable effect of improving his teaching. Second, self-instruction with the aid of a machine puts the chief responsibility for learning on the student, which is where it belongs.

Important as is the progress represented by the audio-lingual emphasis in language teaching and by the proper ancillary use of the language laboratory, television, and programmed self-instruction, it is rather in another area that we can hope for a more important new advance in language learning. In giving our attention to the bilingual child, we have perceived the importance of solving serious educational problems for those of our children whose first language is not English. It is precisely in this area, I believe, that we have our best chance to score a real educational breakthrough.

Dr. Joshua A. Fishman has estimated in his recently concluded report on "Language Loyalty in the United States" that in 1960 there were some nineteen million native speakers of European languages other than English in the United States, or 11 percent of our entire population. The figure would be considerably increased if it included speakers of all other languages. We have, at a guess, speakers of more than fifty different languages. Italian is spoken, according to the conservative 1960 census figures, by more than three and a half million. Spanish is spoken by nearly three and a half million; German is spoken by over three million; Polish is spoken by over two million; and French is spoken by over one million. Also spoken are such languages as Eskimo (in Alaska), Chinese, Japanese, Hawaiian, Vasayan, Tagolog, Portuguese (in Hawaii), and more than a dozen American Indian and Asian languages, in addition to the European languages that are spoken in the United States. It is a matter of national as well as professional interest for us to preserve these languages and to provide their speakers with an education which takes them properly into account. In this vital and complex undertaking, modern language teachers have a central role to play, but they need the help of colleagues in the social sciences — linguists, psychologists, anthropologists, and sociologists — and in professional education and politics. For, as Joshua Fishman has written in the last chapter of Volume III of his report, "the preservation and revitalization of America's non-English language resources (even for the purpose of cultural bilingualism) require, first and foremost, several planned modifications in the goals and processes of American society."

Without dwelling too long on our past and *present sins in foreign-language education,* let us rather select *seven "deadly" sins* which most urgently need correction and which bilingual education, if well conceived and executed, can help us eliminate.

Let us first try to put behind us the almost *useless two-year sequence of foreign-language study in our high schools.* Our need of language competence in this shrunken world is surely as great as that of European nations, where foreign languages — and usually more than one — are studied from four to ten years. In pleading for a six-year secondary school sequence of study for a modern foreign language, I should like also to plead for a four-year sequence for Greek and/or Latin. The present two-year sequence serves only to guarantee a slow death for the classics, for it fails to provide a reservoir of students from which must be recruited future classics teachers. The classics today are as badly off as were the modern languages in 1930 after the notorious Coleman Report had "settled" for a two-year sequence of study in high school.

The *late start made in learning modern languages in school* is the second sin which needs to be eliminated. Most pupils begin this study at the age of fourteen or fifteen when the human mind is least receptive to this kind of learning. If European children can continue foreign-language study for as much as ten years, it is because they begin at the age of ten to twelve, or even earlier. Justification for an early start, resting on psychological, neurological, social, political, and economic grounds, is to be found in a report published by the UNESCO Institute for Education in Hamburg in 1963, entitled "Foreign Languages in Primary Education: the Teaching of Foreign or Second Languages to Younger Children."

The *nonexistence* in many communities *of public kindergartens and nursery schools* is sin number three. Educational psychologists are so well aware of the sensitiveness of three-, four-, and five-year-old children and therefore of the educational importance of these early years that one is surprised not to hear more frequent protests against this educational waste. These years would be particularly valuable for language learning, for we know that children of this age can, under ideal conditions, absorb as many languages as are spoken in a given environment. The exploratory language class, which was doomed to fail in our junior high schools, belongs here with the very young if it belongs anywhere.

Our *traditional misconception of language* almost exclusively *in terms of grammar, reading, writing, and "belles lettres"* is the fourth sin which is crying for elimination. Without for a moment underestimating the value of literacy and literature, teachers who understand the nature of language and the process of language learning believe that the *learning of speech should precede that of writing,* especially for the young learner; that the learning of usage by direct imitation of authentic models should precede the formal study of grammar; and that literature should be studied not less intensively but in relation to other aspects of a culture.

Our sin number five is our *preference to hire John Smith over Juan Suarez for a Spanish teacher vacancy* for which both are otherwise equally well-qualified but for which Juan Suarez offers an additional qualification: his authentic Spanish. Just as a student needs an authentic speaker as a model, so he needs as a teacher an authentic, well-educated representative of another culture if he is to be imbued by direct experience with some intimate understanding of this culture. We should there-

fore reserve on our teaching staffs a larger place for well-qualified native-speaking teachers of foreign languages. In Texas,
where Spanish is widely taught in the schools — though not ex-
tensively enough — and where at least one Texan out of seven
speaks Spanish natively, only about one out of four teachers
of Spanish is a native speaker of Spanish. One out of two would
be a better ratio to aim at immediately. I know of one high
school in a non-Spanish-speaking area which has reached the
ratio of two out of three, to the satisfaction of all concerned.

Our inflexible, credit-counting education of teachers constitutes a sixth sin. *Certification should be no substitute for qualification,* especially now that we have the Modern Language
Association Foreign Language Proficiency Tests for Teachers
and Advanced Students to help us to measure proficiency as objectively as possible.

Coming a little closer to home, we must confess to our seventh
educational sin: *our failure to encourage Spanish-speaking children to speak Spanish,* a sin which we commonly commit in
school and on the playground, and our failure to respect the
great Hispanic culture of which our Spanish speakers are modest
representatives. This is part of an unthinking, inconsiderate,
and self-defeating national policy to destroy non-English languages and cultures in the United States — whether French, German, Spanish, Eskimo, Navaho, or Hawaiian. While paying
generous lip service to respect for individual differences, we
have, until the present, made little effort even to understand
the special needs of our non-English-speaking citizens. In this
connection let me call to your attention an unpublished paper
by my colleague, Dr. Mildred Boyer, on the subject of "Individual Differences and the War on Poverty," which is calculated to deepen our understanding of this problem. *We show
our disregard for other languages by not learning them.* We
tend to equate Hispanic culture, for example, with the underdeveloped, disadvantaged standard of living of Spanish speakers
among us without taking thought as to what is responsible for
this depressed living standard. It is the culmination of irony
that where Spanish-speaking children are at an age that would
make it easy and relatively inexpensive to help them to maintain and improve their language, we do all we can to destroy it.
And when we do find that we need adult citizens in great num-

bers who can understand and speak Spanish or other languages, we must through legislation repair at great cost the damage we have thoughtlessly done.

Since both theory and previous experiments, described, for example, in the UNESCO publication, *"The Use of the Vernacular Languages in Education,"* suggest the rightness and the effectiveness of using a child's mother tongue to begin his formal schooling, I suggest that it is most logical that Spanish-speaking children and their parents be oriented for school and be greeted in school by teachers who speak Spanish natively. Instruction should be done in Spanish and in English in such proportion as to build the child's sense of security. For the child whose experience has been exclusively or nearly exclusively in Spanish and who therefore understands and speaks Spanish within the limits of this experience, the teacher's first educational objective is to teach by means of spoken Spanish and to begin, when the child is ready, to teach the elements of reading, writing, and grammar, as well as an understanding of the literature and culture of his heritage. The *ultimate objective* would be thorough literacy in Spanish, as well as in English, *the development of a sense of pride in identifying with Hispanic culture,* and an active *desire to maintain and cultivate the Spanish language and culture,* while at the same time cultivating skill and pride in American speech and culture.

Since at the outset the average Spanish-speaking child will know little or no English, he should be introduced to English very gradually and with great care so as not to destroy his security and confidence.

Those who have seen adult college students in despair, because they cannot with their deficient knowledge of English penetrate the barriers of intellectual and even physical isolation, can well realize the terror which must beset a small child entering upon his first schooling without even the warming comfort of an understanding and affectionate word in a language which previously served him thus.

There need be no apprehension concerning a child's ultimate capacity to speak English. The main medium of instruction in most schools will be English, so that the Spanish-speaking child will normally have ample opportunity to hear and, when ready, to speak English. How long he will require to develop a readiness for reading and writing in English will have to be determined experimentally. However, as soon as he is ready, perhaps in the second grade, he should begin and thereafter receive steadily increased instruction and opportunity to practice.

The development in each language should be sequential, properly paced, and should proceed in such a way that each reinforces the other. Theoretically, the best results may be expected in schools having approximately equal numbers of English and Spanish speakers. English-speaking pupils can learn to understand and speak Spanish while the Spanish speakers learn to understand and speak English. In this situation the children will teach each other informally but perhaps even more effectively than can the teachers.

Since such a language program should have for its goal *not only to teach* English as a second language to Spanish speakers and Spanish as a second — hopefully no longer a foreign — language to English speakers, *but also to safeguard our children's mental health* and to correct popular misconceptions concerning the nature of language, the process of language learning, and the nature and content of culture; the parents and indeed the whole community would need to be brought into the program. In this somewhat new extension of the usual educational process, language teachers and educational administrators will need the help of social scientists and even public relations specialists. In an operation of this kind educators cannot afford to keep the community ignorant of what is happening lest the old misconceptions, prejudices, or lethargy destroy our efforts.

Clearly, in all this the language teacher plays a central, though only a partial, role. For this reason it is urgent that teacher-education institutions begin early to recruit and to prepare teachers with the necessary wisdom, personality, knowledge, and skill to carry out such a program. Such teacher candidates, who may already understand and speak Spanish competently, should not be delayed by being forced into a lockstep program of teacher preparation. Following the "Standards for Teacher-Education Programs in Modern Foreign Languages" issued by the Modern Language Association as the result of a conference at its administrative offices in New York on December 13, 1963, the most promising teachers or teacher candidates should be sought out and prepared in a flexible, almost individual, program and licensed to teach at the earliest possible moment on the basis of demonstrated proficiency, however acquired. Such a pilot program is in its initial stage at the University of Texas, under the direction of Dr. Joseph Michel.

These then, in conclusion, are the possibilities facing educators in bilingual areas. We have really been discussing two subjects. First, we need to correct our present miseducation of Spanish speakers in the South and Southwest; second, once we have learned how to manage the language education of bilinguals, we need to apply the same principles to language education in general. A new focus on the bilingual child could well serve to trigger an important revolution in American education.

Language Instruction and Intergroup Relations*

MANUEL H. GUERRA

THE OBJECTIVE OF THIS STUDY IS TO EXPLORE the diverse language instructional programs addressed to Spanish-speaking learners throughout the state of California, and to clarify and define the basic philosophy, goals, and purposes of such programs. There will be an endeavor to elucidate what social implications are inherent in the environmental teaching situation and their correlation to the basic purposes and aims of each respective program. Moreover, this study is concerned with the total educational program insofar as better intergroup relations are concerned and specifically how the language program may contribute vitally to the democratic processes of integration and involvement in the classroom.

It should be stated at the outset that much confusion exists among the lay public concerning the aims and purposes of language programs (both Spanish and English) and those to whom these programs are geared. It also should be stated that present Spanish programs addressed to all children, (Anglo, Negro,

* An original paper, printed by permission of the author and the Bureau of Intergroup Relations, California State Department of Education, Sacramento, California.

243

Spanish-speaking, etc.) often entertain lofty educational ideals of "world understanding," "cultural enrichment," or "world brotherhood," while the problems of the local community are overlooked; the opportunities to use community resources are bypassed; and, what is even more important, the need to make classroom recitation and interaction a dynamic experience in democratic living remains unfilled. In other words, the basic philosophy and goals of the Foreign Language program in California 92 to 94 percent of which is devoted to Spanish) is not oriented toward the betterment of intergroup relations in the classroom, in the school, and in the community.

FOREIGN LANGUAGES IN THE ELEMENTARY SCHOOLS (FLES)

The mandated Foreign Language Program in the elementary schools in California (Education Code 7604.6), concerning sixth, seventh, and eighth grade instruction, does not specify the language of instruction. This is left to the individual school board and district. Between 92 and 94 percent of this instruction is Spanish.

The basic purpose of this program, outlined by the professional societies to which the State Department of Education of California subscribes (such as the Modern Language Association of America), as well as the Spanish Curriculum Committee of the State Department of Education, is to teach a second language in all four skills (listening, speaking, reading, and writing) in the New Key — the audio-lingual method. The object of instruction is bilingualism — or the closest approximation to it. Culture and civilization are introduced to reinforce learnings and understandings about the life, art, and people of the society studied.

All children may participate in this instruction, regardless of ethnic background, intelligence quotient, or academic level. Some FLES programs start before the sixth grade; some are addressed to only the highly motivated and culturally enriched children; some exclude the Spanish-speaking child under one of five exclusion clauses of the "Casey Bill" which authorized the program. Many methods of instruction are used, including television, specialist teachers, self-contained classroom teachers, and audio-visual aids. What is important to state here, as it has been said before, is that the social value of FLES has seldom become an integral part of the program, either in objectives or practices, and the opportunity to teach better intergroup relations escapes the attention of many administrators and teachers. The latter do not know what to do with Spanish-speaking children during the Spanish program, and in many instances these youngsters are excluded from the program entirely.

ENGLISH AS A SECOND LANGUAGE

There are two basically different programs of English as a Second Language (ESL). In one the teacher uses the Spanish language as a bridge to teach English, thereby strengthening the learners' self-respect and cultural heritage. In the other, the teacher does not use the native tongue, or perhaps uses it only incidental to instruction, and he is not concerned with bilingualism or the social problems of this learner — he is only concerned with linguistic achievement in English. Both programs are professionally defensible on purely linguistic grounds, but it is unfortunate that in many instances "what" we teach is emphasized at the expense of "whom" we teach. The social goals of our society are not considered legitimate problems of the classroom, which contains children of diverse ethnic and language backgrounds.

SPANISH FOR SPANISH-SPEAKING CHILDREN

This program is a relative newcomer in some parts of California, although in New Mexico and Texas there have been various programs and experiments in this subject for several years. This program has two parts:

1. Spanish language and culture instruction for the Spanish-speaking child to develop fluency in the language of his heritage, to develop pride in his culture as well as help him socially to identify for emotional and psychological reasons, to cultivate the language talents and capabilities this youngster has acquired at home in order to broaden his humanistic understanding, to develop world awareness and contribute substantively to the mainstream of American life, be it in the community, the Peace Corps, AID, other government programs in Central and South America or Spain, or for his own personal enrichment.

2. To broaden the base and establish psychological rapport be-

tween teacher and learner in order to begin English instruction, using Spanish as the familiar frame of reference, that is, Spanish as a bridge to learn English. This approach differs from the ESL approach in that the social philosophy predominates and linguistic goals are a means to an end — bilingualism and biculturalism — in which the ultimate objectives are language development in two equal spheres of articulation and social integration of Mexican heritage in the mainstream of American life. Cultural pluralism is to be respected and sought; that is, the ability of the Mexican American child to function effectively, competitively, and happily in both language and culture environments should be our goal.

THE PROBLEM OF LANGUAGE SEGREGATION

Segregation of Mexican American children or any group of Spanish-speaking youngsters in a homogeneous educational situation is often carried out as an attack upon a mythical villain, "Spanish," as an expedient way of bringing together children with a similar "problem," or as an isolation of the contaminating malignancy of children whose citizenship remains somewhat foreign or uncertain. It is most unfortunate that good intentions cause such bad results, partly because of a lack of knowledge concerning America's Spanish-speaking societies, and partly because of a blindness which loses sight of our educational democracy. Most of the children in question are American citizens, or will be some day, and practices of segregation along linguistic lines stand in the way of the very goal which they endeavor to achieve. If the classroom cannot be an example of the American democratic process, it defeats its own purposes. Isolation and segregation of children for the purposes of instruction deny interaction and exchanges among children of diverse backgrounds. They rob the child of the opportunity to see himself and his neighbor in a realistic environment in which social differences coexist and to respect one another in social harmony. This adulteration of the classroom with its corresponding weakness and myopia penalizes all children: the Spanish-speaking child because it deprives him of making a contribution among his peers; the Anglo child because it deprives him of the benefits to be derived from exchanges with his Hispanic classmates; the Negro child because it denies him the opportunity to gain from this classroom interaction and learn that language differences discriminate as does color; and other youngsters because they are cheated out of the experience of belonging to a society of many ethnic and social differences. The classroom should prepare all children of every background for the challenges of community living. Thus, if the classroom does not convey a realistic picture of American society, our children will not be prepared to live a healthy and happy life in a community fraught with ignorance, prejudice, and fear.

Perhaps an effective substitute for homogeneous grouping would be to bring the Spanish-speaking children together for language orientation, English phonetics, and the appreciation of both bilingual and bicultural abilities. Then move these children into the Spanish FLES classes and integrate the Spanish program in the elementary school with both Anglo and Mexican American youngsters. Such children could exchange their skillful use of Spanish for assistance in English and reading. Using Spanish in the classroom would give them new pride, new status, and new incentive. Moreover, Spanish instruction could become more and more bilingual, until what is presently termed the "Spanish program" would in reality be a "Spanish and English" program. When Spanish and English are used without restraint in the classroom, without stigma and without apologies, the classroom atmosphere will lead to better learning of both Spanish and English. By implication, the dignity of children who come from Spanish-speaking homes will be enhanced, and their psychological desire to learn English will be greatly strengthened.

Our concern for intergroup relations embraces all children in the classroom, school, and community. But we are equally concerned that the opportunity to study another language is not abridged by our concern for the Spanish-speaking child and the English and Spanish programs addressed to him. Therefore, we would not like to see the programs of French, German, Italian, Chinese, Japanese, or any other language suffer because we wish to improve the quality of education in one area. In a smaller degree, the social purpose of language instruction exists among Chinese-Americans, Japanese-Americans, Portuguese-Americans, and Italian-Americans in California, just as the Filipino, Puerto Rican, Cuban, and Central and South American groups in California society are helped in the Spanish program. When we improve the Spanish program among Spanish-speaking learners or non-Spanish-speaking learners, or the English program among Spanish-speaking learners, let us make provisions for the teaching of other languages.

SUMMARY AND RECOMMENDATIONS

The teaching of Spanish to Spanish-speaking learners and the teaching of English to Spanish-speaking learners represent the same coin viewed from both sides. Language instruction, both English and Spanish, among the Spanish-speaking population of California is a complex and serious problem. This problem has not been clarified or resolved as of this date because there is not a program which vigorously addresses itself with initiative and imagination to the Spanish-speaking learner. Moreover, the severity of the problem is counterbalanced by the advantage and talent of the bilingual person, either because he possesses language ability or because he possesses the potential for language ability. Thus, the widely misunderstood "problem" of the Spanish-speaking learner is also a gift and an asset.

But language programs in the public schools of California, particularly as they refer to Spanish instruction, fail to take advantage of an excellent opportunity to improve intergroup relations. Despite their sophisticated goals and objectives, they overlook community problems and needs. It should be stated that international understanding begins at home, in fact, in the classroom. Such programs should incorporate in their humanistic outlook the critical needs of our community. World understanding and cultural enrichment are noble goals of humanistic endeavor, but they are meaningless if ethnic tensions and racial discord destroy the integrity of the school. There is a vital need to make Spanish instruction a vehicle of intergroup understanding in the state of California, and English as a second language a means to that end.

Segregated classrooms defeat their own purpose. Language segregation among Spanish-speaking learners is undemocratic, unrealistic, and retrogressive. Psychologically, the Spanish-speaking learner develops a resistance to English instruction which later he finds is impossible to overcome.

It would be well to reflect and understand that language

learning is the key to the door of happiness and success, or to the door of reticence and failure, depending on whether we lose sight of the human being to whom we gear our teaching and the vision of a better society.

The Implementation of a
Program of Bilingual Instruction*

HAROLD C. BRANTLEY

As I ATTEMPT TO DISCUSS THE IMPLEMENTATION of a program of
bilingual instruction, I am sure that a great deal of what we
have actually been doing will creep into the discussion. As we
study how best to implement a program of bilingual instruction, we find that several things need attention before the program actually gets under way. I should like to use an outline
suggested by Bruce Gaarder:

1. The analysis of the school population

2. Meeting state accreditation and legal requirements

3. Orienting the board of trustees, the community, the staff,
and the students toward such a program

4. The financial requirements of such a program

5. Solving the problems of scheduling involved in a bilingual
program

6. Provision for evaluating the program

* A paper presented at the October, 1966, Symposium at Tuscon, Arizona.
Sponsored by the National Education Association Committee on Civil and
Human Rights of Educators, the program was implemented in the United
Consolidated School District of Webb County, Texas.

ANALYSIS OF THE SCHOOL POPULATION

Why should there be a bilingual program of instruction or any other program of instruction other than the one that has been used for many years? To find the answer to this question, there must be a sensing on the part of the chief administrator that the program that has been used for all these years might not be doing as much for the students of his school as he had assumed it was doing. But when the administrator looks at his school population and sees a large number of overage children coming into the junior and senior high school and he begins to see that there is a high correlation between the number of these overage children and the number who have Spanish surnames, then he begins to ask himself these questions: What is the chief problem of these children? Why are they several years overage when they come into the junior high school? What have been the results of the methods that we have been using to teach these children who come from a different cultural and language background? I say when an administrator looks at his school system and finds some of these things to be true, he then begins to sense that there might be some other way of meeting more adequately the needs of these children whose native language is other than English. It is then that the administrator will make the decision as to whether he will implement a program of bilingual or some other method of instruction.

Of the students of the United Consolidated Independent School District, Webb County, Texas, 52.76 percent have Spanish surnames. These students are divided among the different schools as follows: In the high school 47.73 percent have Spanish surnames; in one elementary school 42.72 percent have Spanish surnames; in another elementary school 94.18 percent have Spanish surnames; and in the third elementary school, 87.5 percent have Spanish surnames. This school population index indicated to us something that we already knew — that Laredo is situated where two different cultures meet and mix continuously. We therefore felt that we had a sympathetic community environment for the implementation of a bilingual program.

ACCREDITATION AND LEGAL REQUIREMENTS

Before releasing in the community anything as different as the idea of a program of bilingual instruction, we felt that it would be wise to clear the program with the accrediting agency of the Texas State Department of Education. Then we felt that it was necessary to clear it with the attorney general's department of the state, because it has long been illegal to give instruction in the state of Texas in any language other than English. As we reviewed our proposed program with the people of the Texas Education Agency, they not only manifested great interest, but they offered hearty encouragement for the implementation of such a program. In addition, the agency gave us the assurance that the legal aspect of such a program could be sanctioned and approved, inasmuch as the program would be deemed an experimental one.

ORIENTATION TOWARD THE PROGRAM

After clearing with the official agencies regarding accreditation and state law requirements, it would appear that the next step would be a full explanation to the board of trustees, to the people of the community, and to the staff members and the students involved of what a program of this type would entail. In all probability this would be pursued in the order mentioned.

In the explanation to the board of trustees it would appear that a full background should be given for the reasons why the chief administrator thinks a different program of instruction might need to be tried. In addition, it would seem that the administrator and members of the board of trustees would need to meet in a very informal session in which all present would feel they had been given a full explanation of all ramifications of a program of bilingual instruction, and in which all would be given full opportunity to ask any questions regarding such a program. Following this free discussion, it would seem wise to invite a linguistic expert to appear before the board and to give a full explanation of the program from his point of view, giving all the information required in the implementation of such a program. Such linguistic experts can be found on the staffs of most colleges and universities.

Next, and at the onset, it would be wise to brief the parents of the students who will be involved in the bilingual program. In the case at United Consolidated we took advantage of every Parent-Teacher Association meeting to give a full explanation of the program and what would be expected of these children who were to be involved. In addition, we called special meetings in different parts of the school district for the express purpose of explaining to these parents how the program would work and how it would affect their children. We proceeded on the assumption that if there were to be objections to the initiation of such a program, these objections would come from two sources; first, from the parent of the English-speaking child who might feel that her child would be shortchanged in the amount of first grade work he would be able to cover, and second, from the Hispanic parent who was striving to become identified with middle-class Anglo culture.

After a full explanation to the people of the community, we next had to orientate all the members of the staff. We felt every staff member, regardless of the position he occupied, would sooner or later be affected by the results we hoped to attain by the implementation of this bilingual program of instruction. Again, we invited language specialists to talk to the staff members, and to answer their questions. Following these meetings, we involved the staff members who would actually be working in the bilingual program in a series of work sessions. A full explanation of the objectives of such a program, how the program would be scheduled, and how the teacher would be expected to perform in such a program was given.

In attempting to prepare the children who were to be involved for this new type of experience, everyone was made to feel from the very first day that he was very much needed in the classroom and furthermore that he had a very definite contribution to make to the life experiences that were to take place in the classroom that year. The policy adopted by the local board of trustees two years prior to the implementation of this bilingual program of instruction included a statement to the effect that all children were encouraged to become bilingual. Therefore, the students were not told, "Now, children, you have started to school, and everybody is going to speak English," for this would have been a direct contradiction to the policy. The children were told that they would spend part of their school day speaking in English and part in Spanish. They were made to feel from the very beginning that each had a language he could be proud of, and a language the rest wanted to learn.

FINANCIAL REQUIREMENTS

If a school district is contemplating the organization of some form of bilingual program, it would be well to consider how much more such bilingual instruction would cost, over and above traditional, routine instruction. Such things as adequate planning, workshops, in-service training sessions, and consultants' services need to be taken into consideration. Adequate instructional materials must also be provided. In the light of our experience, we have found that one of the biggest costs has resulted from developing, borrowing, and adapting instructional materials from our neighbors to the South. When we started our program, there were few if any instructional materials available on the market. More are appearing year after year, and it is hoped that in time adequate materials not only will be available but will be furnished by the state. And since a program of bilingual instruction is more expensive, we have a right to assume that we can expect a greater dividend from it.

PROBLEMS OF SCHEDULING

In attempting to answer the question in the mind of the administrator as to how to go about scheduling such a program of instruction, a brief description of how we began in 1964 in the first grade follows. At that time no attempt was made to divide the children in the first grade on the basis of their intelligence quotients, their racial origin, or which section of the school district the pupils came from. We wanted children of both Anglo and Hispanic background in the same classroom. From the very first day these children spent approximately 50 percent of their time in English-speaking experiences and 50 percent in Spanish-speaking activities. Of course, every opportunity is given for each child to learn more about the second culture with which he is associating. This is done by providing opportunities for the children to learn from one another their little songs, games, and other activities from both cultures and in both languages.

The amount of time we have scheduled for instruction in English and the amount of time devoted to instruction in Spanish differ from the schedule of most programs of bilingual instruction. Most programs begin with a relatively large percentage of time devoted to instruction in Spanish and a relatively small amount of time devoted to instruction in English, and as the program progresses through the months and through the years, gradually the percentage of time devoted to instruction in Spanish decreases whereas the percentage of time devoted to instruction in English increases. In our program we are not interested in completely phasing out the instruction in Spanish. We feel that at the end of the six years of elementary school, we would like our students to be equally at home in either Spanish or English, regardless of their ethnic background. This we feel can be accomplished only if we devote approximately the same amount of time to instruction in each language.

EVALUATING THE PROGRAM

One of the most important phases of implementing a bilingual program of instruction is the matter of providing for its adequate evaluation as it progresses. The evaluation of the program needs to be taken into account when the overall cost of the program is being considered. This is one of the main weaknesses of the present program which we instituted at United Consolidated. Whereas the school district has been able to provide most of the materials needed for such a program and has been able to meet the other expenses involved, it has been unable to secure adequate financing for such an experimental program. As a result, we have been unable to acquire the statistical data we otherwise would have at this point.

However, there are some generalizations we have been able to observe in the light of the experience we have had with the program during the first two years of its existence. We have been able to see from the very beginning that the child who comes from the different cultural and language background is definitely happier in school. In addition, we have been able to observe that the native English-speaker and his parents not only have accepted this new program, but they also are excited about what it can do for the native English-speaking child. We also have observed that the entire class moves at a much faster pace, since from the very beginning the native Spanish-speaking children know what is going on in the classroom, and consequently the native English-speaking children do not have to wait for the native Spanish-speaking child to figure out what is going on. The teachers gladly work in such a program because they are able to see the pleasure derived by all of the students when everyone can make a contribution and can feel that he is actually a part of the life experiences taking place in that classroom. Rarely in this program does a child develop withdrawal traits.

CONCLUSION

We have attempted to recount some of the problems that would need to be thought through before implementing a program of bilingual instruction. We are aware that mistakes have been made. However, the important thing is that we have made the start; we have not been satisfied to continue the methods used in the past. We are not willing to take the easy way out, and we feel that, so far as the Spanish-speaking child is concerned, the changes we have made in the methods of instruction constitute a significant improvement over what we have done for him in the past.

Teaching the Bilingual Child:
Research, Development, and Policy*

A. BRUCE GAARDER

WE DO NOT NEED TO OBSERVE THE CAREERS of such brilliant men as Julian Green, Salvador de Madariago, and Joseph Conrad to know that bilingualism can be an invaluable intellectual and social asset. Innumerable cases attest to this truism. Nor do we need to observe many illiterate speakers of two languages to know that in some cases bilingualism correlates negatively with a full measure of personal development. This paper assumes that whether the bilingualism of a child is to be a strong asset or a negative factor in his life depends on the education he receives in both languages. The child in this case is the native-born American youngster whose mother tongue is not English. The concern is for both that mother tongue and English. Since it has been our public school tradition either to ignore that mother tongue or to discourage its use, this paper is concerned chiefly with research efforts designed to strengthen and maintain it, on the further assumption that strengthening and maintaining the mother tongue will contribute powerfully and directly to the development of the personality and intellect and

* An original paper printed by permission of the author.

in turn increase the student's ability to learn English and learn through English.

In these assumptions the most important issue is unmistakable: At what age, by what means, to what degree, and in what relationship to his studies in English should the child achieve literacy in his mother tongue?

An international "committee of experts" convened in 1951 by UNESCO to discuss the use of vernacular languages in education declared that a child's mother tongue is the best medium for teaching him. The committee included in its report a worldwide survey showing that it is indeed generally conceded that every child should begin his formal education in his mother tongue. Nevertheless, educational practices in the United States support the "ethnocentric illusion" that for a child born in this country English is not a foreign language, and virtually all instruction in schools is through the medium of English. It would seem, therefore, that among the research projects most needed is a series of classroom-based studies to test as a hypothesis that statement which the rest of the world considers axiomatic.

CLASSROOM-BASED RESEARCH

This research would be undertaken simultaneously in a number of typical situations described below, and with the conditions approaching those noted in each case.

Basic plan for bilinguals

In actual practice, there are anomalies in the foreign language development policies in American education which approach the fraudulent. One of these is the situation in the American high school which results, for example, in the bilingual French-English-speaking child's making the lowest grade in the French class. This anomaly, commonplace whether in French, Spanish, or German, is easy to explain if not to justify; the teacher has only a smattering competence in the foreign language, and her attempts to communicate in it embarrass both herself and the native speakers in her class.

I have heard teachers explain this inability to communicate with Mexican American pupils in New Mexico by saying that the Spanish they taught and spoke was "Castilian." In addition, the teacher is using a book and methods geared exclusively to the supposed needs of the monolingual majority of the class. Consequently, the bilingual students, who in most cases have more knowledge and mastery of the tongue than the teacher or their classmates will ever have, are confused and neglected, and they, too, often conclude that there is something wrong with the language they speak and with themselves for speaking it.

The same anomaly pervades the program called FLES (Foreign Language in the Elementary School) and every other level of language teaching; the federal government encourages a multimillion-dollar expenditure annually for language development (in both the "common" and the "neglected" languages), but no part of the effort is directed specifically to the further development of these same languages in the more than one in ten Americans who already have a measure of native competence in them. Rather, at best, our generally unformulated national policy is to ignore, at worst to stamp out, the native competence while at the same time to undertake the miracle of creating something like it in monolingual ability.

Development, rather than research, is called for here: the application of long-known methods in many and varied experimental settings at every level up to age sixteen, to make each student's bilingualism all that it can be. Specifically, the experimentation here recommended focuses exclusively on the development of a high level of literacy in the non-English mother tongue (N-EMT). This is not "foreign language" or "second language" study as these are traditionally conceived and organized and does not involve monolingual speakers of English except as noted in item 5 below. In brief, each "experiment" is simply the provision of at least one class daily in mother-tongue language study, and study through the mother tongue for all N-EMT students.

Some specific suggestions are necessary to help avoid the worst of the mistakes that mar experimentation of this kind.

1. The teacher should be a vigorous, literate, native speaker of the standard variant and, if possible, of the student's variant of the language. For work at the upper elementary school level and above, the teacher should have learned through the medium of the N-EMT the subject matter to be taught. His competence could be determined and his certification based on the results

of proficiency tests such as those which the Modern Language Association has prepared for the five common languages. Pennsylvania and New York have already used these tests for this purpose. For languages lacking such standardized tests, examination of teacher candidates could be by examining committees.

2. The N-EMT pupils would, for the most part, follow the normal curriculum in English. Their schedules would be adjusted, however, to provide at least one period daily in the N-EMT.

3. The N-EMT would be the exclusive medium of instruction in all N-EMT classes. From the beginning, instruction would be focused on the language per se for only a minimum part of the time. The major emphasis would always be on the regular subjects of the curriculum such as mathematics, science, and the social studies, learned through the medium of the non-English language.

4. Only native "speakers" of the non-English language would be admitted to these classes, with the single exception noted in item 6 below. The minimum requirement for classification as a native "speaker" would be sufficient proficiency in listening comprehension to understand normal conversation and simple explanations.

5. Given the widely varying background of such native speakers, there might be need for a pretest for placement purposes. Such a test for speakers of Spanish has been developed by the public schools of Albuquerque, New Mexico.

6. At the high school level, monolingual students who are learning the same second language could be admitted to these classes of native speakers as a special honor if they demonstrate unusual aptitude for such learning.

7. When administratively possible, double academic credit should be granted: for the foreign language study per se and for the work in the subject field taught through the foreign language. For example, a class in geography studied in Polish could earn credit in Polish and in geography.

8. One class period daily would suffice for this instruction. Experimentation could be directed to the question of whether these weekly periods would be sufficient to develop a high enough level of literacy.

9. Experimentation of this kind could begin without loss at

any academic level, with any number of students from two to thirty-five in a class. If the number of non-English mother-tongue speakers in a school is quite small, the children may well be grouped on levels of competence without too much regard for grade level. Thus, pupils in grades 1, 2, and 3 could be together, or those in grades 3, 4, and 5, or those in grades 4, 5, and 6.

10. The section in this paper on corrective analyses-teaching materials is pertinent here. Particularly important is the emphasis on learning through the language rather than concentrating solely on the language itself.

11. Basic to the two-language development program under discussion is the need to reinforce the non-English ethnic group's self-image as speakers of their native language. Irrespective of the extent to which their speech deviates from "cultivated standards" — and in some cases there may be virtually no deviation — they are likely to regard their language as somehow inferior, unsuited for use in one or more domains strongly dominated by the official language, and themselves as weakly representative speakers of the tongue. Here the concept of linguistic relativity, sometimes exaggeratedly espoused by descriptive linguistics, should be strongly emphasized. Whatever the speaker's dialect and idiolect, it should not be suggested that he is to give it up and thereafter speak and write in another, different, "better" way. (Common observation shows that he will never forget it and will be able to return to it at will throughout his life.) Rather he is to learn another, a *third* language or language style which will be more appropriate and effective in other situations in which he might aspire to take part.

Basic plans for bilingual schools

The program set forth on the accompanying chart is most applicable in schools where at least half of the pupils at all elementary grade levels are N-EMT speakers. It is intended to develop bilingualism in both English mother tongue (EMT) and N-EMT pupils. It is modeled closely on the Coral Way elementary school bilingual program established in 1968 with Ford Foundation support in Dade County, Florida. The director of this particular Ford Foundation Project was Pauline M. Rojas.

First Grade	Second Grade	Third Grade
Oral English—English reading with grouping by ability—English writing	Oral English—English reading—English writing	Oral special studies in English—English writing
Oral Spanish—Spanish reading with grouping by ability—Spanish writing	Oral Spanish—Spanish reading—Spanish writing	Oral social studies in Spanish—Spanish writing
Mathematics in English—Art in English	Mathematics in English—Art in English	Mathematics in English—Science (oral) in English (demonstration)

Fourth Grade	Fifth Grade	Sixth Grade
Social studies in English with readings —English reading— English writing	Social studies in English with reading and writing—English reading—English writing	Same as for Fifth grade
Social studies in Spanish with readings —Spanish reading— Spanish writing	Social studies in Spanish with reading and writing—Spanish reading	
Mathematics in English—Science in English with reading and writing	Mathematics in English—Science in English with reading and writing	

Each language group should be at least one third of the total group at each elementary grade level. All pupils are together at all times except for ability grouping in grade 1. Teaching should be in Spanish approximately one third of the day by highly literate, trained, native-speaking teachers; in English two thirds of the day by a different person of equal qualification. Playground supervision should be alternated daily, using teachers of the two languages.

Points to be kept in mind:

1. All teachers responsible for a second language as a subject should be trained as second-language teachers.

2. All other teaching is done by normal elementary school teaching methods.

3. Is the N-EMT group as proficient in the use of English and

in other learnings as a comparable group which received no instruction in the mother tongue?

4. Is the EMT group as proficient in the use of English and in other learnings as a comparable group which received no instruction in a second language?

5. The non-English language instructors should be highly literate in that language and should have studied in that language the subjects they are to teach through it.

6. It seems reasonable to suppose that the best reading (or listening or discussion) material for any child is that which is related to his own life experience so that he can recognize himself in it and identify with the material. For this reason many teachers begin the teaching of reading by using simple stories composed by the students themselves.

Variables affecting language learning

In Montevideo, Uruguay, there have long been K-6 second-language schools. Cranden Institute is a specific example. The case is cited from personal observation by Miss Elizabeth Reesee, Specialist for Foreign Languages, United States Office of Education. These schools in Montevideo have the following characteristics:

1. All instruction is (for example) in English at all levels.

2. Classes of about thirty students are under the charge of a single teacher.

3. All playground and out-of-class speech is in Spanish. (Virtually all students are native speakers of Spanish or prefer that tongue.)

4. Parents and students are highly disposed to foreign-language learning.

5. Most students are from the upper or upper-middle socioeconomic class.

6. All teachers are natively competent in the school language and well trained for their work.

7. Highly literate, native-like use of English by all students is the result.

There are similar schools in Texas where all, or virtually all, of the pupils are native speakers of Spanish and where English is the sole medium of instruction. The analogy with the Montevideo situation weakens at items 4, 5, and 6, which, it may be reasonably hypothesized, contributed much to the achievement of item 7. These three variables should be investigated, with the objective of modifying the school situation so as to offset or overcome deficiencies attributable to them.

Analogy and inference vs. analysis

A major question besetting foreign-language teachers is the shifting interrelation between learning by analogy and learning by analysis at each stage or maturity level from infancy to adulthood. Traditional language teaching methods have relied heavily on analysis; audio-lingual methodology purports to depend heavily on analogy. If all pupils began language learning in grade one, there would be no problem. Since there are, in fact, beginning groups at ages six to twenty-five and older, one pattern cannot fit them all. An approach to this problem could be made by a study of the age of onset and relative strength at each age level of the components of language-learning aptitude isolated by Carroll, the motivational and attitudinal factors described by Lambert and his associates, plus the ability to reason by analogy and inference basic to all first-language learning. Armed with the results of such a study, the language teacher could better adjust his dosage of analogy (pattern drill, over-learning) and analysis (rules, explanations) to suit his learners.

Since analogical reasoning (I walked, I talked, ergo, I looked) and inferential determination of meaning (for example, each of us knows thousands of "words," but only a few score or hundreds were learned consciously by dictionary or other word study) are basic to first-language learning and in lesser degree to second-language mastery, there is need for a study of these two processes and for the development of teaching procedures which will (1) make students aware of their function, (2) give step-by-step practice in the conscious application of both processes, and (3) exploit both processes at every point in the language course.

Foreign language, literary studies, and other academic fields

The traditional curricular pattern in American colleges and universities and in secondary schools offering more than two years of foreign language study has produced a mutually supporting relationship between language study and only one other academic field: literary studies. This has meant that after the "introductory" and "intermediate" courses (and sometimes a bit of "advanced composition" or "conversation") the only further formal courses involving foreign language have been courses in the corresponding literature. This practice leaves out of account the possibility that some students might wish to do advanced study in a foreign language applied to specialization in an academic field other than literature.

Notable deviations from the language to literature tradition are found in those institutions which offer work in the "neglected" languages. It is not unusual for the courses in such languages as Chinese, Arabic, or Persian to have been introduced at the insistence of "area" specialists as a means of strengthening advanced offerings in their fields. This is not the case with the more commonly taught languages.

It seems particularly important to provide the opportunity for bilinguals at the college level to capitalize on their non-English language by professional specialization in, for example, political science, international law or relations, anthropology, or economics, related specifically to foreign regions where that language is spoken. This would require developing the same strong, mutually reinforcing relationship between foreign language study and other fields as now exists only for literary studies. A good deal of preliminary work along this line has been done at Goucher College in Baltimore for majors in International Relations and Political Science, including the expansion of library holdings, indices of periodicals, preparation of a tape library of speeches and other works, presentation of portions of courses through the foreign language, requirement of oral and written reporting in the language, and portions of tests and final examinations to be written in the language.

COOPERATION WITH ORGANIZED ETHNIC GROUPS

Nationwide there are ethnic groups, societies, churches, and parochial schools with a strong commitment to the maintenance and development of competence in a language other than English. Judged in the light of a policy which considers competence in modern foreign languages as a national asset, the efforts of these groups should be strongly encouraged, supported, and coordinated where feasible with those of the public schools.

Within the limited context of this paper the salient needs are two:

1. Language materials and instruction-through-language materials for such teaching.

2. Standardized tests suitable for use in grades 4, 6, 8, 10, and 12 to measure achievement in the four language skills.

COMMUNITY AND REGION-BASED RESEARCH

Any effort to develop the full potential of the bilingualism of native American speakers of a language other than English could profit from answers to two questions:

1. What is the range of dialect variation within the entire community of American speakers of that language?

2. How does the dialect variant of the particular group of speakers under consideration differ from the standard variant which you want them to learn?

This information is essential to the production of teaching materials, particularly for use in secondary schools and above. The most casual observation will show marked differences, for example, between the Spanish spoken in the northern Rio Grande Valley and that of San Antonio. Are these regional differences marked enough to warrant different teaching materials for students in the two areas?

Languages in contact

Much needs to be done to clarify the changing status of the two languages in contact in the bilingual community at every level. Of particular interest in the context of this chapter — apart from basic linguistic surveys of each bilingual speech community — are linguistic interference, borrowings, and switching. If a strict domain separation becomes institutionalized so that each language is associated with a number of important but distinct domains, bilingualism can become both universal and stabilized even though an entire population consists of bilinguals interacting with other bilinguals.

Sociological studies of peoples in contact

Because it is constantly changing, the dynamics of a two-language community, whether a neighborhood, an entire town, or a region, can never be sufficiently studied. Research of the kind done by Oscar Lewis and his associates in Tepoztlan (Mexico), if performed in the typical American setting where two peoples, each with its own mother tongue, come in contact exclusively through only one of those languages, the socially dominant one would help the teacher, the school administrator, and the policy makers to act more wisely. To be most useful this research should show both the anthropologist's concern for the dynamics of belief and behavior systems under stress and in contact and the scientific linguist's awareness of language as a factor in interpersonal and intergroup relationships.

Research on the conflict of two languages within the individual personality requires first that the investigator realize that for a child whose mother tongue is not English, English is a foreign language. The difficulty of grasping this point is typified in the Kobut-Lezea research. These highly sophisticated researchers — referring to the twenty-five Polish, three Norwegian, and two Greek-speaking children they worked with — concluded that the subjects of their study acquired a dual language system because they heard the second language used in the home as a part of their everyday experience.

Attitude formation

The work of Wallace Lambert and his associates strongly indicates that the mastery of a second language depends on two independent sets of factors — intelligence and aptitude, on the one hand, and on the other hand, a complex of motivation and attitudes vis-à-vis the people and culture represented by the second language. In the light of this theory there are in the American Southwest, Louisiana, and Canadian-French New England marked ethnocentrism and authoritarian orientation and unfavorable attitudes in both the English and non-English groups of speakers. There is more than a suggestion of a cruel dilemma if Lambert's "integrative" attitude (studying as if one desired to become a member of the other group) is required in order to produce the highest degree of second language mastery. In this case the research need is prompted by the fact that psychologists are currently working on the problem of changing attitudes. Additional studies and experiments directed toward the formation of more favorable attitudes and motivations in the Lambertian sense might be fruitful.

Bilingual dominance configuration

Without denying the likelihood that most speakers of a given age and socioeconomic level in an area of stable population will speak alike, it must be recognized, too, that members of a minority group may also differ widely among themselves in the use of both their native language and the dominant one. These speakers of a subordinate language are in a period of linguistic transition where youngsters sometimes cannot communicate with their grandparents. They are in areas of marked urban vs. rural differences (some of them traversed annually by uneven waves of illiterate or semiliterate foreign national migrant speakers of the same tongue). They find themselves subjected on every side to forces of acculturation, all attending schools of greatly varying excellence and where all instruction is given in a dominant language. All of these situations are a part of an increasingly mobile society. Therefore, the bilingualism of these people will show wide variations in pattern, quite apart from the relative excellence of their use of the language. They will differ with respect to their active or passive control of the language (Does the "bilingual" think in the language? Does he both understand and speak it? Can he write, or does he only read it?); with respect to the situation where the language is used (Home? Church? Club? Work? In public? With his children or only with his parents? With his boss as well as his subordinates?); and with respect to topics and styles of usage (Can he discuss religion, the malfunctioning of his automobile, or his profession, in both languages? Can he send and receive at each stylistic level as well in one language as in the other? Are there technical or stylistic gaps in his vocabulary?). All of the above is to say that there is immediate need for the construction of a survey instrument which will determine the bilingual dominant configuration of a given group or individual.

It is important to know the "dominance configuration" of any bilingual group that becomes a subject of study, for at least these three reasons: (1) With such knowledge those charged with the education of the bilingual child or adult are better equipped to appraise him and prepare a course of study for him. (2) The dominance configuration, determined periodically and combined with tests of language proficiencies, would be the surest means of determining changes in the status of language maintenance and language shift in bilingual-speech communities. (3) It seems likely that an accurate index of bilingual dominance would be a powerful weapon in support of the position that "balanced" bilinguals will not score below monolinguals in tests of both verbal and nonverbal intelligence. Provided with an adequate instrument for determining bilingual dominance configuration in any of our bilingual areas, we could duplicate, in effect, the Paul-Lambert study of bilingual ten-year-olds in Montreal which gave strong evidence that if the children are equally well educated in both languages, i.e., "balanced" bilinguals, they are superior in both verbal and nonverbal intelligence to monolinguals and also appear to have a greater mental flexibility, a superiority in concept formation, and a more diversified set of mental abilities.

RESEARCH BASED ON THE BILINGUAL INDIVIDUAL

Despite conditions of learning which do not favor the development of highly literate "balanced bilingualism" in Americans who enter school with a mother tongue other than English, some individuals do achieve this goal. It is hypothesized that a study of a representative sample of such persons would produce information of value to educators concerned with the bilingual child. The need here is for a survey instrument with which to conduct interviews in depth of adults identified as "highly literate balanced bilinguals." "Balance" in this case cannot be expected to mean absolute parity, since this is always impossible. Rather, it would mean a relatively equal number of important domains associated with each language, and relatively equal literacy in each. The difficulty in identifying such persons except by personal observation suggests that this research might follow the development of the index of bilingual-dominance configuration noted elsewhere in this paper.

Study of second-language acquisition

There is urgent need for a study of second-language acquisition under "natural" (coordinate) conditions on at least three age levels, such as infancy, six years, and fifteen years, to determine the sequence of learnings in the three language units: phonology, morphology, and system. Each such study should be conducted with the assistance of a person who is competent in descriptive linguistics in order to note the complete process of developing phonemic discrimination. By "natural" conditions is meant total immersion in the second-language environment in a school and play situation, e.g., a monolingual American child placed in a French-language boarding school in France. Such a study could provide invaluable insights into the sequencing of second-language learning materials.

Along with this day-by-day study of the acquisition of a second language to the point where the basic structures of the language have been mastered, there is need for longitudinal studies of the development of bilingual children through the twelfth grade.

Bilingualism and a third language

There is much informal, usually subjective, evidence to support the belief that bilingualism acquired by natural means facilitates the learning of a third language. It is also quite common for the second language to be taught in such a manner as to facilitate the later acquisition of a third. This is especially significant, because although most Americans have little opportunity in school to study any language other than French, German, or Spanish, many might find in later years a greater need for Chinese, Polish, or Twi. The research indicated in this connection is on two levels: (1) the development of objective evidence (possibly through case studies of individuals) of the relationship of bilingualism to third-language learning and the conditions and mechanisms by which the relationship manifests itself, and (2) the application of these conditions and mechanisms to the formal school learning of a second language in order to facilitate maximally the learning of a third one.

TEACHING MATERIALS

For the development of adequate teaching materials, the immediate need is for a study of the range of dialect variation. Thereafter, work should begin on an analysis of the standard form contrasted with each dialectical variant to facilitate the production of teaching materials. The next step would be the development of the teaching materials themselves that would be designed for presentation through that language and with at least the following features: (1) intensive oral drill from re-corded patterns, (2) extensive reading and listening to recorded literature, (3) extensive use of sound films on technical and other subjects to broaden the student's horizon and sense of his own possibilities, (4) controlled composition, and (5) in-creasing emphasis on learning through the language rather than learning the language as an end in itself.

A body of materials should be assembled in both printed and recorded form, consisting of short selections. Usually these should be paragraphs of exposition, narration, or dialogue, graded by difficulty, and each presented in variant forms corre-sponding to the appropriate levels of style. Such materials would not completely fill the stylistic gaps in the vocabulary of "un-balanced" bilinguals, but they could be used to develop an awareness of those levels.

An Analysis of the Need
for Bilingual Legislation*

AUGUSTUS F. HAWKINS

INTRODUCTION

Is THERE A NEED FOR CONGRESS to create special legislation to assist state and local agencies in developing bilingual education? To answer this question properly, we should consider the following:

1. Are non-English-speaking children currently receiving the same educational opportunities as English-speaking children? If non-English-speaking children are not receiving the same educational opportunities as English-speaking children, what is the magnitude of their problem? Is it of national concern?

2. What is the significance of bilingual education? Are bilingual programs successful in alleviating the problems of the non-English-speaking child?

3. Have the state and local authorities adequately confronted the problems of the non-English-speaking child? Are bilingual programs currently being developed by local school districts?

* Testimony presented before the General Subcommittee on Education, of the Committee on Education and Labor, House of Representatives, June, 1967, pp. 90-98. Reprinted by permission of the author, a Representative in Congress from the state of California.

4. Can the needs of the non-English-speaking child be met under current law; for example, are the funds provided under the various provisions of the Elementary and Secondary School Act of 1965 sufficient to meet the bilingual needs of non-English-speaking children?

THE PLIGHT OF THE NON-ENGLISH-SPEAKING CHILD

"The most signal failure in American education," states Monroe Sweetland, consultant for the National Education Association, "[is] our failure to provide equality of educational opportunity for the non-English speaking child." Tragic statistics bear out the fact that our schools have failed in the vital area of providing equal educational opportunities for the child from a non-English-speaking background.

U.S. Commissioner of Education Harold Howe states:

> Clearly our schools must give greater attention to the special needs of non-English speaking children. The median years of school completed by the Mexican American in the Southwest is 7.1 years. The median for the Anglo child in the Southwest is 12.1 years. For the non-white, it is 9.0 years of school completed. These statistics make their own case for special programs for the non-English-speaking child.

More statistics provide proof that educational programs for the non-English-speaking child have been inadequate; in fact, in most cases, nonexistent. "The educational system in California [one of the most progressive states if not *the* most progressive state in the field of education], as throughout the Southwest," states Miguel Montes, member of the California State Board of Education, "*has not* been able to solve the perplexing problem of educating the Mexican-American child." Mr. Montes offers us the following statistics "that serve as testimony to the magnitude of the failure. The Mexican-American has an educational level of 8.6 grade in California as compared with the grade level of 10.2 for the Negro and 12.1 for the Anglo." Thus the Mexican-American child lags three and a half years behind the average Anglo child in the state of California.

According to Dr. Julian Samora, professor at Notre Dame University, "The biggest problem to date in the Spanish-speaking community with regard to education is the dropout problem." In the state of California, according to State Board of Education member Miguel Montes, the Mexican-American has a higher rate of dropout than any other group of children. As stated in the National Education Association publication, *The Invisible Minority,* many of the 1.75 million Spanish sur- named children of elementary and secondary school age "ex- perience academic failure in school. At best, they have limited success. A large percentage become school dropouts." A Cali- fornia study found that as of 1960, more than 50 percent of the Spanish-speaking males and nearly 50 percent of the Spanish- speaking females fourteen years old and older had *not* gone beyond the eighth grade. By contrast, only 27.9 percent of the males and 25 percent of the females over fourteen in the total population had not gone beyond the eighth grade. Thus, as stated by author and educator Herschel T. Manual, "the pro- portion of school dropouts among the Spanish speaking is far higher compared to the English speaking."

Why do Spanish-speaking children drop out of school in such large numbers? The major cause of the Spanish-speaking child's failure in school is the *language barrier.* A California study known as the Lindsay Report states:

> These children [Mexican-American] start school with a decided handicap [they are unable to speak English], fall behind their classmates in the first grade, and each passing year finds them farther behind. They are conditioned to failure in the early years of their schooling and each passing year only serves to reinforce their feelings of failure and frustra- tion.

Professor Sharp, of Texas Western University, states that

> during the two or three years of primary school while the [non-English speaking] pupil is acquiring a minimal knowledge of English, he falls seriously behind his English speaking contemporaries in ... the community. This loss in subject-knowledge is seldom made up by the time he enters high school, where he finds himself unable to compete scholastically with his Anglo-American schoolmates.

Our failure to provide adequate education for our Spanish- American children continues on into the vital field of higher education. According to Miguel Montes, at UCLA, situated where over 800,000 Mexican Americans reside, "Only seventy students out of [over] 25,000 [now there are over 27,500] are Mexican Americans. . . . Since the educational system has not met the educational needs of the Mexican-American child, few are prepared and encouraged to proceed on to higher education." In a current article (April, 1967) entitled "Educating Mexican-

American Children: A Contemporary Problem," Professor Donald Melcher from the University of Texas states:

> Only about 1,400 of the 200,000 Mexican-American children [or .47 of 1 percent] entering the first grade this year will complete one or more years of college at the current rate of attrition. This figure is [frightfully] small when compared with the rate of the total population, where about 21 percent of the entering first graders will attend college. This comparison reflects the degree to which education has not met the needs of Mexican-American children.

We must not forget that our inability to provide equal educational opportunities for the non-English-speaking may very well be a major cause of the high degree of poverty among our non-English-speaking people. The tragic record of unemployment, low income, and social disparity among the non-English speaking is ever present. "The problems of the Mexican-American," states Dr. Frank Cordasco, Professor of Education at Montclair State College and Educational Consultant to Migration Division of the Commonwealth of Puerto Rico, "include all of the interrelated complexities of low income, unemployment, . . . school retardation, low occupational aspirations, delinquency, [and] discrimination. . . . The Mexican-American child classically demonstrates that an almost inevitable concomitant of poverty is low educational achievement." U.S. Commissioner of Education Harold Howe stated at a recent House subcommittee hearing that "These [non-English-speaking] groups . . . are groups who have suffered all the problems of deprived minority groups in our society: the problems of poverty, the problems of prejudice, the problems of economic exploitation. . . ." The Spanish-speaking provide an excellent example of the plight that befalls the non-native speaker in our present culture. We find poverty far more prevalent among Mexican Americans than among Anglo-Americans. In the five southwestern states, 21 percent of the general population had an annual income of less than $3,000 in 1960. For Mexican-American families for that same year the percentage of families with average annual income below $3,000 was 34.8 percent. Edward Roybal, the distinguished representative from California, at a recent subcommittee hearing stated the following statistics:

> The median income of the Spanish speaking that reside in the Southwest is $2,804 a year. In the urban communities, [their] median income is $3,197. In the rural non-farm areas, [their] median income is $1,871. . . .

As we review these amounts that are received annually by the Spanish speaking people of the Southwest, we find in almost every instance they are below the so-called poverty level. . . .

Let us insert again that an almost inevitable concomitant of poverty is low educational achievement.

All the statistics I have just cited reflect the plight of the non-English-speaking child. Not only has the non-English-speaking child experienced educational deprivation, but, in most cases, social and economic deprivation as well. His plight is ever so real; his needs ever so neglected.

A NATIONAL PROBLEM

The Mexican American is our largest linguistic minority group (about 70 percent of the total non-English-speaking are Spanish-speaking), but let me emphasize that the problem of educating the non-English-speaking child includes many language groups other than the Spanish-speaking. Scattered throughout the nation, there are over one million non-English-speaking students of school age (six to eighteen years old) that do not speak Spanish who represent some thirty different language groups. The problem of educating the non-English-speaking child is of national concern; it is a problem not merely affecting a single language group or the Southwest, but it is a problem affecting the entire nation.

Herman Badillo, President of the Borough of the Bronx, at a recent subcommittee hearing presented some important statistics on the problem in New York. Of a total school population in New York City in 1963 of 1,045,554, more than 8.4 percent or 87,782 were non-English-speaking pupils. Of the 586,046 elementary school pupils in New York in 1963, more than 11.5 percent or 67,506 were non-English-speaking pupils. Dr. Bernard Donovan, New York City Superintendent of Schools, points out that in New York City alone 226,000 children are of Puerto Rican origin, of whom 100,000 are non-English-speaking and another 126,000 speak some English but have serious difficulty with the language. As Dr. Donovan reminds us ". . . this is a very sizable problem."

Dr. Cordasco presents us with more glaring facts. At a recent subcommittee meeting he stated:

How the Puerto Rican child has fared in the mainland schools is best illustrated in the experience in New York City where Puerto Ricans have the lowest level of formal education of any identifiable ethnic or color group.

Only 13 percent of the Puerto Rican men and women twenty-five years of age and older in 1960 had completed either high school or more advanced study. Among New York's non-white—predominantly Negro—population, 31.2 percent had completed high school; and the other white population—excluding Puerto Ricans—did even better. Over 40 percent had at least completed high school.

The dropout problem is a tragic fact among the Puerto Ricans of New York. States Dr. Cordasco:

> In 1960 more than half—52.9 percent—of the Puerto Ricans in New York City twenty-five years of age and older had less than an eighth grade education. In contrast, 29.5 percent of the non-white population had not finished the eighth grade and only 19.3 percent of the other whites had so low an academic preparation.
>
> [Furthermore] a 1961 study of a Manhattan neighborhood showed that fewer than 10 percent of Puerto Ricans in the third grade were reading at their grade level or above. The degree of retardation was extreme.

And let us remember that the problem in New York City is not just with the large Puerto Rican school population. Mr. Badillo points out that out of 1,045,554 pupils in the City schools in 1963, 179,223 were Puerto Rican while 45,330 were foreign, mainly from Western European countries. The stark, cruel facts in the Southwest and New York are quite clear; the schools have not been able to provide adequate educational opportunities for the non-English-speaking child.

Important to remember is that the bilingual legislation before us is tailored to meet the needs of *all* non-English-speaking children scattered throughout the nation (with the exception of Senator Yarborough's bill). Along the United States-Canadian border, there is a large contingency of French-speaking children who are in need of bilingual education. William Hathaway, the distinguished representative from Maine, states that in Maine there are communities where there are concentrations of Canadian children who speak Canuck French. And in the South, in Louisiana, there is a large contingency of French-speaking children who are also in need of bilingual education. Bilingual legislation will also provide educational opportunities for our children of Oriental ancestry chiefly located on the West Coast and in Hawaii. Mr. John Belindo, Director of the Washington Office of the National Congress of American Indians (an organization representing over 400,000 American Indians), reminds us that 80,000 American Indian children are submerged in the statistics and they, too, need bilingual instruction. Bob Eckhardt, the distinguished representative from Texas, reminds us that

> In the central portion of Texas . . . there are a great number of Czechs whose first language is their own. In certain portions of central Texas, there is a considerable colony of Swedes whose first language is Swedish. . . . There are a great number of Germans who . . . still in many areas of Texas speak German as their first language. . . .

As the distinguished representative from New York, Mr. Scheuer, stated: "This legislation will be for Polish kids in Buffalo and Chicago, and . . . for Japanese kids in Denver, for Chinese kids in San Francisco, and for the whole wonderful heterogeneity of foreign speaking kids in our country." This legislation will be for all the nation's children.

THE SUCCESS OF BILINGUAL EDUCATION PROGRAMS

Educators and experts throughout the nation overwhelmingly agree that the answer to the plight of the non-English-speaking child in our schools lies in bilingualism. Bilingual demonstration projects reveal that bilingual programs are highly successful. Herman Badillo, President of the Borough of the Bronx, stated at a recent subcommittee hearing: "Programs for non-English-speaking children, to be successful, must utilize the native language skills of the students. There is ample evidence that much more can be accomplished much faster and more effectively by making use of the bilingual abilities of these students."

Mr. Badillo fervently believes that the utilization of bilingual educational techniques for New York City "is a vital necessity." Dr. Donovan, New York City Superintendent of Schools, at a recent subcommittee hearing stated, "We believe in New York City in a bilingual approach . . . we need the bilingual approach. . . . It is part of our general philosophy."

In the state of California, the State Board of Education has been interested and concerned with the education of the Mexican-American child. The Board has approved various programs using bilingual education in an effort to increase the caliber of education for the Mexican-American child. Various members of the California Department of Education have investigated and visited various bilingual programs throughout the country. The results of their investigations have been very encouraging; they seem to be sold on bilingual education.

U.S. Commissioner of Education Harold Howe summed up the significance of bilingual programs quite well when he stated in a recent subcommittee hearing:

> Bilingual education projects . . . show great promise in meeting the special needs of non-English-speaking children. These projects, which involve the use of both English and the children's mother tongue to teach the entire curriculum, have been the subject of considerable research and experimentation in the United States, Puerto Rico, Canada, Mexico, and South America. It is generally agreed that bilingual projects tend to eliminate the handicap suffered by children whose native language is not the language of the school. Some of these experiments show that children in bilingual programs do better even than those taught in their mother tongue.

To be more specific, let me briefly mention a few schools in the United States that, at this very moment, are using bilingual approaches very successfully. Coral Way and Central Beach elementary schools located in Dade County, Florida, have transferred completely into bilingual schools. Coral Way and Central Beach are two schools designed to help educate the some 200,000 Cuban refugee children enrolled in the Dade County public schools, and the some 300 refugee children per month, speaking no English whatsoever, that are seeking admission and integration in the Dade County schools. In a recent subcommittee hearing, U.S. Commissioner Howe commented on the success of Coral Way Elementary School:

> In Dade County, Florida, a model bilingual public elementary school is now finishing its fourth year of operation. This highly successful school provides us with some pertinent information: At the fifth grade level the children are able to learn equally well through either of their two languages. This is better than can be expected in even our best college-level foreign language programs. . . .

Thus, the solution by the Dade County schools of absorbing so many native Spanish-speaking children was to develop two bilingual schools in which native American and Cuban refugee children would learn two languages. As Claude Pepper, the distinguished representative from Florida, states:

> The result [in Dade County] has been a highly unique and successful program, fully integrated both racially and culturally, in which children of neighboring cultures have been enabled to share their separate backgrounds and thus to broaden their abilities and their understandings.

"It worked so well," states author Bert Collier ("Miami's Decision: A Blend of Culture," *Southern Education Report,*

October, 1966), "that today there is no 'Cuban problem' in the Dade schools."

On the northern flank of Arizona's Black Mountain, there is another school based solely on the bilingual-bicultural approach. As Paul Conklin states in his recent article, "Good Day at Rough Rock," *(American Education,* February, 1967) :

> An experiment has been started that could change the entire structure and philosophy of Indian education in America. Here, in a bleak setting of desert, rock, and sagebrush, near the country's largest reservation— 25,000 square miles—that is home to 105,000 Navajos, Robert A. Roessel, Jr., director of the Rough Rock Demonstration School, is applying a community control approach that could hold promise for poor, uneducated people everywhere. His [Dr. Roessel's] thesis [is]—that Indians ought to be able to be Americans and Indians, too. . . . For Rough Rock children, happiness is the chance to learn the white man's ways and to be Indian at the same time. . . .

Dr. Roessel states: "We want to instill in our youngsters a sense of pride in being Indian. We want to show them that they can be Indian and American at the same time, that they can take the best from each way of life and combine it into something viable."

So today, at Rough Rock Demonstration School, the Both-And approach — both white and Indian — is being developed very successfully. The Both-And philosophy places importance on the mastery of both English and Navaho. English is taught formally twice a day and informally at all times. At Rough Rock, a new spirit in education is emerging: a bilingual-bicultural program that "has ramifications far outside the Indian world," that to thousands and thousands of non-English-speaking children can mean a better, fuller, and more fruitful life.

In the Southwest, there are a few schools developing bilingual programs. The NEA-Tucson Survey Committee observed "encouraging and exciting programs" that are being developed specifically to educate children living in bilingual-bicultural communities. The Committee observed a wide variety of innovative bilingual teaching practices including bilingual programs in Laredo, Texas; El Paso, Texas; Albuquerque, New Mexico; Pecos, New Mexico; Merced, California; Pueblo, Colorado; Tucson, Arizona; and Phoenix, Arizona.

In Laredo, Texas, a community of some 65,000 people, the United Consolidated Independent School District serving an area of more than 2,440 square miles, bases its entire program on bilingualism. Students, Anglo-American as well as Mexican-American, are encouraged to become truly bilingual — speaking, reading, and writing fluently in both English and Spanish. English instruction and Spanish instruction go side by side. At Nye Elementary School in Laredo, Texas, involved, absorbed, enthusiastic children gain skills in both English and Spanish and gain common understanding of the people and the cultures of the two countries whose common border lies in Laredo.

Most important to remember is that bilingualism has not always been the theme of the United Consolidated Independent School District of Laredo, Texas. As stated in the NEA publication, *The Invisible Minority:*

> Significantly, in the early 1960's the district tried it the other way. It tried outlawing Spanish—educating the Spanish-speaking children in English. The result was frustration and failure, a heavy proportion of dropouts among Mexican-Americans, tension between the Anglo- and Mexican-American communities. Then a concerned conscientious school board sought administrative leadership which would build a staff believing in bilingualism. The goal of the district ever since has been to build a program along such lines. In September, 1964, there thus began what the district described as "an experimental biliteracy program."

The results of the program: a high degree of pride in both Mexican and American cultures and success in speaking and learning in both languages — achievements which could not be attained under the outmoded system tried in the early 1960's.

In Merced, California, bilingual programs have been extremely successful. After the first year of using bilingual programs, "a majority of students in the Merced schools showed marked improvement in all skills — reading, writing, and speaking. Overall, the average gain in Spanish proficiency was 50 percent. Moreover, significant improvement had taken place in the children's general attitudes and self-concepts." In El Paso, Texas, bilingual programs have been carried on in the high schools for many years and with a great deal of success.

All indicators suggest that bilingualism aids the non-English-speaking child in receiving the basic education that he has been entitled to for so long a time. The National Education Association

> believes that the introduction of bilingualism in the schools is a major step in solving the education problems of Mexican American children. . . .

> The Laredo program and other similar programs . . . —plus our own experiences and independent studies—have persuaded us *beyond any doubt* of the validity of bilingualism.

Bilingualism also has great national and international significance. The National Education Association states: "Bilingualism is a potential national asset of tremendous value — if we will but develop it as such." Senator Yarborough believes, "Bilingualism can mean a better approach to national and international affairs. It can offer a broader base for understanding among all people. It can allow for a free flow of expression among individuals and among nations." Monroe Sweetland, at a recent subcommittee hearing, summed up the national and international importance of bilingualism when he stated:

> The modern teacher views a native language as a great national resource to be conserved and developed, to be a great strength to our nation in its role of world leadership. . . . it is the national and international aspects of bilingualism which make this particularly the responsibility of Congress, and we in NEA look to you for funds and policy to make our local schools more effective for the children themselves and for the nation.

We also must remember that bilingualism is not only a great asset to the non-English-speaking child, but also provides great opportunities for the English-speaking child. For example, the Mexican-American child offers the monolingual English-speaking child a unique opportunity to learn the language and traditions of another culture. Jack D. Forbes, in his work *Mexican-Americans: A Handbook for Educators,* describes the assets which the Mexican-American youths often bring to the school:

> Mexican-American youth bring to the school a varied background of experiences and skills which can be utilized as mediums for both the development of the Mexican-American pupils' potential and the enrichment of the school experiences of non-Mexican scholastics. . . . Those educators who recognize the value of linguistic training can certainly enrich the total program of their classroom or school by making full use of the Mexican-American child's language advantage. A truly bilingual learning experience can be produced which will not only allow the Mexican child to develop both of his languages but which will make it easier for monolingual English speaking children to master a second tongue.

Furthermore, statistics have shown that bilingual students — those students who can speak and learn equally well in two languages — actually do better in school than monolingual students. Thus, we see that bilingualism in our schools will serve not only our non-English-speaking children, but it will serve all the children of our nation.

Educators and experts throughout the nation agree that bilingualism is essential in combating the educational deficiencies of the non-English-speaking child. The most crucial question now is: Why haven't the schools provided adequate bilingual programs for our non-English-speaking children?

INADEQUACY OF STATE AND LOCAL AUTHORITIES TO PROVIDE PROGRAMS

I believe my remarks so far have made two points quite clear. One, there is a definite problem in our nation of educating the non-English-speaking child; the schools, beyond a doubt, are failing to provide adequate educational opportunities for the non-English-speaking child. Two, bilingualism seems to be the answer to the problem; bilingualism is the tool which enables the non-English-speaking child to receive the educational opportunities that he is so greatly in need of. With these two points quite clear, why have our schools failed? If we know we have a problem and if we know the answer to the problem, then why has not the problem been solved? This leads us right into why we do need special bilingual legislation. State and local authorities have not been able to provide bilingual programs for our non-English-speaking children because of the avalanche of other priorities that they feel they must provide for. State and local authorities have simply not put an emphasis on bilingual programs and on solving the tragic problems of the non-English-speaking child.

Dr. Bernard Donovan, New York City Superintendent of Schools, spoke of the limitations of local authorities, at a recent subcommittee hearing, when he stated:

New York City has tried to tackle this problem [educating the non-English-speaking child]. The schools have not neglected it. But we have tried to tackle it in conjunction with many, many other problems that are before us. . . . But with all of the things we have tried to do we still have just about made a dent in the problem and therefore the bilingual legislation pending before the Committee is of extreme importance to us. . . . Title I [of the Elementary and Secondary School Act of 1965] money, despite the fine effect it has had on us, is really, as far as the city of New York is concerned, so limited in its amount [that] to spread it over every problem we have of the low income and disadvantaged child is almost impossible.

. . . the choice of English as a second language program sometimes falls by the way when we look at health problems, and basic reading, and all these things that affect children of disadvantage. . . . It is a matter of not having money enough to go around for all high priority needs of which this bilingual education is one. Therefore, if we had directive legislation of this nature, it would help us in the allocation of our funds.

Title I funds of the Elementary and Secondary Education Act of 1965, which provides financial assistance for educational agencies for the education of children of low-income families, have not even begun to alleviate the educational problems of the non-English-speaking child. U.S. Commissioner of Education Harold Howe states:

> Only seven million dollars of Title I is now going into what you would call English as a secondary language project nationally. . . . In other words, a very small proportion of Title I is now being used locally for projects.

Roman Pucinski, the distinguished representative from Illinois, commented at a recent subcommittee hearing:

> Public schools have been able to experiment in this area [of bilingual education] with some asistance under Title I and Title III of the ESEA. However, demands for other services available under these Titles have prevented any one educational body from meeting the requirements of bilingual education. . . .

According to Mr. Pucinski, the Office of Education reported that in Fiscal 1966 only one twentieth or only 5 percent (142,000 children out of an estimated three million) of the youngsters needing special bilingual education were being reached by bilingual programs under Title I and Title III combined.

Miguel Montes, at the subcommittee hearing, made some important observations concerning the relation of Title I funds and the bilingual legislation being considered. He stated that (1) Title I funds are not as plentiful as the need; the ratio of dollars per child is becoming alarmingly low. (2) Since Title I funds are earmarked for disadvantaged students, the program developed by the school district may not be, and in most cases has not been, related to the problems of the bilingual student. (3) The lack of expertise in the development of bilingual programs is one reason for the lack of utilization of Title I funds for bilingual programs.

U.S. Commissioner Howe, before the subcommittee, stated:

> Any school which serves a significant number of non-English speaking children, and which fails to provide special programs to meet the needs

of those children, is not fully meeting its obligation. When Title I projects are funded in such a school, it would seem to me that some kind of bilingual program should *automatically* [italics by the author of this paper] be at the top of the list of priorities. . . . Unfortunately, in too many instances, the necessary measures have not been initiated.

The fact of the matter is quite clear — state and local agencies have not given bilingual education high priority. Commissioner Howe states that at "any school which serves a significant number of non-English-speaking children . . . some kind of bilingual program should *automatically* be at the top of the list of priorities"; in reality, that has never been the case. In most every instance, state and local agencies have let bilingual education fall by the wayside while thousands of non-English-speaking children are denied an adequate education and forced to face a life of frustration and hopelessness.

Though funds are available to state and local agencies through the Elementary and Secondary Education Act, the National Defense Education Act, and the General Co-operative Research Act that can be used for bilingual programs, bilingual programs are not being developed. A major reason why programs have not been developed by state and local agencies is the lack of trained bilingual teachers. Special training arrangements are needed to provide schools with bilingual teaching staffs. Training procedures to develop bilingual teachers are nearly nonexistent. Because of other priorities and a lack of funds, local districts cannot afford to develop special training programs, nor can they afford the special bilingual books and library materials that are needed to carry out programs.

U.S. Commissioner Howe further stated that "A major difficulty faced by Mexican-American children has been that school programs have not been able to respond fully to their special needs," and he listed the six "chief difficulties" facing local schools. Four out of the six "chief difficulties" listed by Commissioner Howe had directly to do with the lack of teachers and teacher-training programs, and the lack of designed curriculum. The list presented by Commissioner Howe is summarized as follows:

1. Inadequate understanding between local school districts and the Spanish-speaking community of the need for special attention to the needs of Spanish-speaking children, especially in the earlier grades.
2. Lack of local funds to attract higher quality teachers or teachers who may be trained to teach Spanish-speaking children to become bilingual.

3. Lack of curriculum designed for Spanish-speaking children.

4. Lack of teachers who are bilingual or trained in teaching non-English-speaking children.

5. Lack of teacher-training programs needed to develop and train teachers to work in the schools located in Mexican-American communities.

6. Shortage of trained guidance counselors who speak Spanish and understand the cultural differences.

Teachers trained in bilingualism are a necessity for any bilingual program. State and local agencies, in most every instance, have not responded to the need for bilingual teacher-training programs.

State and local educational authorities, in general, have made bilingual education unjustly a low priority item. Now is the time for Congress to encourage local areas to do something specifically about bilingual education. Local areas have failed, and they have admitted that they have failed, to fulfill the needs of non-English-speaking children. Now we must provide the guidelines so urgently needed by which local agencies, if they so desire, may develop bilingual programs and be assisted by the federal government.

Speak Up, Chicano*

ARMANDO M. RODRIGUEZ

I SAT QUIETLY AND LISTENED as fifteen Mexican-American citizens who had gathered in a crumbling adobe community center in San Antonio's oldest slum talked about their schools. As director of the U.S. Office of Education's Mexican-American Affairs Unit, I was there to learn what the local citizens and school people felt were their most pressing educational needs.

"We ought to be consulted more about what goes on in our schools," the president of the Mexican-American Community Club said heatedly. "Our high school needs a Mexican-American on the counseling staff. But the school people say they can't find a qualified one to hire. Over 60 percent of the kids are Mexican-Americans and most of them have trouble speaking English. Yet we have only five Spanish-speaking teachers, and not a single person in the school office speaks Spanish. Is it any wonder the kids drop out like flies? The hell with the requirements. Let's take care of these kids' needs, and one of the first is to get somebody who can talk to them."

"Now wait just a minute," interrupted the school district's assistant superintendent. "We have to follow state regulations,

* From *American Education*, May, 1968.

you know. You can't put just anybody in the counseling office. You tell us where to find a qualified Mexican-American teacher or counselor and we'll be delighted to hire him."

"At least you could have Mexican-Americans in the school as aides, couldn't you?" asked a neighborhood representative on the community action program board. "But you folks downtown made the requirements so high that none of our people could get a job. Why?"

"We have to have qualified people to work with the youngsters," answered the director of instruction.

"Qualified?" the president broke in. "What could be better qualifications than speaking the language and understanding the kids?"

"Well, we haven't seen much show of interest from the parents," countered a schoolman. "We can't get them out to PTA meetings, can't even get many of them to come to parents' night. We hired a Mexican-American school-community coordinator for some of our schools, but she's finding it an uphill battle getting the parents to take an interest in school matters."

And so it went at meeting after meeting that I attended with Lupe Anguiano and Dean Bistline, my co-workers in the Mexican-American Affairs Unit. We visited seventeen communities on our three-week tour of Arizona, California, Colorado, New Mexico, and Texas. Both Mexican-American community leaders and school people — some seventeen hundred altogether — poured out their frustrations, and we learned a great deal about what the people want and need and in what priority.

In those five states alone, there are more than 5.5 million people of Spanish surname. Eight out of ten live in California or Texas. Their numbers are constantly reinforced by a stream of immigrants from Mexico. Add the 1.5 million other Spanish-speaking people — Cuban, Puerto Rican, Central and South American, and Spanish — who live in Florida and the northeast and midwestern industrial cities, and it becomes apparent that the United States has a substantial second minority group. They are a minority whose historical, cultural, and linguistic characteristics set them apart from the Anglo community as dramatically as the Negro's skin sets him apart. Few people outside the Southwest realize the degree of discrimination this difference has brought about.

For me the introduction to discrimination began thirty-seven years ago when my father brought the family to California from Durango, Mexico. I was nine years old when we settled in San Diego in an extremely poor but well-integrated community of Mexican-Americans, Negroes, and poor Anglos. The trouble was in school. I knew only a dozen words of English, so I just sat around the first few weeks not understanding a thing. I was not allowed to speak Spanish in class. But after school each day I played with neighborhood kids, so I soon picked up enough English to hold my own on the playground. Then I made this smattering of English do in class.

It didn't occur to me or my family to protest. In those days people didn't talk much about ethnic differences or civil rights. The Chicanos (our favorite nickname for fellow Mexican-Americans) pretty much stayed "in their place," working as domestics and laborers in the cities or as wetback stoop laborers in the fields and orchards. Only a few became professionals or businessmen.

I remember being advised by my high school counselor to forget my dreams of going to college and becoming a teacher. "They don't hire Mexican-Americans," he said. Then World War II came along. When I got out of the army in 1944, the G.I. Bill of Rights saw me through San Diego College. I got a teaching job and eventually became a junior high school principal in San Diego. But my experience was a rare one for the times.

Since then, conditions have changed a good deal. There is spirit in the Mexican-American community now. On my recent trip I saw a pride in the young people that was not so evident when I was growing up. The Chicano today is proud of his role as an American. Many parents, even those who are illiterate, as were mine, are determined that their children will not be like them. And they see education as the means. But along with their determination has come a new impatience. Gone is the meek, long-suffering separateness of the Chicanos. They are beginning to stand up and make their voices heard.

"Head Start is great," said a parent-businessman at one of our meetings. "But it isn't enough. Some of the programs are only for the summer, and our kids need a whole year if they are to have a chance to start out even with the Anglo kids."

"Many of our kids go to school hungry," another complained. "Why can't the schools use more of their government money for food and health services?"

As we listened to their grievances, I realized that our most valuable role at these meetings was as a bouncing board for their ideas. With us present, both school and community leaders found themselves saying things to each other they had heretofore said only within their own group. Inevitably, though, they looked to us, the spokesmen for the government, to "do something." Of course, that was not our role. We were there to help them establish lines of communication and to explain to them the ways in which the U.S. Office of Education can support their efforts. But we had to make clear that it is they, the state and local school people and the community, who must design the programs and carry them out.

Nationally there is a growing amount of concern about Mexican-American affairs that has generated much real help. In evidence is the recent series of conferences at Tucson, Pueblo, and El Paso sponsored by the National Education Association. Also, the federal government created three new agencies with specific responsibilties to the Mexican-American. The Inter-Agency Committee on Mexican-American Affairs assists in development of services that cover the wide range of government activities. The United States-Mexico Commission on Border Development and Friendship is charged with creating programs to improve cooperation on both sides of the border. And the U.S. Office of Education's Mexican-American Affairs Unit seeks to bring some expertise to bear on the education of the bilingual-bicultural citizen and to develop a focus on the effort. This unit is now supported by a newly created Advisory Committee on Mexican-American Education. Still another evidence of concern and help is passage by the United States Congress of the Bilingual Education Act (Title VII of the Elementary and Secondary Education Act). It authorizes funds and support for schools to develop programs in which both English and the native language of the student can be used as teaching tools until a mastery of English has been achieved.

These are a healthy start, as is the rising involvement of the Mexican-American community itself in directing attention to educational issues. Still, some major obstacles remain in the way of the Mexican-American's progress toward educational equality. Of prime consideration is the shortage of teachers qualified to cope with the Mexican-American's particular situation. There are only two thousand bilingual teachers in the elementary and secondary schools today. Equally distressing is the lack of teachers who are even aware of the Chicano's cultural background and recognize his language as an asset. It is a striking contradiction that we spend millions of dollars to encourage schoolchildren to learn a foreign language and, at the same time, frown upon Mexican-American children speaking Spanish in school. The impression they receive is that there must be something inherently bad about their language. This, of course, leads to self-depreciation. To make the situation even more ridiculous, they are often asked to take Spanish as a foreign language later in school.

Only bilingual teachers can correct this situation — teachers who can treat the Chicano's Spanish as an asset while the student is learning English. And that will require a tremendous effort in teacher education. As a starter, the Teacher Corps, cooperating with the Mexican-American Affairs Unit, has set up a high intensity language training component for a group of interns teaching in schools with a number of Spanish-speaking students. This program lasts six weeks and gives considerable attention to cross-cultural values as well as to language instruction.

A second obstacle to a comprehensive education for the Chicano is the lack of well-integrated curricula. As I toured the Southwest, I saw good programs here and there for preschool youngsters, some good adult basic education going on in one place, a good program to educate the whole migrant family in another. But in no single place did I see a school district whose curriculum and instructional program correlated with the needs of the Mexican-Americans from kindergarten through high school. There were glimpses of hope, though.

In San Antonio, Texas, I was impressed with a program developed by the Southwest Educational Development Laboratory of Austin that used linguistic techniques to improve the fluency of Mexican-American youngsters in oral language as a foundation for reading. Intensive instruction is given in English as a second language, and an identical program of instruction is given in Spanish. The program was started two years ago in nine schools and is in formal operation in the first two grades in San Antonio with plans for continuation in grades three and four. The first group of youngsters in the program are now equaling national norms in reading, and some are even achieving the fifth-grade level. Traditionally Mexican-American boys and girls in southern Texas have lagged at least a year behind the national norms.

San Diego, California, has developed a demonstration center for English as a second language to help school districts create specialized educational programs for students who initially learned a language other than English. One of its bright features has been the large number of parents who worked with the professional staff in designing these programs for non-English-speaking parents and youngsters alike.

The Foreign Language Innovative Curricula Studies at Ann Arbor, Michigan, used funds from Title III of the Elementary and Secondary Education Act to develop a bilingual curriculum program with materials for language arts instruction. The program has been aimed at the Spanish-speaking youngster — both migrant and permanent resident — whose linguistic handicaps severely limit his educational achievement. The program is for the primary grades and stresses the development of materials which are exciting to all youngsters and are suitable for use by teachers with a minimum of specialized training.

By sharing their experiences in these innovative programs, school districts can help one another. And a wealth of good ideas are emerging from conferences such as the one sponsored by the Advisory Committee on Mexican-American Education and the Mexican-American Affairs Unit in Austin, Texas, recently. Here at the Office of Education we have a special task force that works closely with the eight bureaus in considering funding proposals for projects aimed at improving educational opportunities for the Mexican-American.

A third obstacle to the young Chicano's educational success is a lack of models — "heroes," if you will. The school needs to put before him successful Mexican-Americans whom he can emulate as he sets his educational goals. A teacher, a counselor, a principal who is Mexican-American can do the trick. Discrimination in past generations has, unfortunately, limited the number of such persons. In many heavily Mexican-American schools, there is not a single Mexican-American teacher, let alone a counselor or administrator. Now, however, with the Chicano's education improving and discrimination diminishing, I am hopeful that more and more of today's children will have the career models before them that they need.

If my impression of all this activity and promise is correct, the Mexican-American is about to see the dawning of a new era. He will become a far more productive member of society. His cultural and linguistic heritage will be turned to good use.

Although the Chicano has suffered and lost much in the last one hundred years, he now intends to do what is necessary to win his fight for educational equality. And he will do it today. Mañana is too late.

Part 5
ROLE OF
EDUCATIONAL INSTITUTIONS

The Death of Miss Jones*

VINCE VILLAGRAN

"BENNY, WILL YOU TELL US why Jim's dog would not pull the cart?" Miss Jones looked up from her teacher's text and waited for the little boy to respond. Benny stared intently at the book and then sheepishly said,

"I don't know, teacher."

Miss Jones smiled and the children, especially Benny, relaxed a little.

Dozier Elementary School was in the heart of East Los Angeles, and Miss Jones had been there only a few weeks — a new teacher, fresh out of college. She was tall and attractive, and as she gazed out at the nervous faces of her fifth grade class, her eyes were kind and helpful.

"All right, Benny," she said, "please read the paragraph on page 32. That will tell us about Jim's dog."

"Jim, t,t,t . . ." the boy began.

"That's fine, Benny. You know the first sound. The word is took, just like look and book."

Benny gave his book a determined look and continued. "Jim took his c,c,c, . . ."

* Con Sajos, vol. 1 (1968), pp. 43-45. Reprinted by permission of author.

"Benny, if you cover up the "c" with your finger, you will see a word you know. What is it?"

Benny stared and wrinkled his brow in concentration. He did as she said and discovered the familiar word. "Art! Art!" the boy cried out triumphantly. "Jim took his cart and l,l,l, . . ."

"That word is loaded." Miss Jones closed her book, looked at the clock on the wall, and announced, "Well, boys and girls, time does fly. It's lunchtime. Please close your books and get ready for dismissal."

The children hurriedly slammed their books shut and were perched on the edge of their seats as the bell rang, and Miss Jones dismissed them.

As the last child walked out of the room, Miss Jones sat down wearily at her desk, resting a moment before going to the cafeteria for lunch. The room seemed eerily quiet to her now, after the din and shuffle of the children's hurried departure. She stared out at the empty seats facing her. As usual, she felt as if the brown, eager faces were still seated before her. It always happened. As soon as the room was emptied of its tiny pupils, Miss Jones remained for a few minutes believing the sudden quiet was an illusion. For her the children were still impatiently waiting to be dismissed. Miss Jones smiled. "So what?" she was thinking. "What if I do picture their faces after they've gone? What's that prove? It only proves how fond I am of them." And with this positive reflection, she got up, pleased with herself, and went to lunch.

The teacher's lunchroom was buzzing with chatter as Miss Jones carried her tray to an empty seat near a group of new teachers. At the table Mrs. Bender, the school's old-timer, was describing the school to the group. Miss Jones listened awhile and then, during a lull in the conversation, addressed herself to the elderly woman.

"Uh, Mrs. Bender? Why is it that two thirds of my class is reading below grade level? Could you suggest something for me to help them improve? What have you done with your kids?"

"Let me give you a piece of advice, honey," Mrs. Bender said. "You'll live a lot longer if you just stop worrying about it. Believe me, better people than you have tried to do something about your so-called reading problem, and they've gotten nowhere. Just as you will unless you forget about it."

Miss Jones was about to answer, but Mrs. Bender continued, her voice louder now, for the benefit of the other teachers at the table. "We're doing a hell of a job as it is, Miss Jones. I've been here twenty years, and the problems these kids have get progressively worse. We used to have some good students here once — Russian and Armenian kids — "

Miss Jones interrupted her now. Her voice was tense and irritated. "Excuse me, Mrs. Bender. But do I follow you correctly? Are you telling me — us — that there's nothing to be done about the problem? That not being, ah, Russian and Armenian makes some kind of difference?"

Mrs. Bender sat back in her chair and glared a moment at Miss Jones before she answered. "You're new here. You don't know anything about the problems. But since you ask — yes, that's precisely what I'm saying." Her voice was shrill now. "Have you seen the homes these kids come out of, Miss Jones? Have any of you?" She looked challengingly around the table. No one answered. "Well, I have," she continued. "And good heavens, we're lucky we can reach these kids at all. Both parents work, and as many as eight kids live in a two-bedroom shack."

Miss Jones spoke again, her voice angry. "Mrs. Bender, do you mean to say that there is little or no hope for these kids? Why, that's ridiculous. Surely, someone with your experience should have some solutions to these problems."

"Look, Miss Jones," the aged teacher announced, "You and the rest of the teachers had best understand some damn basic hangups you're up against. The damage is done in the home. You'll find out how much parents care when you send your first notices out for parent conferences. They won't show, believe me."

Miss Jones' blue eyes flashed under an angry frown. "Mrs. Bender, have you tried house calls? It may have helped, you know!"

Mrs. Bender got to her feet. "If mama can't find time to be here, that's her problem! Besides some of these people don't even speak English! You'd think they would at least learn that after being here for all these years from Mexico." At this Mrs. Bender, deliberately snubbing and embarrassing Miss Jones in front of the other teachers, went over to a nearby table and sat with some of the school's veteran teachers. Miss Jones stared after her, then finished her lunch in silence and left the cafeteria.

Outside in the corridor, as she headed back to her classroom, Mr. Carlson, the school principal, stopped her. "Why, hello, Miss Jones," he said, "how're you getting along?"

Miss Jones could only shrug.

"Is something the matter?" he asked, noticing her lack of response.

She hesitated a moment, then spoke. "Why ah, yes. Something is very much the matter. Do you have a minute, Mr. Carlson? There's something I'd like to speak to you about. But not here. In your office. Would you mind?"

Mr. Carlson looked puzzled, but finally said, "Certainly. Would you come with me?" He led the way to the office and Miss Jones perched on the edge of a sofa chair. He sat behind his desk.

Miss Jones' pent-up emotions burst forth and she spoke rapidly, excitedly. "Mr. Carlson, I really don't know how to say this, but I'm afraid I'm going to be very candid. I like it here and I love the kids. I happen to feel these children have potential and can succeed, but some of the other teachers feel otherwise. They've given these children up for lost causes — all because they — "

Mr. Carlson interrupted her. "Relax, Miss Jones. I couldn't agree with you more, and I'm darn pleased that you feel your kids can be a success, believe me. But, look, Mary — you don't mind my calling you by your first name, do you?" He continued before she could answer, "I know, however, that we're a long way from solving the problems we have here at Dozier. But I'm confident that we're doing as much or more than anyone else."

"But, Mr. Carlson, I've got kids in my class who can barely read, and they've been in this school since kindergarten. Most of them don't speak Spanish — as their main language, that is — so their poor performance in reading can't be blamed on that! That's what I'm concerned about. What can we do about that?"

"Well, Miss Jones, let me set you straight on a few things. I've been here for ten years — by choice — and I've learned much about this district. You know, Miss Jones, that we have a budget to work with, and I can only do with what I have. What you seem to be suggesting takes money, more than we have. You apparently overlook this because you're new — and I might add, a little idealistic. Idealism is good, don't misunderstand me. However, we do have to look at cold, hard realities, too, Miss Jones."

"What cold, hard facts are you talking about, Mr. Carlson? Can't you be specific?"

Mr. Carlson leaned forward over his desk. "I hardly need to explain anything to you, Miss Jones, but perhaps I can illuminate a few things. We can do wonders here, but we get little support from the parents, and the attendance problem these kids have is atrocious."

"But, Mr. Carlson! I have kids in my class who've excellent attendance records, and they can't read either. How do you explain that?"

"There are exceptions, of course, Miss Jones. You know that as well as I. We're simply trying to do the best we can. That, Miss Jones, is what I'm trying to tell you."

Miss Jones became thoughtful a moment. "Actually, Mr. Carlson," she said finally, "I wanted to talk to you about a reading course I'm in the middle of at U.C.L.A. I wanted to ask you to recommend instituting the techniques here at Dozier. We're talking about various methods of extending the reading time beyond the normal one hour. I know it isn't the whole answer, but maybe we could organize a program like it here."

"Great idea, Miss Jones, but I'll need to clear this with the reading supervisor as well as with the curriculum section downtown." He stood up, hand extended to Miss Jones. "Tell you what," he said, "let me talk it over with the grade-level chairman before we do anything. If the teachers aren't behind this, it just won't work. We'll get together in a few weeks. How's that?"

Miss Jones returned his smile and shook his hand. "Thank you, Mr. Carlson. I'm sure it'll be for the good of all concerned."

"Fine, fine. Bye now, don't forget; I'll let you know what develops."

"Thanks again," she said and left the office.

The next few weeks were busy ones and Miss Jones found that she kept reminding herself to find out what Mr. Carlson had determined, but her schedule forced her to continue putting it off.

Finally, some months later, she was able to speak to him about it at one of the school's faculty meetings. Mr. Carlson appeared to have forgotten their meeting. Miss Jones reminded him of their conversation, but he indicated nothing had been decided. For the first time in her brief stay at Dozier, Miss Jones felt useless. During the semester, she had argued with the other teachers innumerable times about the poor quality of the reading techniques being provided the children. But now she realized that their almost unanimous acceptance of the old guidelines used to teach reading were as much a part of the school and faculty as the cement cornerstone around which the school was built. And she felt useless. But in spite of the feeling, Miss Jones continued adamantly to believe that her relationship with the children had not been affected. Even when she caught herself tense and cross with her class, she would brush it off as being due to her exacting schedule. She knew and felt deep within herself that her relationship with the children remained unchanged. She loved them still — and she knew they loved her.

One Friday, Miss Jones stopped by the corner grocery store to buy some milk. She was just closing the refrigerator when she heard familiar voices. From behind the refrigerator she could hear Carlos and Benny, two of her students, talking. They were at the candy machine.

"Hey, Benny," she heard, "you still like Miss Jones?"

"Heck, no!" she heard Benny answer. "She used to be nice and everything, but now she acts mean like all those other teachers. She ain't like before."

Then Carlos' young voice came back to her ears.

"Me, too, man. I can't take her no more. All she does now is holler and everything. I used to like her. But now she looks all bored and lazy. I'm gonna go to the railroad tracks tomorrow — the heck with school and Miss Jones. She looks all *muerta*."

"Yeah," Benny echoed, "she is all *muerta*. I'll go with ya tomorrow." The boys walked away eating their candy.

Miss Jones left the store and drove home slowly, and she was crying.

How Sharp Is the Focus?*

ARMANDO RODRIGUEZ

THE MIDWEST OFFERS A REAL CHALLENGE to the Mexican-American, Spanish-speaking people to become a vigorous entity in rapidly growing urban areas in the industrial center of our country. Well over 80 percent of the Mexican Americans now live in urban communities and their struggle to survive in such an environment far exceeds the expected fight. Tragically, many of the young people are caught up in the battle of poverty and are losing that battle to crime, drug addiction, and social rejection. When the nation thinks of poverty, far too often its thoughts go to the Negro in the urban ghetto, the southern rural area, or to Appalachia. Actually, the American people should be made aware that the most vicious poverty is in the *barrios* of hundreds of communities throughout the Southwest and in many *barrios* in industrial centers of the Midwest and Northeast. Poverty and its companions have lived with the Mexican American for well over a century.

For the sake of defining a problem, the term "Mexican American" will be used. Included in this designation are Americans

*Revised and edited by permission of author.

303

of Spanish descent, Spanish Americans, Hispanic Americans, the Spanish surnamed, and the Spanish-speaking.

Three resource units with specific responsibility have been set up to work on the needs of the Mexican American. The Interagency Committee has the authority to work on problems at the cabinet level and across departmental lines. The United States-Mexico Commission on Border Development and Friendship has been set up to work specifically on problems common to both governments along the border. Constructive programs are being created and implemented by this group. The Mexican-American Affairs Unit carries on its operation in the Office of Education. The Unit has the responsibility of advising the Office of Education, the Department of Health, Education and Welfare, and other agencies on programs related to the education of the bilingual-bicultural citizen. One example of the activities of the Unit was the survey of the educational needs of the Mexican American. This survey has produced data which has been instrumental in determining some changes in emphasis on funding by the Office of Education.

These three operating units are making the first adjustments in sharpening the focus of the federal government on the Mexican American. They have been able to correct faulty vision in four vital areas. Previously there was:

1. No systematic record of the activities of government agencies with the Mexican American.

2. No organized program for dealing bilingually with the Mexican American.

3. No consideration of the employment of bilingual Mexican Americans in professional and policy-making positions.

4. No attempt to correlate existing programs with the highly visible needs of the Mexican Americans.

The focus may still not be intense in these areas, but there are very few governmental agencies today that do not include in their operating principles a concern in these four areas, *and more and deeper attention is coming.*

How do these changes relate directly to Mexican Americans? What resources in education are designed to meet Mexican-American needs? What are these needs? They can be framed in two general areas.

First, there is the inability of the school (both public and private), and therefore the community, to provide equality of opportunity in education for the bilingual-bicultural student. Second, there is the lack of sufficient visible achievement in the Mexican-American community to motivate Mexican-American youth to continue their education. Both of these factors must be met in an aggressive attack carefully coordinated to maintain an equal pace of accomplishment.

This job can be tackled in four thrusts:

1. Giving direction to those persons at all levels who are interested in creating solutions but who do not "know quite what to do."

2. Identifying some basic characteristics and elements of promising programs.

3. Providing bases for dissemination and transmission of appropriate information.

4. Encouraging the development of more programs directed toward the needs of the Mexican American.

As a means of giving substance to this effort, a task force must be organized in each of the bureaus in the Office of Education with the specific responsibility of giving leadership and force to a constant consideration of every project proposed which deals with the Mexican American. Such proposals must receive the closest scrutiny and must be appraised by a person who is knowledgeable in the Mexican-American culture. The employment of Mexican Americans must be supported in quality and key positions in the Office and the Department. The basic role of packaging a better product for support of educational programs for the Mexican American is becoming a reality through this approach.

There were fifty-three million dollars in federal funds directed toward the improvement of Mexican-American education during the 1967-1968 fiscal year. That only amounts to about twenty-five dollars per pupil, whereas about 250 dollars per pupil is needed; but it is a start. There is the Bilingual Education Act, which can be a powerful tool for effective changes in the concepts of teaching the bilingual-bicultural student. But it had only five million dollars during fiscal 1969. In addition, the Dropout Act was initiated with its thirty million dollars and an opportunity to focus on the most devastating problem facing many of our youth. Some time could be spent discussing the

Education Profession Development Act which can be a vital tool in preparing teachers and administrators for coping with the challenges of our bilingual-bicultural society. One could dwell on the plans for using the Teacher Corps as a vehicle for developing a High Intensity Language-Training Program which will give language competency in Spanish to the new interns in six weeks. This can be a real breakthrough in what may be considered a must goal for America: 100,000 bilingual teachers in the next three years. It can be done if the same kinds of commitment and resources are placed behind this need that were placed behind the need for new mathematics teachers only a few years ago. And this step must be taken! Not too many children dropped out of school because of mathematics, new or old, but no end of students are dropping out because of the school's failure to meet their linguistic and cultural needs.

The writer has attempted in perhaps much too brief a manner to outline what is happening that is good. But one would be less than honest if he did not speak out about those things of which one is less than proud.

Equal educational opportunity for the Mexican American is still a myth. There is not a single coordinated program in a school system today that deals with the total Mexican American. What seems to be developing is a patchwork of programs, dealing with deficiencies, not strengths, and still being placed in the school environment which is designed to educate the Anglo and to some extent, now, the Negro. The Chicano is expected to perform in this atmosphere. But he just is not able to do it. And he will not be able to do it. If one is not convinced, he should look at the Chicano's achievement level, which is at least one, and more often two, grade levels behind Anglos of his age in reading. His dropout or pushout rate is as high as 70 percent in parts of Texas. In some of the schools in Los Angeles where the students have been demonstrating, the dropout rate is over 40 percent. *Compensatory education programs which bandage a little here and there, but never reach the source of the illness, result in nothing more than a delayed death for the Chicano!*

The church schools are as bad as the public schools. Their programs do not reflect the need for making culture and language an inseparable part of the curriculum and foremost in the instructional techniques. And one might even say that they are worse offenders, since they receive so much support from the Mexican American and return so little benefit in the form of educational programs which recognize his needs. It is inexcusable for any school to fail to make its program meet the needs of its students, and to force the student into whatever shape the school sets for all who attend. The failure of the parochial school to display leadership and vision in this matter is most distressing.

The bilingual programs in San Antonio and Laredo show some promise. English as a Second Language in the San Diego Demonstration Center has a most hopeful component of meaningful community involvement. The refining of Head Start and the introduction of its cousin, Follow Through, have the potential of breaking through some of the psychological and sociological hang-ups which have burdened so many Mexican-American youngsters in their formative school years. Still, most of these activities are developed and put into operation without a great deal of attention to the cultural attitudes of the children. Unless there is a significant correlation of the learning experience with the child's cultural concepts, sooner or later he — even if he has a competency in English — will experience serious doubts about his worth, his self-image will be challenged, and his feeling of being a vital part of a total society will be measured and found wanting. At about that stage he will ponder a moment, turn aside, and seek solace in the less hostile sanctuary of his family or his companions who have made the same decision: *to give up!*

What direction must be taken? Until America is prepared to make a national commitment that reaches deeply into the attitude of the Anglo and Negro society, realizes that cultural and language isolation is wrong, supports that commitment with financial resources and leadership, there is nothing but disaster ahead. The determination for some change now by the young Chicano is so great that incidents like that of Cesar Chavez, who went on a twenty-five-day fast as a means of demonstrating to his young "Benito Juarez" that violence is not the path to victory, will be repeated over and over.

This country must accept cultural and language integration just as it must accept racial integration. It is this cultural and language integration that will demonstrate to the Mexican American that our country and all of its people are committed to equality in education through an active program now. Now is the time for Juan to say proudly his Pledge of Allegiance to his country in his language. Just as proudly, his classmate John will be standing beside him respecting and honoring him. This unity will signify the replacement of cultural and language isolation with cultural and language integration. This, more than anything else, will take Juan out of the *barrio* where he can join his Negro friends out of the ghetto, and together they can join their Anglo friends in a total society.

The Negro has moved out of the cotton field, even in the textbooks. The Chicano is coming out of Tortilla Flats, in one way or another. The textbooks do not yet have him out, but they had better hurry, for he is not going to wait much longer.

The focus of the federal government is sharp and is getting sharper every day. The tools of financial resources and leadership are available, but no great progress will occur until the support of the whole community is secured. Equal educational opportunity for the bilingual-bicultural child must be a total community project. But with the support of all or not, the implementation of the commitment of the federal government in the schools of America will be demanded and secured.

Throughout the entire nation there is a deep stirring in the Mexican-American communities. Interest, concern, participation, organization — yes, even cooperation — are making action the first order of the day. The focus of this action is heavily on education. The young Chicanos recognize the importance of education far more than is suspected. If one analyzes the basic issues of the demonstrations which were held in Los Angeles, he will find that the student demands were for realistic and well-designed changes for better educational opportunities. And they are right!

If education is the main vehicle for social and economic mobility, the community must assert its need for membership in the policy levels of administration of public education. If the leadership in the Mexican-American community does not take this step, *it will find itself trampled by those coming from younger ranks who will.* Only in this way can the focus which the federal government has created and is sharpening be realized in the classroom. Only in this way can Mexican Americans secure for their youngsters what they know is now being denied them and for which they are prepared to fight.

The image of the Mexican American is changing. The change is not fast enough, but it is coming. No longer does America look at Mexican Americans as passive, unmotivated, and somnolent. It is now coming to be realized that the Mexican American is a tough character! And so he is!

In the crusade for change are many suggestions for solutions to the problems. The ways of making these solutions effective are fewer. Nevertheless, resources for a new life for the Mexican American are coming to the fore almost daily. But the extent to which the effect of these resources reach all Mexican Americans depends upon how well they are implemented and pressed.

When Mexican Americans sharpen their focus in the community and bring it into line with the national focus and resources, a working partnership can bring changes. *But, do not ever forget that education is a local matter!* The ultimate characteristic of the change Mexican Americans may make will be determined locally. What is wanted can be obtained if it is sought out, if the avenue of communication is forcefully used, and if action is taken to influence the local school organization. Mexican Americans can be no stronger than the schools in which their children are taught. No important change will occur unless Mexican Americans make it happen.

Unless Mexican Americans are in the driver's seat, such changes that are now possible with the intensified focus of the federal government will be slow in coming — or may not come at all!

All Mexican Americans must continue to press, push, cajole, and fight for improvement in educational opportunities. But the only really important effect of the fight must be the change that takes place in the child's classroom. This suggests that one must realize that only in the local community will the focus be important. Are Mexican Americans saying to their local educational leaders, *"¡Ya Basta!"?* Mexican-American leaders are needed to analyze the basic needs of their youngsters. Mexican Americans are needed to analyze the basic needs of their entire community. They must be present and heard when priorities are determined, and they must insist on the full utilization of available resources in a continuous and forceful thrust of action and change.

This nation is now going through a period of torment and agony. Never in modern history has the turbulence of terror and fear been so great. The nation is pulling apart racially, socially, economically, and spiritually. The contrasts in direction are tremendous. Arthur Goldberg talked about a pluralistic society. He may have been talking for foreign consumption, but over eight million citizens listened and their hopes and dreams rose. These eight million citizens had bilingual-bicultural assets. There is a great opportunity for America to fulfill its promise to mankind.

The National Advisory Commission on Civil Disorders has said, "Our nation is moving toward two societies, one black and one white — separate and unequal." Where does this analysis leave the largest ethnic, linguistic, cultural group in America? Must Mexican Americans choose sides? Is there no place for the brown? Is a pluralistic society not possible? For Chicanos the die may soon be cast.

Mexican Americans must keep cool. They must not be swept into support or condemnation of the course of others. Whatever course the rest of America may take, there is only one direction for Mexican Americans. They must remain resolute and dedicated to a single principle, to one compelling goal. They must be confident that this country is based on the rights and the dignity of man and that education is the one catalyst that can preserve that principle and achieve that goal. The dignity of self-respect, faith in mankind, and a belief in equality is really what education — race and education, language and education, and culture and education — is all about. The Mexican American must show the rest of America's troubled peoples that through a vigorous pursuit of quality and equality in education, differences and doubts and suspicions can be removed from our society.

This pursuit is a dangerous and difficult mission for Mexican Americans. It will require all the toughness and determination which any people have been asked to provide. Through dedication to education as the only bridge which can span the gulf now developing in our explosive biracial society, the Mexican American may well be able to bring reason and trust to this hostile atmosphere. Chicanos must make education work for their people; if they fail, Mexican Americans will be swept into the arena of hatred and distrust. Then Chicanos must make the focus on education a commitment by all people, for the survival of a nation. If it can be demonstrated that education is the means by which the burdens of discrimination, isolation, rejection, and contempt can be removed from the Mexican American, then Chicanos have the most powerful weapon for taking the arm of the white man and the arm of the black man and saying to them, "Grow up, get with it, become a part of Everyman's society."

Victor Hugo's observation, "No army can withstand the strength of an idea whose time has come," shall be the base for action. Let us take education and make it a tool for becoming the force that welds America's torn society into a unified civilization. This can be done; and, more important, Chicanos must do it. How sharp is the focus? It has never been sharper. And it never has given so much and never has asked so much as it does today. Education and the Mexican American may well determine the destiny of a nation.

Pattern Transmission in a Bicultural Community*

THE DATA PRESENTED IN THIS PAPER were obtained during a three-year field study of an Anglo/Mexican American community in the Southwest. The study was an inquiry into the persistent patterns of ethnic cleavage which characterize such communities and the social and cultural dynamics of pattern maintenance. As a consequence, the inquiry focused intensively on the institutions presumed to be responsible for transmitting core-culture content to young members of the village community.

The village of Rosario is located in one of the rich agricultural valleys of the southern half of California. Village economic life centers on the growing and preparation for market of a variety of fresh vegetables and fruits. Of the population of about 1,800 people, approximately 40 percent are "Anglo" or "American" as they are locally termed, 55 percent are Mexicans, and 5 percent are of miscellaneous racial and cultural backgrounds. The social structure of this community approaches what Simmons has called the "Caste Pole" of a ranking continuum: the Anglo and the Mexican villagers are differentiated according to

*Printed by permission of Bureau of Intergroup Relations, California State Department of Education.

ethnic identification and "racial" or physical characteristics, the critical visibility symbols of which are language, color, and possession of Spanish surname. Each group is highly endogamous, and there are strong avoidance patterns between them. Contacts between the two groups occur almost wholly within the economic structure which is dominated by Anglos and in which relationships are impersonal. Anglo villagers control political and economic power and are dominant in nearly all relations with Mexicans. Institutional and organizational associations are segregated, with the Anglos using deliberate exclusion practices to maintain segregation. This situation was found to be particularly true of two major institutions in the village — the church and the school.

The rank system of the village is not completely closed and cannot, therefore, be considered a true caste situation. This is because of the Anglo notion of the possibilities of assimilation in the dim future and their willingness to enter into certain social relationships with those "high-type" Mexicans who approach Anglo ideals, i.e., a person who is light-skinned, aggressive, speaks unaccented English, is economically successful, and educated. Few such persons are to be found in Rosario. The four Mexicans who do meet these Anglo qualifications have been socially redefined as "Latin" and are admitted to some Anglo social activities which are held in public places but *never* to those held in private residences. Indeed, the patterns of residence and of inter-residence visiting reveal that the social cleavage between Anglos and Mexicans is virtually complete.

The ethnically differentiated social structure of the village is supported by mutually reinforcing images and expectations by means of which Anglos and Mexicans define the character of members of the other group. These images and expectations take the form of stereotyped beliefs according to which villagers organize their perceptions of, and behavior toward, one another. They are *de*scriptive in that they define the characteristics of members of the out-group, and *pre*scriptive in that they indicate the need for appropriate behavioral adaptations to the defined characteristics. The patterned adaptive responses then constitute the norms governing social relations between the two groups. The data suggest, moreover, that the antithesis of the characteristics imputed to members of the out-group is precisely the profile of characteristics attributed to the members of one's own group — and therefore to oneself. (From the Anglo point of view, what the Anglos *are*, the Mexicans are *not*, and vice versa.) Thus these patterned beliefs appear to support both the sociocultural system and the psychocultural system within the population, and to be an important linkage between the two.

In general, Anglo informants believe the Mexican villagers to be immoral, violent, superstitious, animal-like in their sexuality, physiologically and mentally underdeveloped (or less advanced on the evolutionary scale), improvident, irresponsible, lazy, black, and childlike. Mexican informants characterize Anglos as being unsympathetic to members of their own group as well as to outsiders, aggressive, harsh, demanding, "cold," interested only in themselves, always worrying, and unconcerned about important human values. The reciprocal and self-sustaining nature of these belief systems is illustrated by the fact that the appropriate adaptive behaviors to which they respectively give rise are construed as realistic evidence of the validity of the beliefs. Thus Anglos behave toward Mexicans consistently with their beliefs about Mexicans; patterned Mexican responses to Anglo behaviors provide evidence to reinforce Anglo beliefs and lead to Anglo adaptive responses; these in turn provide evidence to support the Mexican beliefs about Anglos which structured their original responses to the Anglos. The dynamics of these reciprocating subsystems define the content *and* form of the larger, community-level system. The stability of the community system depends upon the degree to which individuals learn the patterned attitudes, beliefs, and behaviors of their own subsystems — and how these articulate with the functioning whole. This implies, of course, that each individual develops a cognitive and dynamic awareness of self, subgroup, and community.

One incident which I observed provides a clear and dramatic illustration of how Anglo beliefs about the immoral and violent nature of village Mexicans structure their perceptions of real situations and their behavioral adaptation to them. During the course of the field investigation, my wife and I attended several of the Mexican dances held in the village. These dances were usually held on Saturday evenings, and when possible, in the community center. Other than my wife and I, I know of no Anglo who has ever attended one of these dances.

Anglo villagers, however, claim to have intimate knowledge of what happens at the dances. They believe that the dances are orgies of fighting, drunkenness, and sexuality. To "contain the violence," as one influential Anglo put it, Anglo villagers take up a collection among themselves and hire a half dozen private police to come over from the county seat and cordon off the area immediately surrounding the community center. Because of the expense of this practice, the Anglo chamber of commerce, which controls the calendar for the use of the center, permits the Mexican villagers to use the recreation hall only infrequently. Toward the end of one evening, I stepped outside the building for a breath of cool air. There were six people outside the hall: my two male companions and myself, a Mexican girl and her boyfriend, and the Anglo private patrolman who had been stationed outside the front entrance. The Mexican man was drunk, but quiet and very formal in his relationship to the girl. As the couple walked by the side window of the building, the man stumbled and in falling threw his hand into a glass window. The glass cut his hand and arm, and he was bleeding profusely. At that moment a man emerged from the building; seeing the accident, he rushed over to the couple and began to give aid. While trying to stop the bleeding with his handkerchief, the newcomer was speaking rapidly to the girl in Spanish, asking her what had happened, and remarking that that was what comes of being so drunk. Hearing the excited talk, the Anglo patrolman turned away from his car where he had been listening to the shortwave radio. Seeing the group on the sidewalk, he rushed over, seized the injured man, and dragged him to the patrol car. The injured man and the girl said that they wanted to go home, but the patrolman held them there and radioed for help. The man who had tried to help stepped back into the little crowd that had begun to gather, and he offered no more assistance. As more people emerged from the dance hall, the crowd grew larger, but there was little talking and little movement. They stood there silently watching. The girl began to argue with the patrolman, asking to take the injured man home. The more she argued the more agitated the patrolman seemed to become; he even unhooked the flap of his gun holster. The young man was standing, bleeding, shaking, and growing visibly weaker, but saying nothing. A police ambulance soon came and drove the injured man and the patrolman away. The girl was taken home by a cousin who was attending the dance. The crowd quickly dispersed. No further incident occurred that evening. Other than I, the only Anglo to observe the entire sequence of events was the patrolman who had been hired by the village Anglos to curb violence.

The next day the Anglo villagers were very much excited about the "big brawl" that had taken place at the Mexican dance. Many said that there had been another slash fight with razors and pointed to the blood on the pavement as evidence. One prominent Anglo, telling the "news" to a group of friends outside the church, said that a bunch of Mexicans got into a knife fight over a girl and that two or three were badly stabbed. He said that he was going to put pressure on the chamber of commerce to "do something to stop all this violence." The newspaper account which appeared two days later further substantiated the Anglo stories by stating that the Mexican man arrested for fighting at the Mexican dance had been fined $100 and given fifteen days in jail. Upon reading the newspaper version, several friends of the injured man gathered in the local cantina and discussed ways they might help their friend. Their discussion was noisy, but inconclusive. Later, Anglo villagers were saying that the "Mexes" were planning to "get" two of the Anglo men in retaliation against the jailing of their friend. At the same time, the Mexican villagers were saying that the Anglos are aggressive, hard, always having their own way, and therefore were to be avoided.

Incidents such as these are important means for transmitting and maintaining village ethnic patterns. Discussion of the event provides an opportunity for reinforcement of existing belief/value systems through agreement with others, through the emotional commitment built up during the repetition of a highly charged story, and by the appeal to the "objective evidence" which such discussions often include. As the saying goes, "A picture is worth a thousand words." And, for days following the above incident, villagers were to be seen standing on the sidewalk before the community center and pointing to the bloodstains on the concrete while they discussed the meaning of the stains.

Throughout their lives, villagers are exposed to constant

verbal instruction in and reinforcement of the ethnic world view. Frequently, this consists of stories and explanations of the nature of the other group and their activities. More often, however, it is expressed in the *Because . . . Therefore* formula which is the form in which most village stereotypes are stated. The *Because* portion of these statements expresses a belief about the characteristics of a group, and the *Therefore* portion indicates the adaptive behavior which is considered to be an appropriate response to the particular characteristics identified. The adaptations are generally in the form of withdrawal or exclusion. Let me give three examples taken from ordinary backyard gossip situations:

"[Because] Mexicans are not reliable, you can't be sure they will ever do a job right. [Therefore] I always get an American when I have something important I need done."

"[Because] a bunch of Mexicans joined up and I am afraid they might gang up on him or give him something [a disease], I [therefore] don't let my boy go to that scout pack anymore."

"Jess wanted to play Little League with the American boys, but [because] if he didn't play too good, he might get into trouble. A lot of these parents get real mad when their boys' team loses a game. They always blame the Mexican boys and make trouble. I [therefore] told him it would be better if he played with the Mexican boys."

One particularly salient form of verbal instruction is that which is given in the weekly sermons in the Catholic church to which 1400 of the 1800 villagers belong. Delivered by the Anglo priest, these sermons closely reflect the Anglo stereotype. Because the sermons are primarily a means of public instruction, they probably reinforce both the stereotypes and the social arrangements based upon them. Inasmuch as these sermons are delivered *ex cathedra* with all the aura of dogma and sanctity that this implies to Catholics, the influence these sermons have on the thinking of the villagers is probably very great indeed. Their influence is probably greatest when they are delivered to the whole village on one of the many special days when there is only one Mass which is heavily attended by both Anglos and Mexicans. One such sermon included the following:

You Mexicans need to learn the prayers of the church. We try to teach them to you in religious instruction classes, but we don't often get very far. You should keep trying to learn the prayers because this is the way you can get closer to God. You parents just let your kids run wild. If you would keep your children together at home and teach them the prayers of the Church and then pray regularly with them, maybe you wouldn't have so much trouble. Boys who pray at home with their parents and who come to church regularly will not be the ones who are out fighting with knives and getting into trouble. . . . Remember, when you pray to Heaven you must have clean thoughts. You can't make a good prayer if you are thinking about getting a girl or planning some thrill. You have to think about Our Lord and not about yourselves. . . . And when you pray you should be truly sorry for your sins. God doesn't listen to the prayers of people who are sinful. He *does* listen to people who are sorry. If you could try to know when you are sinful and be truly sorry, He will listen to your prayers.

The twice-yearly confirmation ceremony is an example of some of the more subtle means by which the church reinforces village ethnic patterns. These ceremonies are important social events in the village and are attended by large crowds of Anglos and Mexicans. According to local custom, the Mexican villagers tend to sit toward the rear of the church and the Anglos sit toward the front. In the confirmation ceremony, Anglo youth are given precedence over the Mexicans: They march in first, sit in front of the Mexican youth, are confirmed first, and lead the recessional march. In Rosario the bishop customarily questions each child on some point of doctrine, and he does so as part of the confirmation ceremony itself. He begins with the Anglo boys. As his turn comes, each boy stands and waits for his question. Once he has answered, he sits down and the next boy stands. When all the Anglo boys have been questioned satisfactorily, the bishop turns to the Anglo girls and the process continues. On those occasions when an Anglo boy or girl hesitates over an answer, the bishop waits until the answer is given. At times, however, he may help the child by giving hints or by asking related questions.

Once the Anglos have been questioned, the bishop turns to the Mexican boys and then to the Mexican girls. The question process here, however, is not as smooth as it is with the Anglo children. The bishop repeatedly admonishes the Mexican children not to "mumble," and if the children hesitate or become confused in their answers to questions, he becomes quickly impatient and calls for one of the Anglo children to "volunteer" to "help" the distressed Mexican child. Usually he selects a volunteer who he is sure has the right answer and praises the

Anglo child for knowing that which, presumably, the Mexican child does not know. Since there is always a relatively large number of Mexican children who need "help," a considerable portion of the ceremony is taken up by this question sequence in which the bishop (as an authority of the church) repeatedly demonstrates the validity of the villagers' ethnic images and expectations.

The use of Anglo "helpers" in question sequences is a practice that is widely employed in the village school as well as in the church. Nine of the eighteen Anglo teachers were observed to follow this procedure *whenever* they worked with Mexican children. Asked about this, one long-time village teacher said: "If I didn't, I would spend all day waiting for the Mexican children to give out with the answer. Most of them aren't awfully smart and they need help. It wouldn't do any good to ask one of the Mexican pupils to help out with an answer because he wouldn't know it either. Most of the time you can be sure that the American kids will know the answers. I think that it is better if the Mexican kids get help from an American kid who knows what he is talking about than from another Mexican who doesn't. Besides, it is good educational practice to have the American children help the Mexicans. It draws them out and gives them a feeling of importance."

To me, it seems that this and a wide variety of similar classroom practices in the village school contribute to the maintenance of ethnic patterns by putting the Mexican pupils in a subordinate position in the classroom, by reinforcing the Anglo stereotype of the unintelligent Mexican who needs the guidance of a superior and paternalistic Anglo who knows "best," and perhaps more significantly, by structuring public opportunities for Anglo and Mexican children to enter into prototypes of their adult relationships.

Within the school, the verbal expression of ethnic beliefs is much less open than it is in the general community. Because they are usually occupied with school matters, the children do not appear to state their beliefs and interpretations as frequently or openly in school as they do outside. Whereas the teachers *do* express the Anglo beliefs frequently among themselves, they rarely ever make direct reference to them in the classroom. Instead, they structure the classroom groupings, sequence the instruction, and both verbally and symbolically *demonstrate* to the school population and the community the validity of these beliefs and the appropriateness of the patterned adaptive responses. The ability-grouping program separates Anglo and Mexican pupils into ethnically distinct groups and publicly demonstrates the "fact" that Mexicans are less intelligent and ambitious than Anglos. This "fact" is further proclaimed in the policy of posting pupil-achievement charts in the classroom. It is all too obvious that the Anglo names are the ones followed by the gold stars or pink bunnies, and that the Mexican names are usually not so adorned. That these charts influence pupil perceptions of one another was evidenced in the fact that pupils regularly used them as points of reference in making judgments about classmates.

In addition to the grouping procedures, teachers carry out a number of other practices which structure the social contacts of Anglo and Mexican pupils. In the choosing of monitors, game captains, and special representatives, the teachers habitually place Anglo children in "charge" of Mexican children. When they see a group of Mexican children misbehaving, teachers very frequently reprimand the whole group and then ask an Anglo child to take "charge" and "show" everyone how to act. The following interview from the field data illustrates both the practice and its meaning:

Interviewer: Do you remember the group of boys that you stopped from running out of the room the other day? I am thinking about the group that made a rush for the door at noon on the day that I visited your classroom. I have been wondering why it was that you selected Johnny to take the lead of the group.

Mrs. S.: Oh, yes, I remember. Well, I try to follow the strict rule in my room that no one is to leave the room until everything has been put away and the class is excused.

Usually the kids are pretty good, but that day those boys were in a hurry to get out to the playground. There was some kind of activity going on during the lunch hour; I think that was the day they were putting some new blacktop on the yard. I remember thinking that the Mexican boys were going to make trouble if I didn't catch them. You know, they just can't follow directions. You always have to tell them what you want done. They seem to have a hard time remembering the rules. Anyway, I thought that if I told Johnny to take the lead, they would have a good example of how to act.

Interviewer: Was there some reason why you chose Johnny specifically?

Mrs. S.: Yes. He was right there, of course. Besides that, I think that Johnny needs to learn how to set a good example and how to lead others. His father owns one of the big farms in the area and Johnny has to learn how to lead the Mexicans. One day he will by helping his father, and he will have to know how to handle the Mexicans. I try to help him whenever I can. You ought to meet Mr. F. He came here with practically nothing and could only speak Italian. Now he is one of the important men in the community. He is an example for everybody to follow.

Interviewer: Do you mean that the Mexicans need somebody to direct them?

Mrs. S.: Definitely.

Interviewer: Why?

Mrs. S.: Well, they are just not very bright. Besides that, they are lazy. No ambition at all. You should hear some of the boo-boos that the Mexicans make around here.

The data obtained in this study reveal that the ethnically differentiated social patterns and associated stereotypes are learned quite early by village children. After the second grade, Anglo and Mexican American children increasingly restrict their social choices to members of their own ethnic groups. By the time they reach the upper elementary grades, there is virtually complete social separation between the two groups. That the children are aware of Anglo dominance is reflected in their leadership and prestige choices. Both Anglo and Mexican American children chose Anglos as sources of prestige, and both groups made significant choices of Anglos for the positions of leadership.

One of the most impressive features of the village social structure is the high degree of functional integration exhibited by its major institutions in the maintenance of the traditional ethnic patterns. Whether they are at home, in church, at school, on the playground, shopping with parents, attending Scout meetings, or watching the Harvest Festival activities, children are provided with examples of the social positions they are expected to occupy and the roles they are expected to play. They are frequently shown that Anglos are best in everything and the Mexicans are the worst. Mexican children are rewarded in school and in church when they look and act like Anglos and punished (or ignored) if they look and act like Mexicans. Anglo children are allowed to joke and talk freely with teachers, the priest, and adult Anglos, but Mexican children are expected to maintain a decorum of respect and formality. The ideal of ethnic separation is demonstrated and taught to the children through the fact that they *are* separated by the grouping practices of the school, by the class seating assignments in the church, by the Scout arrangements, etc. The examples and teachings of their parents further reinforce these learnings. Adults find the same consistency in social expectations as they move from their homes to the church, to their jobs or in the community at large. The beliefs which support these patterns are communicated unofficially through conversation and gossip and officially through pronouncements, warnings, analogies, and stories, made by teachers in school, the priest in church, the newspaper in print, or the chamber of commerce officers in town meetings.

In this brief presentation I have attempted to sketch out some of the ways in which ethnicity structures social and cultural patterns in a small southwestern community and to explore a few of the more overt mechanisms through which these patterns are transmitted and reinforced. I should like to end my remarks with a comment about (more properly a reaction to) some of the new federal- and state-supported school programs that are being forced upon communities like Rosario under the banners of "humanity" and "equality." Whether educators or other social reformers working unilaterally through the schools in such communities can ever attain their goals of social reconstruction is extremely problematic. The greater the functional integration of the social and belief/value attitude systems of the community, the greater the likelihood that efforts to produce such fundamental changes will require approaches through multiple aspects of the system.

The power of the school to induce significant social change is probably always very limited, for the school does not have effective, lasting, or broad enough sanctions available to it. In small, highly integrated communities, this power will be even more restricted, for the traditional mechanisms of social control will operate both within and without the school and limit both the teachers' freedom to institute change and the pupils' freedom to accept it. Also, where changes contrary to traditional patterns and concepts are introduced through one institution of such a community, other institutions may be expected to attempt to correct and/or compensate for these changes. Thus, as in Rosario, when the child comes home from school with a notion contrary to accepted patterns, he will be corrected within the home, the church, and other nonschool institutions. Even massive community-wide efforts to produce basic sociocultural changes of the type required to bring about assimilation of the Anglo and Mexican groups in the Southwest would require substantial periods of time. Such changes occur only within the span of generations, not on a short-term basis.

Elementary and Secondary Education*

EDWARD V. MORENO

No longer can any federal agency or department hide behind a mantle of ignorance or innocence. Nor can they continuously ask: What are the problems? What are the needs? Never before have there been available so many studies of facts, figures, and statistics. A few sources include:

1. California State Department of Education, "Racial and Ethnic Survey of California Public Schools; Part One: Distribution of Pupils"; "Part Two: Distribution of Employees," Fall, 1966, Sacramento, California, 1967.

2. California State Department of Education, "Survey of Mexican American Pupils in the Schools: Their Strengths and Their Needs," Sacramento, California.

3. California State Department of Industrial Relations, Division of Fair Employment Practices, "Californians of Spanish Surname: Population; Employment; Income; Education," San Francisco, California, May, 1964.

4. Colorado Commission on Spanish-Surnamed Citizens, "The

---

*A paper presented by the author to the Cabinet Committee Hearings on Mexican American Affairs, El Paso, Texas, October, 1967.

Status of Spanish-Surnamed Citizens in Colorado," Denver, Colorado, January, 1967.

5. Walter Fogel, "Mexican American Study Project — Advance Report I — Education and Income of Mexican Americans in the Southwest," The Regents of the University of California, November, 1965.

6. Hearings before the Special Subcommittee on Bilingual Education of the Committee on Labor and Public Welfare, United States Senate, Ninetieth Congress, First Session on S. 428, Part I; Bilingual Education, Washington, D.C., May 18, 19, 26, 29, and 31, 1967; Part II, June 24 and July 21, 1967.

Narratives from ESEA (Elementary and Secondary Education Act), Title I and Title III projects, further detail needs and concerns. For example:

1. Mexican American Research Project of the State Department of Education, "Bilingual Education for Mexican American Children," Marysville, California, October, 1966–June, 1967.

2. Stockton Unified School District, "A Demonstration Bilingual Education Project," Stockton, California, June 1967.

Additional narratives and documentation are certainly available to the Office of Education from a variety of programs, projects, and proposals.

Therefore, I want to suggest some solutions to the problems that face the Office of Education and to insist that the Office of Education (1) offer technical assistance to congressional committees writing educational legislation and (2) assume a leadership role in rewriting guidelines, making recommendations, and advocating and supporting funding to improve the quality of education for the Spanish-speaking people of the Southwest.

COMMITMENTS

Appreciative and cognizant of previous and current efforts on the federal level, the following statements define and demand the involvement and commitment of the Office of Education to Spanish-speaking people:

1. The commitment of the Office to long-range funding and operation is imperative for permanent, effective, educational programs. *Ad hoc* one-year projects and funding are inadequate. We are committed to long-range funding.

2. The education of the Mexican American child is only one aspect of his total need. Only the commitment of the Office to long-range comprehensive programs from early childhood through adulthood and including the education of migrant families will produce optimum results. To such programs we are committed.

3. Only a coordinated, integrated multi-agency commitment by the Office will insure maximum performance of services, manpower, and funds and, in addition, will render long-range comprehensive programs possible. We will support this effort.

4. The commitment of the Office to flexible implementation with accountability and with final decisions at the state or regional level will meet the diverse needs of this target population. We are committed to this approach also.

If the Office of Education is sincere and concerned in meeting the needs of the Mexican American population of the Southwest, it must be committed to the preceding statements.

Then a joint commitment — on the part of the Office of Education and the Mexican American communities — will provide competent bilingual and bicultural citizens for this nation. This valuable Mexican American citizen has served, and in the future will participate even more fully, in the affairs of this nation at home and abroad, especially with Spanish-speaking countries.

The potential and resources of both the Anglo and Hispanic communities and the positive values of each will have to be utilized in every area of involvement.

CRITERIA

Before meaningful practices in education are listed, the Education Committee of the Pre-White House Conference and the membership of the Association of Mexican American Educators demand that programs funded under federal titles be reviewed with us in light of the following questions. The answers to the following questions will provide the Office with a better understanding of what is being done and will provide the Mexican American community with a better understanding of what is being done and will also provide the Mexican American community with a better understanding of how it might be able to assist the Office and the local school districts.

1. In an effective educational program, the recipients of the

program must believe in it. This belief is generated by involving the recipients in the planning and execution of the program. An otherwise effective program, prepared by experts with positive intentions, may fail because the participants do not appreciate the necessity, relevance, or importance of it.

How, then, are the children and their parents being involved in the decisions, policies, and implementation of their educational program?

2. Recipients of a program cannot be brought into it after major plans have been made. They must be involved from the beginning and must continue their involvement.

How long, then, have the recipients been involved in the planning of their program?

3. An educational program must be related to recognized needs of the learners involved as they perceive their needs. That program must take into account the assets, attitudes, skills, and personalities of the learners for whom it is intended. It is necessary to specify in detail the characteristics of these learners and to define carefully the population of learners who are the targets of the program.

How relevant is the program to the target population?

4. It is not enough to provide a program and have children receive it. It is necessary to select children for a program based upon evidence of their need and their possession of prerequisite attitudes and skills. Selection must be carried out by using instruments that unequivocally answer the question of needs and prerequisites.

What evaluative devices are being utilized to determine the selection of participants for the program?

5. An educational program is successful to the extent that its outcome is known. It is essential to state, unambiguously, what the participants are expected to be like after completing the program. This requires defining the behaviors the child is expected to exhibit after finishing the program.

What are the specific behavioral objectives of the program?

6. There must be clear evidence that the procedures making up the program lead members of the target population to exhibit the desired behaviors after participating in the program. Definitive data that show that children in the program achieved the expected objectives are essential.

How has the program guaranteed successful attainment of its behavioral objectives?

7. In some fashion, children must be evaluated after receiving the program to show that they have attained its objectives. Evaluation may involve available tests, specially prepared tests, or specially prepared observational instruments. The form is not as important as the validity of the evaluation.

What evaluative tools are being utilized to determine the successful performance of the children in the program?

8. Recipients of an educational program must be engaged in its planning and execution. In addition, they must participate in evaluating and reevaluating the program to continue their meaningful contributions to the program's success.

How do the recipients convey to the school their reactions and evalutions of their program?

9. Once an effective educational program is operating, it will have ramifications for other areas of instruction. The children will now have different needs and capabilities, and these differences must be taken into account in future educational experiences.

What meaningful adjustments, changes, or improvements are being made in succeeding levels, grades, or classes to accommodate the successful children of the program?

10. Once an educational program has been demonstrated to be effective, it must be made a regular part of the actual school operation. The planning of the program must include provisions (personnel, resources, materials, and financing) for an implementation phase and not just for the research development phase. It has been assumed that an outstanding program would be implemented by the district. Seldom has an educational agency been capable of implementing excellent programs.

How is the educational system incorporating the program as part of its regular services?

11. Frequently, an effective educational program can be beneficial for children other than the target population. Attempts must be made to determine applicability of a program, starting with a critical review of the program to speculate on its potential for different types of participants.

Would the program be desirable for participants other than this target population? For whom? How?

PRIORITIES

In listing practices and meaningful actions, several district and community priorities have been considered:

1. Educational programs must focus on early childhood and adults.

2. Educational programs must strengthen communities and extended family structures bringing resources into the communities and families, thus stemming the exodus of manpower and resources from them.

3. Educational programs must build in preservice, in-service and postservice training for teachers and administrators. Teacher training is crucial, but administrator training is more vitally needed.

4. Educational programs must upgrade skills of the paraprofessionals employed in federally funded projects.

5. Educational programs must accelerate the expansion of bicultural and bilingual projects throughout the Southwest and the nation.

The succeeding statements include only a partial list of meaningful ideas and practices. Each meaningful action must be part of a systematic longitudinal approach to individualizing instruction for Mexican American children, youth, and adults.

GUIDELINES

Guidelines for federally funded elementary programs concerned with Spanish-speaking children must:

1. Provide a program of in-service training that will develop the potential of the indigenous aide from one occupational level to the next wherever aides are used and provide optimum employment opportunities for indigenous people to serve in their target area as part of the total program.

2. Initiate early childhood classes before entrance age in kindergarten.

3. Include English-as-a-second-language specialist teachers in all schools with Spanish-speaking children.

4. Structure maximum parent participation and involvement in all grades.

5. Provide compensation and time from the regular day to permit teachers to attend in-service classes.

6. Provide stipends to community people who are utilized as advisory or resource persons in the schools.

7. Allow time during the regular school day for teachers to visit homes and become involved in the community life.

8. Encourage sensitivity training for teachers and administrators plus information on the cultural and value systems of the Mexican American of the Southwest provided by the Mexican American community.

9. Utilize bilingual proficiency tests for proper placement of children, and for adequate adjustments of classes in follow-up programs.

10. Provide for additional bilingual classes for grades K-9 for both Spanish-speaking and English-speaking youngsters.

11. Recommend teaching in the child's own language with transfer to the English language skills in a sequentially designed curriculum. The Spanish program would continue to develop bilingual children.

12. Structure counseling and guidance to children and their parents by persons sensitive, concerned, and trained to do so.

13. Insist on maximum participation of a target population in the development of their program.

14. Insure in every project and program, or component thereof, that the self-concept of the child is paramount.

15. Insist on provision of health and nutritional services to all children.

16. Provide for early childhood programs in child care centers.

17. Recommend extensive use of paraprofessionals in all grades.

18. Emphasize serving and strengthening the total family structure.

Guidelines for federally funded secondary education programs must:

1. Provide for counseling in a nonschool environment by a counselor and/or school community coordinator, or a student in school.

2. Design continuous in-service training for administrators, teachers, and counselors during the school day in schools with a high density of Mexican American students.

3. Support with extra compensation the services of master teachers and other resource personnel in schools with large numbers of Mexican American students.

4. Design long-range evaluative instruments to measure specific behavioral objectives in classes serving Mexican American students.

5. Expand tutorial services and extended day study centers in *barrios.*

6. Conduct action research in the schools throughout the Southwest.

7. Develop on a national level national norms utilizing culture-free tests.

8. Increase bilingual programs for both the Spanish- and English-speaking youth of this nation.

9. Provide criteria for investigation and evaluation of teaching materials for children of Mexican American background.

10. Recommend school-community coordinators in every high school in a Mexican American community.

11. Stimulate interest in developing scholarships, loans, and grants to retain adolescents in high school.

12. Encourage apprenticeship programs through vocational education that lead directly to employment upon high school graduation.

13. Provide specific behavioral objectives for each program in order to insure administrative and teacher commitment in the implementation and evaluation.

14. Encourage private industry to set pilot and experimental learning centers in the *barrios.*

15. Outline post high school and adult education for dropouts and adults that leads to formation of food, gasoline, and clothing cooperatives and self-help housing.

16. Provide legal aid service for parents to deal with undesirable school conditions.

SUMMARY

In conclusion, we request that the Office of Education be committed as the Mexican American communities of the Southwest are committed to the following:

1. Only long-range programs
2. Only comprehensive programs

3. Only coordinated integrated multi-agency efforts

4. Only flexible implementation

Moreover, we will ask, and look in federal guidelines, for the reflection of the following questions:

1. How are the children and their parents being involved in the decisions, policies, and implementation of their educational program?

2. How long have the recipients been involved in the planning of their program?

3. How relevant is the program to the target population?

4. What evaluative devices are being utilized to determine the selection of participants for the program?

5. What are the specific behavioral objectives of the program?

6. How has the program guaranteed successful attainment of its behavioral objectives?

7. What evaluative tools are being utilized to determine the successful performance of the children in the program?

8. How do the recipients convey to the school their reactions and evaluations of their program?

9. What meaningful adjustments, changes, or improvements are being made in succeeding levels, grades, or classes to accommodate the successful children of the program?

10. How is the educational system incorporating the program as part of its regular services?

11. Would the program be desirable for participants other than this target population? For whom? How?

Inclusion of these questions in federal guidelines will demonstrate the degree of involvement and commitment to improving the education of the Mexican American child.

Lastly, when the practices outlined previously are common in the schools of the Southwest, we will know that the Office of Education has fulfilled its duty.

In Southern California, I will begin to generate the political pressures that will help both the Office of Education and the Mexican American communities to bring about the changes so necessary to improve the education of Spanish-speaking children and adults.

Hopefully, when we meet again, many of the solutions, recommendations, and ideas presented here will be standard operating procedure in the Office of Education.

The Educational Need of Migrant Children*

THIS NATION'S COMMITMENT TO EQUAL EDUCATIONAL OPPORTUNITY for all its citizens faces one of its sharpest challenges in providing for migrant farm families. None of the educational needs of this group are unique or new; the difficulty is that so many needs are combined for these people. They share the handicaps of extreme poverty with all others at the bottom of the economic ladder, the handicaps of segregation with all who live outside the central culture, the handicaps of language with others who speak a different tongue or a form of nonstandard English, and the handicaps of migrancy with the increasingly numerous rootless people whose work requires frequent moves.

Educational techniques are available to deal with any or all of these needs. The problem is no longer in knowing the needs or inventing the educational solutions; the needs are fairly obvious, and the solutions, though sometimes complex, are not too difficult for even the smallest and most remote school, *providing* (it is at this point — in the *provisions* — that the problem lies); for the solutions require facilities, personnel, materials, and

*Published with permission of Bureau of Intergroup Relations, California State Department of Education.

money that schools have not been able to get. More than anything else, the solutions require concern, not only on the part of those immediately affected but on the part of the larger community — concern and commitment that grow from full realization that the development of human potential is as vital to the nation as to the individual, that the greatest untapped reservoir of American talent is in groups such as this which have never had adequate access to opportunity, and that no group of Americans can be left outside the gate. When there is enough concern, the resources can be found for schools to accomplish what they already know how to do.

With new programs and new funds available from both state and federal sources, a significant change is in sight. It is essential that these new resources be used well, so that the value of such support is demonstrated clearly in educational gains. The immediate concern is where to begin in strengthening the present educational program. As background for a discussion of ways and means, this paper outlines some of the educational needs of children, youth, and adults in the migrant group as these are defined by teachers, school board members, and others who work closely with the problem.

SUMMARY OF EDUCATIONAL NEEDS

1. EQUAL OPPORTUNITY. Migrant children, youth, and adults need educational programs which offer them the same opportunity for maximum development as that which is available to any other group.

2 IDENTIFICATION AND CITIZENSHIP. Educational programs should be planned to help migrant people identify with the community and with the country as participating citizens.

3. ATTITUDES FAVORABLE TO SUCCESS. Migrant people need educational experiences planned to develop and strengthen self-confidence and self-direction.

4. RELEVANCE AND MEANING. Educational programs should be directly and immediately related to the experiences, needs, and goals of migrant people.

5. MASTERY OF ENGLISH. Schools should provide systematic instruction in the English language, both for children and youth who speak a different language and for those who speak nonstandard English.

6. VOCATIONAL GUIDANCE AND EDUCATION. Schools should open the way to improved vocational opportunities for members of migrant families.

7. BETTER LIVING. School programs should help migrant people to deal with problems of daily living under camp conditions and to develop the skills and knowledge needed for better living.

8. KINDERGARTEN AND PRESCHOOL PROGRAMS. Young children of migrant families should have an opportunity to attend kindergarten and preschool programs.

9. INDIVIDUALIZED LEARNING PROGRAMS. School programs for migrant children and youth should be based on the individual needs of each pupil.

10. BROADENING BACKGROUND AND INTERESTS. Migrant people need compensatory experiences and activities planned to develop understandings, interests, and expressive abilities.

11. SECONDARY EDUCATION. All migrant youth should be able to obtain a high school education.

12. ADULT EDUCATION. Programs of adult education should be available to migrant families.

13. CONTINUITY IN THE EDUCATIONAL PROGRAM. Schools which educate migrant children and youth need to improve cooperative planning and communication for greater continuity in their education.

14. SUFFICIENT SPECIALIZED PERSONNEL. Fundamental to a good program is a sufficient number of teachers and other personnel trained in the special requirements of the recommended program.

15. ADEQUATE FACILITIES AND EQUIPMENT. Schools in the migrant areas should be supplied with the facilities and equipment needed for the recommended program.

16. FLEXIBILITY IN EDUCATIONAL ARRANGEMENTS. New ways for organizing and implementing educational programs should be developed.

17. SUPPLEMENTARY FINANCING. Additional finances need to be made available for educating migrant children, youth, and adults.

THE NEEDS DEFINED

1. *Equal opportunity.* Migrant children, youth, and adults need educational programs which offer them the same oppor-

tunity for maximum development as that which is available to any other group.

Although this group of people is exceptionally handicapped, the educational provisions for them are frequently meager and substandard. Tremendous improvements have been achieved since the days, not long ago, when "emergency" schools were hastily set up at the beginning of every crop season in barns, basements, tents, and empty churches. But still the children of these families too often spend their school lives moving from one overcrowded classroom to another, being taught by poorly trained teachers, falling behind year after year, until on days between crops they disappear from the public school rolls. Few migrant children survive their first educational experience and attempt high school; those who do face great discouragement with every move, because they are caught in a system of semester units and subject requirements devised for a permanent population. Provisions for adult education are scarce indeed, especially for the man or woman who must adapt his attendance to crop seasons. And so lack of education, poverty, and alienation are perpetuated in the same old cycle from one generation to another.

Equal opportunity does not mean the same school provisions for everyone. Because of their exceptional needs, migrant people should have highly trained teachers, small classes, excellent facilities, liberal materials, good transportation — the best educational provisions that are offered to any group. In addition, to assure equal opportunity to a group so handicapped, special arrangements will need to be made beyond those provided for people without handicaps. The point is that an opportunity should be made available for each child, youth, and adult to become all he is capable of becoming, and that whatever is necessary to achieve this goal should be provided.

2. *Identification and citizenship.* Educational programs should be planned to help migrant people identify with the community and with the country as participating citizens.

Migrant workers and their families almost always live in housing that is separated from the rest of the community. They associate very little with members of any other groups and make few permanent ties even with the other migrant families that share their temporary neighborhoods. They seldom go to church in the community and almost never vote. Living in isolation, they have none of the participatory experiences on which most people build the feeling of identification and belonging which is basic to citizenship.

It is vitally important, therefore, that school programs provide an opportunity for this essential learning. The experience of community is basic. Children should have the opportunity in the public schools to extend their acquaintance with people of many kinds and from many backgrounds, and to become welcome and contributing members of their class and school communities. On no account should migrant children be taught in groups which are separated from the main school population. Somehow provision must be made to give them the special educational help they may need in reading, arithmetic, or other school skills and still maintain their association with the permanent school children; otherwise, they may miss the most essential of all the learnings for which public schools are established and supported — the elements of citizenship.

Through carefully planned school programs at all grade levels, migrant children should also be brought into positive and significant contact with the outside community. This could be achieved by visiting government centers, industrial activities, and public communication and transportation facilities; becoming acquainted with government officials and with people in a wide variety of occupations and professions; seeing at firsthand how the people of a community collaborate in daily life. An organized study of government, history, and all phases of the social studies is especially important for these children who probably will have little out-of-school opportunity for these learnings. Every effort should be made to involve them personally in these studies, emphasizing contributions of various ethnic groups to building America, and relating government activity to their experiences and concerns. Through these experiences and studies, migrant children need to see themselves as Americans, sharing a valuable heritage, participating in the benefits of citizenship, and responsible for contributing to the improvement of American life.

3. *Attitudes favorable to success.* Migrant people need educa-

tional experiences planned to develop and strengthen self-confidence and self-direction.

Poverty, segregation, and alienation can defeat a man — or child — before he starts. Success in school, as in life, depends to a great extent on the confidence with which a person approaches new experiences and the goals which urge him on. Because migrant people often come to school with damaged self-esteem, reinforced by many experiences of inadequacy and failure, the school's first task is to strengthen the learner himself.

Acceptance in the school situation is the first step — acceptance and welcome of the migrant people, as they are and for what they are, both by teachers and by other children, youth, and adults. It should be obvious to the newcomer, when he arrives at the start of the crop season but in the middle of the school term, that he is expected, that there is room for him, and that everyone finds his coming normal and welcome. The responsibility for building this favorable atmosphere belongs to communities, to boards, and to school personnel. Where it is found, this atmosphere is the result of careful planning, provision of supplies and facilities, preparation of teachers, recruitment of sufficient aides, and other measures which allow both teachers and children to meet the influx of migrant pupils with confidence, ease, and goodwill.

A learning program with which he can be successful is the second step in building a self-confident learner; confidence is built through successes. First steps should be easy; difficulty should be increased at such a rate that the pupil finds success, increasing satisfaction, and challenge with each new step.

As self-confidence grows, independence and self-direction should be encouraged. The migrant child or youth, or the adult also, needs to come into control of his own learning program as soon as possible, for he will need to do for himself what good counselors and guidance programs do for most other learners over a long period of time. Fundamental to self-direction is a clear goal, and here the school can make a significant contribution. Because of the relatively limited experience of migrant people with other ways of life, they have little scope for choosing their goals. The school program should include an introduction to a wide variety of occupations, to schools and training programs, and to learning requirements. Exploration of many fields of interest and discovery of the learner's strengths, weaknesses, and preferences should be guided and encouraged, so that the goals he sets may be realistic, neither too high nor too low to serve him as he develops his potential ability.

4. *Relevance and meaning.* Educational programs should be directly and immediately related to the experiences, needs, and goals of migrant people.

School must make sense to the migrant family in order to have its cooperation. Education for its own sake is seldom valued by poor people, especially when school attendance has to compete with wage earning.

The curriculum at every level should really be immediate and usable in terms of what children and young people know and want. This relevance to living should be made clear to parents, as well as to pupils, so that they are willing and eager to make it possible for their children to get to school regularly — an achievement which often calls for considerable trouble and even sacrifice.

The amount and quality of learning are dependent on the meaningfulness of the task and the material. Primary instructional materials which deal with the kinds of situations familiar to young migrant children — for instance, situations with which they can identify and which are charged with meaning and importance for them — involve them in learning as no amount of drill or carefully graded materials unrelated to their experience can do. The principle that learning is built only on what one already knows — that new insights represent extensions, modifications, and interpretations of real-life experiences — is fundamentally important in designing the curriculum for migrant children, youth, and adults at all school levels, because so much that the central culture takes for granted is strange, unknown, or insignificant to these people.

This does not mean that the curriculum necessarily should be either simpler or less sophisticated than that offered to other learners, only that it should be adapted to the interest and lives of the pupils. It is impossible to estimate what any person can learn until his previous experiences and values are understood and taken into account.

5. *Mastery of English.* Schools should provide systematic instruction in the English language, both for children who speak another language and for those who speak nonstandard English.

Opportunity for people living in America lies in an English-speaking world. Mastery of standard English is prerequisite to full acceptance and effective functioning in that world, as well as to education itself.

Because so many migrant children start school speaking no English or speaking with extremely limited vocabularies, it is vital to their future success that they be given as much opportunity and special help as possible at the beginning. This is one of the reasons for the importance of preschool programs and kindergartens. It must be remembered that a large number of migrant children spend their out-of-school lives in Spanish-speaking homes and groups. Because they have so little practice with English, compared with children who live in an English-speaking environment, these children will continue to need special help with language through the primary and intermediate grades and even through high school. Even though they learn to read fluently — at least to say the words fluently — meanings are likely to be improvised or even inaccurate; this is easily understandable to most English-speaking adults who have studied a foreign language.

The program for teaching English needs to be systematic, well-planned, and continued through high school and into the adult education program. All the advances which have been made in the past few years in the teaching of foreign languages for speaking as well as reading competence should be applied to the teaching of English; schools in migrant areas need records, tape recorders, films, and all the other aids usually available for good foreign-language programs; the teaching staff needs to be large enough so that assistance can be given to individuals and small groups as needed.

The educational needs of English-speaking children in the migrant group can be overlooked even more easily than those of children who speak another language. The limited experiences of migrant living lead to a limited vocabulary and a limited ability to express ideas even where the basic language is English; in addition, the use of dialect or nonstandard English can be almost as handicapping as a strong accent or foreign speech patterns. The curriculum for these children and young people should include the learning of standard English patterns, a continued and systematic enrichment of vocabulary in connection with all subjects and experiences, and both guidance and the opportunity for building expressive power in the use of language.

6. *Vocational guidance and education.* Schools should open the way to improved vocational opportunities for members of migrant families.

For people who live as precariously as migrant agricultural workers, opportunity for better paying and regular employment is one of the most important contributions education can make. The connection between school and a better job can be direct, both from the standpoint of school planning and in the view of the migrant family.

Increased mechanization is continually reducing the need for migrant labor, and this trend can be expected to continue. In some parts of the state where large numbers of migrant workers once were employed, there now are practically none, partly as the result of expanding urban settlements and partly because of almost complete mechanization. In other areas, year-round farm employment is open to the more capable, better-trained workers. Some of the agricultural migrants will find their opportunity in better farm jobs, others in work of an entirely different character; in either case, schools should be helping these people and their children to prepare for new kinds of employment.

From the first grades, this vocational objective of schools in migrant areas should be clearly in view for both teachers and migrant families. As young children study their communities, their attention should be directed to the abilities and training needed for the many ways people earn a living. This exploration of vocational possibilities should continue through all school levels. Direct training for jobs should be provided in high school and adult education, with first-rate facilities and programs, and learnings that are immediately applicable in the employment field. The programs offered and the vocational counseling made available should be based on current studies of employment opportunity and actual on-the-job requirements; the training program should be accompanied by a job-placement service for both youth and adult trainees.

Work experience programs and the continuation of education should be developed more widely, with special adjustments made so that young people who need to work can also continue their studies.

Every effort should be made to see that young people in migrant families do not settle for vocational goals which are lower than they are capable of attaining; it is the responsibility of schools to see that these young people have every opportunity possible for continuing with their education — through scholarships, subsidies, or any other means which can be devised — and that if it is necessary for them to leave school before their objective is attained, they be helped to work out a long-term plan for completing their preparation.

7. *Better living.* School programs should help migrant people to deal with problems of daily life under camp conditions and to develop the skills and knowledge needed for better living.

With both parents at work in the fields, young people and older boys and girls often carry a great deal of family responsibility. Under these conditions schools can plan exceptionally useful and meaningful instruction in all phases of practical living. Health and safety programs should center upon the actual conditions of camp living, giving boys and girls immediate help in carrying out their responsibilities for themselves and for younger members of their families. Instruction in nutrition and careful shopping can lead to immediate and valuable improvements in daily living. Help with grooming; selecting, making, and caring for clothing; and taking care of children are all useful, both for young people and indirectly for the education of families and improved standards of living. Both boys and girls should learn to use common tools and make simple repairs.

Migrant families have great need for programs of physical education and school-connected recreation to improve health and physical fitness, to provide resources for constructive use of leisure time, and to bring about contacts to reduce their isolation from the central community.

Schools should also offer instruction for adults of the family during the evening, on weekends, and at other times when they are not working. Sewing rooms, shops, and other facilities needed for a good educational program for children and youth should be used to the maximum, providing the opportunity for adult learning and community activity.

8. *Kindergarten and preschool programs.* Young children of migrant families should have an opportunity to attend kindergarten and preschool programs.

A strong start is the best opportunity a school can provide for a child. Young children from migrant families are usually handicapped in a number of ways: in language development, in experiences and concepts, in self-confidence, in the ability to relate to other people, and in ways of behaving which are different from the cultural patterns of other children. In good kindergarten and preschool programs, they can take a long step toward overcoming these handicaps before they start the first grade.

Such an opportunity to modify early experiences is most effective at three to five years of age because this is the period of most rapid growth in both language skills and concept development. Moreover, the effects of early deprivations are cumulative if they are left unmodified. Children who start school with a language handicap, for instance, are almost certain to meet difficulty as they start to read; with a reading handicap, they have difficulty with all other learnings which depend on reading. When school becomes a struggle, it is soon and thankfully given up.

Classes and groups for young children must be kept small if they are to be useful at all; well-trained teachers, in sufficient number, are essential. If a program for young children is to achieve these important objectives, the professionals in charge must be highly skillful and have the opportunity to relate directly to individual children. In such a one-to-one relationship some significant progress can be made.

Health conditions of children should be checked and correction started as part of preschool programs. One of the most significant contributions of such programs can be the involvement of parents in their children's successful growth, starting with their concern for good health and continuing through observation of other aspects of child development. A successful collaboration between home and school can be established here which may continue throughout the child's educational career.

9. *Individualized learning programs.* School programs for migrant children and youth should be based on the individual needs of each pupil.

Because of their fragmented school experiences, migrant children and youth vary even more widely than other pupils in their accomplishments and their needs for instruction in language development, reading, arithmetic, and other skills. Every school in the migrant areas should have a practical, easily administered program for properly assessing the educational status and needs of each entering pupil. His instructional plan then should be developed specifically on the basis of these findings. Any other procedure must be considered a waste of time for both pupil and school, a waste which neither can afford.

This type of individualized instruction, which pinpoints the learning needs and provides help and practice specifically focused on those needs, often can be carried on within a class situation, provided classes are small and materials are varied and plentiful. In addition, tutorial instruction should be provided for pupils who need more assistance. Preferably, this instruction should be given by specially trained teachers; if this is not possible, then tutors should be used, with competent supervision.

Personalized instruction is at least as important as individualized instruction. Many teachers who have worked individually with pupils find that the personal attention and relationship in the situation seem to be as effective as the actual instruction. Migrant children are likely to lead anonymous lives; to be known as "Raphael," an individual in whose problems the teacher is interested, instead of "you there in the blue sweater," may be the most important educational therapy the school can provide. The role of the teacher's faith in the learner's potential can hardly be overemphasized in this situation.

10. *Broadening background and interests.* Migrant people need compensatory experiences and activities planned to develop understandings, interests, and expressive abilities.

Because the range of experiences available to migrant families is narrow, their understandings, interests, and abilities are frequently underdeveloped. These are the basic materials of which education is made; if migrant children and young people are to realize their potential, schools must provide experiences and activities to compensate in some degree for earlier deprivation. There should be an opportunity to explore in many directions, to build background, to accumulate concepts, to express ideas in many forms, and to try themselves out in a wide variety of situations.

Firsthand contacts are important: study trips to significant places, an opportunity to meet and talk with interesting adults in the community, attendance at concerts and other community events, and observation of industrial processes. Schools should have a wealth of study materials: films, photographs, reproductions of paintings, records, science collections and equipment, books, newspapers, and magazines. Libraries should be excellent; they should be open for long hours, before and after school, evenings, and on Saturdays in areas where the people would have access to them; pupils should, of course, be able to check books out to take home.

The school program should provide many opportunities for expressive activities; a wide variety of art projects; dramatizations and programs; orchestras, bands, choruses, and other musical groups; school newspapers and magazines; much discussion, speaking, and writing; and observing, collecting, organizing, and experimenting in relation to science and social studies.

11. *Secondary education.* All migrant youth should be able to obtain a high school education.

No real opportunity, either for self-development or for economic advancement, is available unless the young people of migrant families are able to obtain a high school education. It should be the responsibility of every school district to make high school attendance readily accessible and practicable for this mobile group. It is vital that secondary schools explore every possibility for flexible scheduling and other adjustments which may be needed to solve the complex problems involved: midsemester transfers, the need for young people to work, special help to overcome deficiencies in preparation, and others.

Elementary and secondary schools should collaborate to assist and encourage young people to make the transition to high school; graduation from elementary school is still very often the culmination of the migrant youth's education. Especially, attention needs to be given to orientation and counseling during the last year in elementary school, with frequent visits to the high school so that boys and girls know the campus and something about the program available and are acquainted with some teachers, and other young people. Even if they are in another district when school opens, the idea of attending a high school will be familiar and they will have some knowledge as to the procedures involved.

12. *Adult education.* Programs of adult education should be available to migrant families.

A major need is to involve adults in the education of their children. Without parental support and encouragement, most young people will not be able to overcome the many difficulties which stand in the way of regular and continued school attendance. Where parents can be involved in actual decision-making roles, as in the planning for preschool programs, their advice is of great value in making the programs practical and useful.

Such involvement in their children's education is often the first step in encouraging adults to seek further education for themselves. The general level of education in this group is very low, and past experience with school has often been frustrating and unhappy. But when adults see the opportunity that is being made available to their children, they sometimes respond with great interest to an extended program of practical adult education. Every elementary school which serves migrant families should be a center for classes adults want and will attend. Included should be such courses as literacy, English, preparation for citizenship, industrial arts, homemaking, crafts, and child growth and development. Counsel of the migrant groups should be sought in establishing these courses and in giving direction to them.

An opportunity should also be made available for adults to obtain vocational counseling and instruction directly related to actual job openings; high schools should work closely with community representatives of agriculture and industry in planning such programs, and when this is advisable, in obtaining the use of facilities outside the school for the training.

13. *Continuity in the educational program.* Schools which educate migrant children and youth need to improve cooperative planning and communication for greater continuity in their education.

The education of migrant pupils is made up of fragments, too often a patchwork with great gaps or wasteful overlapping. Transfer of records or information between schools is sketchy or nonexistent, and each new school must start the educational process again in the best way it can. Pupils who do well with schoolwork are able to fit into the new situation and progress, even though they may miss important learnings, but those who need special help are likely to fall further and further behind.

Solving this problem is a complex and difficult procedure, as schools in the migrant areas know from much experience in trying to improve the situation. Since the families employed at any one stop seldom move along the same route, neither mobile schools nor transfer information can accompany the group. What is needed is widespread collaboration among the many schools involved. Such collaboration should extend beyond the transfer of data to educational planning to coordinate programs, methods, materials, and even philosophy in much the same fashion as this is done within a large school. One of the problems in the past has been a lack of any central staff for coordination; each school has been so busy just keeping up with pressing demands that no one has had either the time or the assignment to work with the total situation. Certainly this kind of planning needs to be statewide; even better would be an interstate project or agency, as extensive as the migrant stream.

Coordination needs to take place between various levels of education as well as among schools at the same level. High schools and elementary schools do not always work together closely for smooth articulation and planning of the program as a continuous unit even within the same geographic area; with the new preschool programs being established by other agencies, it will be important to maintain close working relations between this segment and the kindergarten and elementary school programs.

14. *Sufficient specialized personnel.* Fundamental to a good program is a sufficient number of teachers and other personnel

trained in the special requirements of the recommended program.

Recruiting and keeping teachers and other personnel has always been a problem in the many remote and rural areas where migrant people attend school. Good housing and adequate salaries should be basic provisions. Perhaps even more important for attracting and holding high-quality personnel is professional satisfaction; the opportunity to do significant and first-rate work; availability of facilities, materials, and support for the program; recognition and appreciation for their contribution; and involvement in decision making and in establishing educational improvements.

Because of the need for small classes and supplementary individual instruction, the personnel needs will always be relatively large. To assist teachers, districts will need to explore every avenue for additional aides: parents, older children, community volunteers, and other nonprofessional and semiprofessional helpers who can take care of nonteaching responsibilities or actually assist with tutoring under close supervision.

The classroom program needs to be supplemented with many auxiliary services and with adequate personnel. Principals should be both efficient administrators and knowledgeable instructional leaders. An instructional supervisor or consultant should be readily available to work directly with teachers to analyze problems, to make recommendations, to obtain materials, and to help in establishing programs. Attendance and child welfare personnel should be provided to make immediate and direct contact with new families as they move into the area, helping children to enter school with as little loss of time as possible. Nurses are needed to check and care for health needs. Every school in the migrant areas should have a cafeteria, providing a nutritious lunch, and even breakfast if children come to school hungry. Counselors, social workers, psychologists, physicians, and other specialists should be available as needed.

Special training programs should be established for all the people who work with migrant families through both intensive workshops and courses during school vacation periods and in-service activities during the school year. Teachers working in these situations need many specific techniques to enable them to realize the school's goals for the educational program; they also need deep insight into the cultures of their pupils as well as exceptional understanding of child growth and development. Such a program of continued study serves both to improve the school and to bring about the increased professional rewards which hold teachers in the program.

15. *Adequate facilities and equipment.* Schools in the migrant areas should be supplied with the facilities and equipment needed for the recommended program.

The educational program for migrant children, youth, and adults requires more classrooms and other building space, equipment, and materials than are needed in schools where the educational needs are not so great. Adequate provisions have been difficult to obtain, chiefly because they are needed for only part of the school year. Special subsidies should be made available to provide these facilities, and every possibility should be explored for ways in which books, equipment, and other facilities can be shared by districts which serve migrant populations at different times of the year.

16. *Flexibility in educational arrangements.* New ways for organizing and implementing educational programs should be developed.

Both by custom and by law, certain school patterns have become fixed. These standard patterns probably work fairly well for standard situations, but more flexible arrangements would greatly facilitate the education of migrant people. Certainly customs and legal limitations need to be questioned whenever they impede educational solutions. Is there any reason why school has to be held Monday through Friday? Why not on Saturday? Does the school day need to be from 9 to 4 o'clock, or for any other standard period of time? Could the school day sometimes be the school evening instead? Would a summer school period be more useful than a summer vacation? Could some way be developed to use more teacher aides to supplement professional personnel? Do high school requirements have to be in terms of semester units? Might high school and adult programs be organized for long hours during intensive periods of time rather than spread out over a semester or a year? Such probing questions need to be asked constantly as a basis for inventions to make educational opportunity more widely available to the migrant group.

17. *Supplementary financing.* Additional finances need to be made available for educating migrant children, youth, and adults.

The educational program suggested here is expensive and will require that additional funds be made available to districts which educate migrant people. Responsibility for providing equal educational opportunity for this group does not belong to any one local area, but it is a joint responsibility which should be supported on a wide base. Planning for the future must include a system of regular, continuing finance from state and/or federal sources.

Adult Illiteracy*

A. R. RAMIREZ

THE RATE OF ILLITERACY AMONG AMERICANS of Mexican ancestry is unusually high as a result of one or a combination of the following factors:

1. Immigration laws which permit a constant flow of new citizens who are unable to speak, read, or write the English language;

2. Inadequate instruction of non-English-speaking school children due to untrained teachers, inappropriate methods and materials, and, sometimes, to discriminatory practices;

3. Limited educational aspirations of this population which are often a result of frustration brought about by repeated failures at impossible tasks imposed by the school;

4. Limited opportunities for adults to get a second chance to achieve literacy.

A change in immigration laws may not be in the national interest and, in any case, this in itself would not help raise the educational level of individuals already residing in this country. Any permanent solution lies in the improvement of educational

* A paper presented to the Cabinet Committee Hearings on Mexican American Affairs, October, 1967.

opportunities for both children and adults rather than in the control of the influx of this population group.

The typical life cycle of the undereducated Mexican-American develops in this manner:

1. He is reared in a humble home, in a large family. Spanish is the only language spoken, and it is seldom read or written in the home.

2. He lives in a Spanish-speaking neighborhood and at six years of age attends a neighborhood school where all of the pupils come from Spanish-speaking homes. His daily schedule, his books, his tests, and his entire school life are patterned after those of his English-speaking counterparts in the school across town. Academic failure — the repeating of grades or retentions — and eventual dropout constitutes the school record of at least 75 percent of these youngsters. The school has not helped him to achieve literacy in his native language and has insisted that he learn to read English before he speaks it well. At best, he leaves school without marketable skills and with only a slight knowledge of English.

3. He marries a fellow dropout at an early age. They have several children, and the cycle begins anew for each of his children.

This cycle can be broken in the public schools. Better still, it can be broken through a comprehensive program of family education in combination with improvements in public education.

The agency with the responsibility for the education of citizens beyond the public school age must be determined. School districts are reluctant to assume responsibility. Institutions of higher education do not indicate willingness to accept the assignment. If neither local nor state educational agencies willingly provide the funds, organization, and leadership required, perhaps a federal system is needed. We have federal law enforcement, federal employment assistance, federal mail service, federal agricultural assistance, and federal housing assistance — why not a federal educational system for needs not being met by local and state governments?

Probably the most desirable arrangement is one of a cooperative endeavor involving the three levels of government, but there are local authorities all across the Southwest who are not ready to accept this challenge. If all local districts had met their obligations in the past, we would have no need for federal aid — and we would not be discussing ways in which to solve the educational problems of one segment of our population. This may also be the opportune time to state that no blanket indictment is intended by these general statements. There is ample evidence that many of our school boards are committed to quality education for all citizens.

In referring to the life patterns of the non-English-speaking individual, the question of adequacy of instruction was mentioned. Regardless of the sponsorship of adult schools, this problem of instructional methods will still have to be resolved. Materials and methods often employed in literacy classes are those developed for illiterate English speakers. In such cases, there are no guides for teachers, no adequate training of teachers, no texts for teaching English as a second language — hardly any consideration given to the special needs of the Spanish-speaking adult student. This is exactly the same deficiency noted in our public schools. How can we convince our educators that no meaningful instruction in reading and writing can take place until the learner has mastered orally the material he is expected to read and write? Until this gets across, we are going to be stumbling around and creating unnecessary confusion and discouragement. We need to give these learners a series of successful experiences, and we cannot do it with the methods and materials we have been using.

We should consider the possibility of providing Spanish literacy instruction as part of the adult program. For beginning students, part of the evening would be devoted to reading and writing Spanish and the rest of the time, perhaps three fourths, to oral English instruction. By the time the students are ready to begin reading English, they will have acquired skills that will enable them to read *Life, Popular Mechanics, Reader's Digest,* and other English-language periodicals translated into Spanish, as well as newspapers and books also readily available along the Mexican border. Furthermore, most of the mysteries of the reading process will have been cleared up, and the pattern of failures reversed.

While he is achieving literacy in Spanish, the adult learner is taught the sound system and the grammar of English through example and extensive practice. Teachers need special training in this type of instruction. They need guides and tapes, both for Spanish literacy classes and for oral English instruction.

Odd as it may seem, the United States government has done more to help citizens of other countries to learn English in their own lands than it has done for non-English-speaking American citizens in this country. We know that there are texts and tapes and teacher-training programs available through the State Department for overseas use. Why can't these materials be made available to our teachers and students of English?

Above all, we need a planned program that will be adequately financed for several years and that will be broad enough to take into consideration the factors working against us. Evening classes are inevitable but, in a way, desirable. Classrooms and teachers are easier to contract for night classes. All members of the family are available for instruction at that time of the day.

It would be possible to have child-care and kindergarten activities for the children below school age, study and enrichment activities (perhaps Spanish literacy classes) for those of school age, and a full adult education program for the parents. The enthusiasm that can be generated for learning under such a schedule can be of inestimable value in changing the levels of aspiration of our undereducated citizens.

Several teachers of Mexican-American adult basic education classes were asked to make recommendations and suggestions for presentation at these hearings. There was unanimous concern about materials, both for students and teachers. One group of teachers asked for research findings on the suitability of various instructional materials for classes of Spanish-speaking adults and for the selection of materials on this basis. They also suggested that the number of class hours, now set at 120, be increased in order to progress more rapidly.

Now, for a final suggestion: In order to limit the chances of failure, let us have the materials on hand, the teachers trained, the funds assured, the facilities contracted, and the maximum enrollment determined *before* we seek students. Then let us establish enforceable policies concerning age, family size, residence, and attendance that the father will accept for himself and his dependents. Then let us enroll families, teach them, and keep teaching them until they achieve independence as literate bilinguals and as self-sufficient participating citizens.

The Mexican American and Higher Education*

ARMANDO RODRIGUEZ

NEARLY TWO HUNDRED YEARS after the Declaration of Independence, more than a hundred years after the Treaty of Guadalupe-Hidalgo, more than a decade after the first major entrance of the federal government into aid to higher education, Americans should have progressed to the point where all of society could look without fear toward maximum educational opportunity. But, unfortunately, the bitterness that rolls across the campuses of many of the colleges and high schools is born out of the frustration of barriers to maximum educational opportunity.

The drive and determination of young Chicanos to fight their way into maximum educational opportunities is the brightest picture for immediate change for Mexican Americans. Mexican American youngsters in the West and Southwest make depressing and very disturbing observations about the causes of student unrest.

No discussion about higher education for the Mexican American is feasible without taking account of these developments. No discourse about higher education for the Mexican American

*Revised and edited by permission of author.

is realistic without noting that higher education enrollments have increased 58 percent for Anglos in the past five years, and yet less than 2 percent of the Mexican Americans are in college. In the center of the largest concentration of Mexican Americans in the U.S.A., California State College at Los Angeles has dropped in its enrollment of Mexican Americans from 6 percent to less than 4 percent in a single year. Recent figures from the Department of Health, Education and Welfare show a rise of 23 percent in costs of tuition, fees, board, and room at public colleges and universities during the past five years. It is interesting to note that a recent report showed that more than 4,200 Cuban refugee students are attending 365 American colleges with the help of about four million dollars in federal loans. And in the past eight years, an estimated 12,000 needy Cuban students have received more than 50,000 educational loans. At a time when thousands of American students, especially Chicano students, are being turned away or having to drop out of school for lack of financial resources, something seems out of proportion. Also quite disturbing was the following editorial in the *Washington Post* of May 12, 1969:

FEDERAL DISINHERITANCE

There is not going to be much benevolence for colleges or for college students in the 1970 fiscal year if President Nixon's proposed budget is approved by Congress. Perhaps the parsimony has something to do with the widespread student feeling that the older generation really does not care quite so much for education as it likes to pretend it does. At any rate, the Federal aid to higher education cupboard looks pretty bare.

The National Defense Student Loans have been cut by slightly more than one-third from the level promised by the Johnson Administration—from $270 million to $155 million. These low-interest, long-term loans benefit lower and middle-class families; over half a million students now depend upon them. The College Work-Study program, designed to provide decent paying jobs for needy students working their way through college, has been cut by 31 per cent, from $211 million to $146 million. Educational Opportunity Grants have been cut in half. These grants are awarded to children of poor families to help them pay basic college costs. This cut alone would deprive more than 100,000 needy students, intellectually qualified for higher education, of the financial means to attend college unless the already overtaxed colleges themselves can somehow offer them scholarships.

"My Administration," President Nixon said when he was campaigning for election, "will commit itself to the proposition that no young American who is qualified to go to college will be prevented from doing so because he cannot afford it. I will support existing programs which aid needy students, and will call for their expansion when it is indicated. . . .

I intend to make the new Administration one which will not allow men's worlds to remain closed to those who need only money."

It is not only for fiscal 1970 that the Nixon Administration is now closing men's worlds. Funds to promote the Higher Education Facilities Act also have been drastically reduced—a reduction which will mean inescapably that colleges will lack the physical plant to accommodate young men and women seeking higher education in the years ahead. Commissions on Higher Education set up in all parts of the country have recommended substantial Federal grants and loans for construction purposes. Funds for Title I of the Act, designed to promote the building of undergraduate academic facilities, have been slashed to a minor fraction of what the commissions recommended; under the proposed budget, only $43 million is requested for this program. . . The President's budget recommends no funds at all for the construction of graduate academic facilities.

Can this Nation reclaim the trust and allegiance of its young by disinheriting them?

With the possibilities outlined in that editorial, it is difficult to look ahead with high hopes and expectations that the reality of maximum educational opportunity will take place soon. But for the Mexican American the problem is not solely financial aid. It is necessary to look squarely at the earlier levels of education that have so much to say about who gets a higher education.

It is true today, as it was ten or twenty years ago, that the elementary and secondary education made available to the Mexican American is utterly inadequate. But one can point to one element of progress: Chicanos are rising throughout the country to insure that this condition will not continue. This nation's conscience is far from clear about the self-defeating, monolingual, monocultural, second-rate elementary and secondary schooling that has been the lot of Mexican Americans and members of other minority groups, including a good number of poor whites. The United States cannot continue to offer inferior education to those who most need excellent education — the neediest, the least powerful, and the most oppressed. For today is different from yesterday, in that those who need excellent education most are going to get it — one way or another. This is what the Mexican American community has been saying from Texas to California to the Midwest.

If there is one single charge to every Mexican American community, it is to bring to the door of the Mexican American every resource, every opportunity, every commitment of the schools — elementary, secondary, and higher — for his participation in maximum educational opportunity. To do less is to deny him, the Chicano, "men's worlds."

There is no more significant question facing education and the country today than the question of whether the nation will continue to maintain or increase, or whether it will dilute, the federal effort to focus available funds on the problems of the poor, the racial minority, and the culturally different. The *Post* editorial raises some serious doubts in the minds of many as to the commitment of a federal effort in higher education. Will Mexican American students have to become political refugees to gain the recognition and support necessary to pursue higher education?

The federal education programs now under way, large as they may seem to be, are really little more than pilot projects when they are seen in terms of the vast educational needs that must be met. Educators are a long way from knowing for certain exactly what should be done to offer quality education to the poor and the racial minorities such as the Chicano. Educators do know, of course, that younger children should be reached earlier. There is need to bring the home and the community into the school environment, and teachers need to be trained differently. There is a need to do these and many other things now, or it will be too late. Unless there is clear evidence of full commitment to existing federal programs, there is real doubt that those already directly affected by such programs will continue to bear the burdens of second-class citizenship any longer.

There is clear indication that the major flaw in the crisis in education is the failure of government to bring the dreams and ideals of blacks and browns, the young and the poor into reality. Educators are confronted with the rising expectation of these groups as to what the United States can become and must become. The major attack is on an educational system whose premise of operation has been exclusion. Public education, from elementary through higher education, at its earliest stage, was created to exclude people who failed to adopt or to share the Anglo-Saxon life style. The present structure of education has done little to eradicate this posture. The stress on this structure is now heaviest at the points of higher education and rural education.

When in 1954 this nation undertook a program of inclusion of all its people, it made a moral and legal commitment which accounts for the fantastic revolution which has shaken the educational establishment. Today educators have created an intolerable environment for a once highly successful, sophisticated system of education. Mexican Americans are now demanding that this system, created for exclusion, become inclusive. To do this is to render that system dysfunctional. No matter how many alternatives are programmed into the present system, its basic design makes functioning in its expected new role impossible.

The educational system of today is capable of denying any group or person its or his individual identity. This simply means that the educational system will exclude all who are not able to embrace the Anglo-Saxon life style and culture. The continuance of this system to carry out the function of inclusion can only result in the total devastation of the system. It is this reality that must be faced. It is this reality that government must accept and must move immediately to change. No government has the right to foster and create revolution. Yet this government has done so by demanding that a system do something for which it was not created. A government cannot moralize; it cannot dream. It does have the responsibility to define reality and to create systems that can function in that reality.

The courses open to government are clear and rather simple: (1) Return to the realities of the past and continue to exclude, or (2) create a system that will carry out the post-1954 concept of education. What today is called the brown and black crisis in education, the urban crisis in education, and the student crisis in education is a result of a government playing at revolution. Fundamentally, a system which is created for the sole purpose of excluding cannot be altered to include that which it was created to exclude.

In the long run, obviously, the strengthening of educational opportunities through a reconstruction of the total system to enable it to function for inclusion will do the most to remove the obstacles to higher education for the Mexican American. But as John Maynard Keynes said, "In the long run we're all dead." No matter what system the schools have been using in the high schools and colleges to recruit and retain Mexican American students, these schools will have to be thoroughly overhauled. Every procedure must be minutely examined to eliminate even the slightest element of exclusion. The name of the game today is "include"! This new game particularly applies to high school counselors, college admissions officers, and financial aid officers.

The time has come for this country to do two things: First, to guarantee that every student who has the ability to pursue a higher education has the resources and opportunity to do so, no matter what his income, race, culture, or past educational track record. And this track record means going beyond this basic guarantee to find ways to offer quality education to those who, because of whatever circumstances, did not receive the academic preparation ordinarily required for the pursuit of higher education. Second, the institutions of higher education must restructure their academic environment so that it is compatible and consistent with the demands of society upon its products. One of the best examples is the demand by the black law students at Howard University for some classes on welfare law. What could be more relevant in a society wherein there are almost as many starving people as those overfed and almost as many welfare people as millionaires? This restructuring also means redefinition of what is meant by quality and standards on the one hand, and ability on the other. There is a need to stop equating ability with performance simply as measured at a given moment and to expand the meaning of that word to include some concept of potential related to motivation, to past deprivation, and to the possibility of rapid change in individual performance through special and intensive assistance.

Quality must more and more measure the ability of colleges and universities to offer genuine learning experiences to different kinds of students, especially the culturally different. An ability must be interpreted in terms that reflect an understanding of the fact that evidence of poor preparation does not necessarily mean innate incapacity. Education cannot start too soon.

There is one other area that is critical in the rising role of the Mexican American in higher education. That is the whole concept of student rights. One of the brightest spots in the drive for increased participation by Chicanos in maximum educational opportunity is that of the young Chicano movement. The forceful determination of United Mexican American Students, Mexican American Youth Organization, Mexican American Youth Association, and other groups to open the college doors for themselves and their younger brothers and sisters is the strongest force right now. But these movements or, for that matter, any student movement must be regarded as a legitimate step to secure economic, political, social, and educational rights until otherwise proven. It is wrong that such actions must be protested under the same laws that protect the rest of society. Mexican Americans are therefore deeply disturbed by the vigorous attempts by segments of the ruling society to isolate and to identify the student movements as forces which must be hampered and restricted by special legal means. Chicano students are only doing things that many before them have failed to do. They are making education a right for all, not a privilege for some. Mexican Americans everywhere should become defenders and supporters of the legal and legitimate rights of Chicano students to promote and to demand a maximum educational opportunity for all.

The federal government should be deluged with proposals that show imagination and courage, and which focus upon inclusion. Skillful programs are needed to bring the high school and the college into constant relations that result in a dragnet of recruitment of Mexican Americans. The Chicano students have already begun, by putting a program for the federal government, the colleges, and the high schools into a model package for immediate and concerted action.

The *Washington Post* raised the question "Can this Nation reclaim the trust and allegiance of its young by disinheriting them?" The National Advisory Committee on Mexican American Education, in its report, *The Mexican American: Quest for Equality,* raised the question, "Is only a monolingual, monocultural society acceptable in America?" The answers to both of these questions confront society today. It is obvious that the melting-pot ideology that is so proudly spoken of has not produced a moral climate in which all citizens are accepted on the basis of individual worth. It is obvious, also, that the educational system has not produced a climate in which maximum educational opportunity is available to all. All Chicanos must join in the fight to make cultural diversity and its richness a catalyst for educational change. Chicanos must become experts in educational revolution in the guerrilla warfare of attitude and behavior change. Chicanos must become experts in the politics of human rights and maximum educational opportunity. All Mexican Americans must play a more active and aggressive role in seeking out and assisting in college decisions, and financially supporting the Mexican American student. It is only through such vigorous movements that the entrance of the Mexican American into the scene of higher education will bring the United States the strong fabric of cultural cognizance and thereby enrich the entire society.

The Chicano is coming out of Tortilla Flats, in one way or another *now*, and universities and colleges must be ready for him, and *now!* Chicanos must lead the way. No one else can or must do it. As all Mexican Americans move forward, they must remember and say — really shout — the challenge of their forefathers:

¡Viva La Causa!
¡Viva los estudiantes!
¡Viva La Raza!
¡Viva toda La Raza!
¡Que dios nos bendiga!
¡Gracias por su atención!

The Role of the State*

JOSEPH BERNAL

THE PREAMBLE TO THE UNITED STATES CONSTITUTION announces that *we* the people of the United States *are* to be concerned with the general welfare. In the tenth amendment we also find that "The powers not delegated to the United States by the Constitution, nor prohibited by it to the States, are reserved to the States respectively, or to the people." But the fourteenth amendment, ratified immediately following the Civil War, provides that "All persons born or naturalized in the United States" shall not be denied "equal protection of the laws."

Education is not mentioned specifically in our United States Constitution, and it is for this reason that for many years some people, including some leaders, have come to assume that education is a responsibility delegated solely to the states. Consequently, we have had confusion, debate, and more confusion on this matter.

The role of the states in education is certainly not to be minimized in any way. On the contrary, it is to be treated with utmost concern, objectivity, and respect. As a case in point, I shall cite my own state which currently spends forty-eight cents

*An original paper printed with permission of the author.

of every tax dollar on education. The Constitution of Texas declares:

> A general diffusion of knowledge being essential to the preservation of the liberties and rights of the people, it shall be the duty of the Legislature of the State to establish and make suitable provision for the support and maintenance of an efficient system of public free schools.

In this declaration, the constitution clearly places upon the shoulders of all future legislators the responsibility of maintaining a system of public education that would meet the needs of the children of Texas.

Although people from Texas, as people from most all of the states, have prided themselves on local control of their schools and have encouraged local initiative to strengthen school programs, the fact still remains that whenever school programs have met the demands of the time, sound working partnership has had to exist between local citizens, local boards of education, and the state legislative bodies. On this we must agree.

Idealistically this situation of partnerships among the people, the school boards, and the state cannot be debated. But unfortunately we are not working under ideal conditions, for it is obvious that situations are unequal as shown in Table No. 1. It may be seen that California had a per capita personal income of $1,000 more than New Mexico but that during that same year New Mexico was spending a greater percentage of its dollars in education than any other state in the union.

A situation of inequality such as we see here brought forth the 1954 Supreme Court decision on desegregation, to protect each citizen equally under the law. Add discrimination to the information on per capita personal income and expenditures

Table 1 [1]

Per Capita Personal Income—1964			Expenditures for Elementary and Secondary Education in 1964-65 expressed as % of Personal Income in 1964		
Delaware	$3,460	1st	New Mexico	5.6%	1st
California	3,103	6th	Arizona	4.7%	8th
Colorado	2,566	18th	Colorado	4.2%	13th
Arizona	2,233	31st	California	4.0%	20th
Texas	2,188	32nd	Texas	3.9%	25th
New Mexico	2,041	38th	Massachusetts	3.0%	50th
Mississippi	1,438	50th	U.S.	3.8%	
U.S.	2,566				

for schools as a percentage of that personal income and you have a problem that the Negro has had to cope with in the South in a much more publicized manner than the sometimes subtle, but no less real, discrimination the American of Mexican descent has had to cope with in the Southwest. The idealistic situation of local and state partnerships has at times (more in the past than now) been adverse to the welfare of the Mexican-American minority of the Southwest.

We have not had to overcome slavery; but oppression, yes! Economic discrimination, yes! Ethnic discrimination, yes! Educational deprivation, yes! De facto segregation, yes! Mix these with cultural and ethnic pride and somewhere you will find the answer to why some people had not been aware that there were problems in the Southwest. That deep-rooted pride has caused us for many years to turn inwardly to find reasons or causes, instead of outwardly to be understood, and to understand.

Most of you know that there is poverty in the Southwest as well as low educational achievements and rankings. Actually, the correlation between the two most important factors of *low income and low education* is 67 percent. Our Mexican-American ethnic group has not only had to overcome the old one-room country school, but the old one-room *Mexican school.* Not only has the Mexican-American had to overcome poverty as the Appalachian citizens are now doing, but he has had to cope with bridging himself from what he has been culturally and linguistically to that which was brought in by an outside force *before* he has been able to overcome his poverty. Whether poverty came first or whether it was low educational achievement which came first is really irrelevant. The truth is that Americans of Mexican descent have been the quiet possessors of both problems for many, many years.

In 1964 the President of the U.S. received a report prepared by Helen Witmer, director of Research of the Children's Bureau of the Department of Health, Education and Welfare, entitled "Children in Poverty." This report declared that a family living on an income of $3000 or less was living under poverty conditions. Then we knew how really economically deprived we Mexican-Americans have been! Table No. 2 shows it statistically.

There are certainly obvious inequalities revealed by these figures.

Table 2 [a]

	Familes with Incomes Under $3,000		Less Than 8 Years of School	
	General Population	White Spanish Surname Population	General Population	White Spanish Surname Population
Arizona	21.3%	30.8%	19.8%	52.3%
California	14.1	19.1	13.5	37.9
Colorado	18.3	35.0	13.0	55.0
New Mexico	24.4	41.5	23.5	50.3
Texas	32.5	51.6	29.8	71.3
Southwest	21.0	34.8	19.3	52.9

Such figures enable us to see the necessity of partnership between the people, the local school boards, and the state legislatures, extending even to the national government. Willing to recognize that local direction and control should prevail, I must accept also the entrance of the national government into the financing of public education to provide adequate educational opportunities. This is another way of expressing equal protection under the laws for all children, regardless of their abilities, their station in life, their ethnic background, or their color. I welcome this last-named partner.

The inequality of education can be clearly understood in my own area where the Edgewood ISD (predominantly Mexican-American) with approximately 21,000 scholars is able to collect a half million dollars in local tax money, compared to Northeast ISD with approximately 22,000 students (predominantly Anglo-American), which is able to collect three and a quarter million dollars locally.

Where we have such inequalities, whether on a local ISD basis or on a state level (compare Delaware which has twice as much per capita personal income as Mississippi), then it behooves us to ask our national partner for financial support. But to do this we must have sensitive leadership, not middle-class teachers teaching middle-class children middle-class values and mores, but quality teachers looking at every individual and helping each child to reach his maximum potential. We need sensitive leadership in education, business, labor, government, and in the newspaper business — yes, in the total community — to ferret out these inequalities in today's system of education.

Wherever possible, poor districts should be consolidated with nearby rich districts. In Texas, for example, the number of school districts has dropped from 4500 to 1300 since 1949. Where such consolidation is impossible because of deprivation in the total community, let us avail ourselves of assistance from our national government. If we cannot clearly define our methods of combating and overcoming our educational deficiencies, it may be because we have become used to not being heard, or still worse, not being able to overcome our fierce ethnic pride.

The LULAC (League of United Latin American Citizens) in Texas started the idea of the Little School of the 400 and the state adopted it. It had as its purpose the preparation of non-English-speaking children for entry into the first grade with a command of 400 basic English words. Some of us consider this program as the forerunner of our nationally successful Head Start Program. We in Texas also take pride in our school for migrants, where we are able to provide the same number of school hours usually contained in a regular nine-month year to those children who are only available to our schools for six months. But is this to say that we are meeting the needs of all these children in Texas? Of course not!

I say we still have to look to a *bilingual approach* in teaching the Mexican-American (as well as others), especially in his formative elementary school years, because we know the importance of the mother tongue both as a medium for concept development and as a means of building the confidence of children whose English is nonfunctional.

We must look to further *consolidation of school districts* and to the creation and support of technical and vocational programs. We must see that the college work study programs reach *all* of the disadvantaged and that colleges in the Southwest ask for direct government grants to provide higher education for capable and disadvantaged Mexican-American youth so that they can go back into those areas which they know and understand better than anyone else to serve as examples of success and leadership for people who need to emulate success and leadership as they see these qualities among their own. We must provide a forum to discuss the Elementary and Secondary Acts so as to plan better how to utilize the programs which can best suit our local needs.

We have to provide for *adequate remedial work* for students with academic deficiencies who have been passed under automatic promotion procedures but who are incapable of functioning satisfactorily at the grade level to which they have been promoted. We need a *diagnostic center* to assist local school systems in identifying individual learning problems with special emphasis on accurately testing the bilingual child who at times may be diagnosed as being retarded when in reality he has ability far beyond that shown by the inadequate testing.

We should create a *regional agency* designated to assist, on a *regional basis,* in the evaluation programs which provide for a continuing reassessment of the needs of local systems, in order to continue planning for more effective use of federal subsidies. This is advisable especially where there are school boards or administrations which are not sensitive to the needs of the disadvantaged in the Southwest.

We should create a *regional system* for the dissemination of statistical information on education so that there may be more cooperative action on the interchange of professional personnel. There should also be a continually current comparative statistical picture of education by districts and states, so that the inequalities among the schools could be appraised more realistically and corrective action could be taken.

When we begin to work on and fulfill some of these objectives, it is then, and only then, that we will be achieving a more perfect democracy, which is one of education's major goals.

NOTES

[1] Lampman, Robert J., *The Low Income Population and Economic Growth.* Study Paper No. 12 prepared for the Joint Economic Committee, 86th Congress.

[2] Manuel, Herschel T., *Spanish-Speaking Children of the Southwest, Their Education and the Public Welfare.* Table 12, Frequency of Low and High Incomes in the Southwest (Census of 1960) (Austin: University of Texas Press, 1965), p. 48.

The Federal Government and Its Role in Education*

FRANK SANCHEZ

THE ENACTMENT OF THE MCATEER ACT in 1963 is a forerunner of what is now known nationally as compensatory education. This program was designed for "disadvantaged" students. At the time of its enactment people were not too sure as to what they were talking about, but there seemed to be a strong feeling that special attention had to be given to many school youngsters. The term "culturally deprived" became popular and the first programs in the schools under this approach were primarily remedial and culturally enriching. The attitude of the school was that the student must be to blame for his educational failures, and therefore educators should bring him up to the school's level by using the school's regular curriculum with some intensification in areas where teachers deem him to be weak; so in many cases educators began extensive remedial reading programs without taking a look at the beginning reading curricula.

By 1965 the federal government got into the action with the Elementary and Secondary Education Act (ESEA). There was

*Keynote speech at the Conference on Strengthening a Developing Institution in the Heart of the Mexican American Barrios, Lake Arrowhead, California, May, 1969. Reprinted by permission of the author.

considerable scrambling during the spring of 1965 to get something underway with that "extra" money. People juggled faculties, created new positions, jumped further into remedial reading, bought lots of hardware, and generally used the money to do some of the things people had said for years should be done. Educators tried to reduce class size, bring in teacher aides, and get more textbooks and supplementary teaching and learning materials. But still there was no significant improvement in the student.

By 1966 many of the educators were saying that the problem did not lie with the individual himself, but in his environment. So, with the Office of Economic Opportunity (OEO) and its programs, people began to say that if a person is poor, has language difficulties, lives in isolation, has a minimum of the experiences which today's schools expect before children come to them, then he will have problems in trying to succeed in the schools. These schools were with few exceptions staffed and operated and controlled by the Anglo-American middle-class society. So a program was begun in order to improve the social conditions of millions of American families. Unfortunately, the schools were not sufficiently involved in these programs designed to achieve this improvement. Head Start, for the most part, remained outside the scope of the school, but some schools did develop a preschool program. *But OEO brought a new element into our society — community participation.*

As community participation developed and community people became experienced in dealing with political and social institutions, they began to say, loud and clear: *It isn't we or our way of life that is the cause of our educational failures — it's the "system."* For it is the system which tells Chicanos to be Anglo in school and brown at home. It then became evident that few notable gains had been made, and for the Mexican American, ESEA was barely holding even. Compensatory education, as used by most schools, was not functional for the Mexican American. The Negro was coming to the same conclusion in regard to his education. The programs, for the most part, were Anglo-oriented, with little significant attention given to curriculum and instructional emphasis on the needs of the bilingual, bicultural, or the racially different child.

In October, 1966, the National Education Association (NEA)

held a conference in Tucson, Arizona, from which came a written report, *The Invisible Minority*. Many important things are said in that work. Of particular importance for teachers is what is expressed in the foreword:

The most acute educational problem in the Southwest is that which involves Mexican-American children. In the elementary and secondary schools of five states in that region—Arizona, California, Colorado, New Mexico, and Texas—there are approximately 1.75 million children with Spanish surnames. Many of these young people experience academic failure in school. At best, they have a limited success. A large percentage become school dropouts.

Little headway is being made against the problem. While teachers and administrators are and have been deeply concerned about it, they are also for the most part perplexed as to just what to do. The traditional approach has been simply to ignore the unique circumstances of children from Spanish-speaking homes, to assume that even with little or no experience in speaking English they would somehow learn as easily as their English-speaking classmates. Obviously, this did not happen. As a result, some schools have attacked the problem directly by grouping all their Mexican-American children in a pre-first grade where they would spend a year learning English and laying a foundation for regular school experiences. Such a procedure has the built-in disadvantage of creating an over-age group of students who must then go all the way through school a jump behind their peers. . . .

Teachers with insight into the problems of Spanish-speaking children have come to realize that two separate but parallel purposes need to be pursued. One is to help the Mexican-American student adjust to [note: it does not say "mold into"] the dominant "Anglo" culture. The other is to foster in him a pride in his Spanish-speaking culture and Mexican origin. These teachers have chosen to recognize the Spanish-speaking ability of Mexican-American students as a distinct asset and to build on it rather than root it out. They have found that Spanish properly used can be a bridge to the learning of English instead of an obstacle and that Mexican-American students can become truly bilingual and bicultural. . . .

To meet the problem fully, however, further legislation and substantially increased appropriations are needed. A more intensive effort to recruit additional teachers from among the Spanish-speaking is another imperative. Additional research, especially of a demonstration nature, is yet another. An extended series of needs could be listed. *But the urgent need is for action and innovation in local school districts almost everywhere.* [Italics added.]

The NEA Conference and the Tucson Report challenged each of the participants to return to his community and state and to sponsor conferences to consider the problem. With this kind of impetus, a number of communities began planning for what is known today as the Texas Conference for Educational Opportunities for Mexican Americans. This was held in San Antonio,

Texas, April 13–15, 1967. It was agreed by the chief planners that the three agencies most responsible for the educational change should sponsor the conference: *(a)* The Southwest Educational Development Laboratory in Austin; *(b)* the Inter-American Educational Center, known today as Region 20 Center; and *(c)* the Texas Education Agency. For the first time, a statewide effort was made for concentration on the issues which NEA had pointed out. As a matter of fact, the opening paragraph of the recommendations and resolutions reads, "the objective is to recognize that a problem exists."

One of the main speakers, Dr. Nolan Estes, then Associate Commissioner for Elementary and Secondary Education, U.S. Office of Education, said some important things which educators can use:

> Today American education is caught up in a revolution of change and growth that has not been matched in the history of this nation. In every state, in every city, in nearly every town there is revolution at work in the schools and in the community. It is a ferment and a stirring marked by a new, intense interest in two concepts—QUALITY EDUCATION AND EDUCATIONAL EQUALITY FOR ALL.

He further added:

> And everywhere—in the South and in the northern cities—the ugly bolt of discrimination and segregation, a discrimination that touched the Mexican American, the Puerto Rican, the Oriental, the Negro, and the poor of whatever race, color or creed. . . .
>
> We have finally turned the corner in education for the Mexican American, for the Negro, and for other disadvantaged groups. . . . Ahead lie our twin goals—quality education and equality of educational opportunity for all.

To attain these goals, Dr. Estes pointed out four things:

> *First:* The Mexican American community—the political, educational, business, and labor leaders of that community—must now make sure that they are taking full advantage of the educational opportunities being offered under the new federal programs. The money and the opportunity are there. The laws and the programs are there. The technical knowledge for solving the problems is there.
>
> *They must now apply the power of community action,* working with their local educational leaders and groups, to make sure they are properly represented in those programs. *This means organization, study, and work. It means joining and becoming active* in the PTA's and other community groups interested in action. *In short, it means developing "school power" —power and influence in the school community to achieve proper representation* and an equitable distribution of the money and programs in which they should share.

Second: We must all work for an end to the law which says that all classes in this state—and all other states—shall be taught only in English. . . . There may have been good reason once for this law, but that reason is not valid today. Our country is blessed with the richness of many cultures and languages: Spanish, German, and many others. It is rich and strong, and it can tolerate differences among us which once it feared.

Third: Bilingualism is a necessary educational tool for thousands of out-of-school children. . . . Education can play a key role in that war on poverty.

Finally: Local, state, and federal agencies must join together in a common crusade in the war on ignorance and educational deprivation.

Education is an intensely local function. It cannot be directed from Washington or Austin. It can only come from a local school and a local teacher. Today, as never before, that local school bears new and heavy responsibilities. For our state and national goals extend far beyond the boundaries of that school district. And these national goals—security, defense, technological development, conservation of human and cultural resources, and equal opportunity—demand a higher allegiance from all our citizens.

In the following month Senator Ralph Yarborough, taking his cue from the Tucson Conference, began the hearings on Senate Bill 428, the first effort on the national level for legislation for bilingual education. The two-volume record contains tremendous support from all over the country. Two introductory remarks are worthy of mention:

The failure of our schools to educate Spanish-speaking students is reflected in comparative dropout rates. In the five Southwestern States of Texas, New Mexico, Arizona, Colorado, and California, Anglos fourteen years of age and over have completed an average of 12 years of school compared with 8.1 years for Spanish-surname students. . . .

We are faced initially with the need to make a concentrated attack in a number of areas in order to produce significant results. Bilingual teachers must be trained; new curriculums and new teaching materials must be developed; large-scale pilot projects must be carried out to provide models which can then be utilized elsewhere.

During the interim other states held statewide conferences, coming up with similar findings. Subsequent to the NEA meeting, the First National Conference on Educational Opportunities for Mexican Americans was held in Austin, Texas.

The planners would have considered an attendance of 800 to be a successful conference. As things turned out, more than 1,100 people registered, followed a few weeks later with nearly 1,000 requests for materials. The resounding success could only be attributed to the national anxiety for constructive action.

As the Texas conference presented various ongoing programs

in the state, the national conference revealed various programs around the nation. Many important topics were touched upon by participants such as this one by Commissioner Harold Howe II:

> I would like to talk about the "education problem"—and it is basically just one problem: helping every youngster—whatever his home background, whatever his home language, whatever his ability—become all he has in him to become.
>
> Such a goal is a lofty one, and it is doubtful that the schools will ever achieve it perfectly. What must concern us is the degree to which many schools fail to come within a country mile of that goal. If Mexican American children have a higher drop-out rate than any other identifiable group in the nation—*and they do*—the schools cannot explain away their failure by belaboring the "Mexican American problem." *The problem, simply, is that the schools have failed with these children.*

Commissioner Howe then quoted a paragraph from Dr. Severo Gomez (to give an idea of the attitude of some teachers toward the Mexican Americans):

> They are good people Their only handicap is the bag full of superstitions and silly notions they inherited from Mexico. When they get rid of these superstitions, they will be good Americans. The schools help more than anything else. In time, the Latins will think and act like Americans. A lot depends on whether we can get them to switch from Spanish to English. When they speak Spanish, they think Mexican. When the day comes that they speak English at home like the rest of us, they will be part of the American way of life. I just don't understand why they are so insistent about using Spanish. They should realize that it's not the American tongue.

Commissioner Howe then went on to add:

> In a hundred subtle ways, we have told people of all origins other than English that their backgrounds are somehow cheap or humorous. The tragic thing is that this process has succeeded. Of the incredible diversity of languages and traditions that the people of a hundred nations brought to this country virtually nothing remains except in scattered enclaves of elderly people who are more often viewed as objects of curiosity rather than respect.
>
> Mexican Americans are one of the few exceptions to this American rule of cultural elimination through cultural disdain. A distinctive Spanish-Indian-Mexican culture survives in the United States.
>
> As you know, this culture has been a handicap, not a blessing, in the attempts of Mexican Americans to prosper. Basic to the success of any such attempt is a good education, and the cultural backgrounds of Spanish-speaking children have produced a staggering amount of educational failure.

In support of bilingual, bicultural programs three points are stressed:

First: Evidence is clear that people learn languages best if they learn them young. It is rather paradoxical that in the Southwest some elementary schools have forbidden children to speak Spanish, while at the same time many of our secondary schools require students to learn another language.

Second: The proper conduct of bilingual programs should produce dramatic improvement in the performance of Spanish-speaking children. (Dr. Knowleton has said: "The majority who fight their way through to a high school level often have the dubious distinction of being illiterate in two languages.")

Third: We note "this advantage for bicultural, bilingual programs for Anglo as well as Mexican children may well be the most important for our country."

The notion of cultural superiority has seriously harmed the U.S. in this century in its dealings with other peoples. In the middle of this century, after nearly 150 years of largely ignoring the rest of the world, we have lumbered into the family of nations as an international force. A position of international responsibility was thrust upon us, and we were ill-prepared to assume it. In fact, one of the great motivations behind the present set of Federal programs for education was the lack of Americans who could speak foreign languages or deal with other peoples in terms of their own cultures. The result was that we often offended people whom we were trying to help or befriend.

If we are to gain the friendship of these new nations and strengthen our ties with much older nations that have felt the strength of American parochialism in the past, we must give our children the ability to move with ease and respect in cultures other than their own.

It was soon after this conference that the Puerto Ricans in New York, representing more than two million people, held their first Educational Conference for the Puerto Rican. Some of the Mexican American leadership was invited to this conference, and it was interesting to hear how similar their problems were to Mexican Americans.

Recently, the U.S. Commission on Civil Rights held its first major hearings on the Mexican American. It took place in San Antonio.

From the educational component of the hearings, important testimony from staff papers, administrators, and other people was revealed. Under oath, the following things were heard:

Mexican American students are isolated by school district, by schools within individual districts, by ability grouping within schools, and by selection of vocational rather than academic programs.

School administration in the area is Anglo controlled. . . . Most Mexican American principals, vice-principals, and teachers are assigned to Mexican American schools.

Although state and federal aid comprise a greater proportion of total revenue in Mexican American districts, per pupil expenditures are not equalized with those in Anglo districts.

Mexican American students perform less well on verbal-oriented I.Q. and achievement tests given in English, which may not validly reflect the potential of those students. Interpreters of their scores tend to assign them to classes for underachievers, or to counsel them away from a college preparatory curriculum.

If students attend schools in a high density area of Mexican American population, the probabilities they will drop out are greater than for Mexican American youngsters enrolled in predominantly Anglo, or ethnically mixed schools.

Because Mexican American districts are financially less capable they suffer from inadequacy of facilities, and noncompetitive teaching salaries. As a result 89 percent of the non-college degree teachers employed in the nine San Antonio school districts are concentrated in the predominantly Mexican American districts.

Less well known, but equally distressing, are the 1960 census figures revealing that nearly one fourth of the Mexican Americans in Texas twenty-five years old or older had not completed one year of education, and that close to 40 percent of the Mexican American adults were functional illiterates having completed the fourth grade or less. Based also on 1960 figures, other sources indicate that while 21 percent of the Mexican American student population graduated from high school, less than 2 percent graduated from college.

A wide variety of educators, community leaders, and Mexican American students were invited to give an explanation for this picture. Some of their testimony was the following:

There are the genetic differences of the Mexican American. [This statement was given by an Anglo junior high principal, San Antonio; you can imagine the excitement this caused.]

Teacher education, textbooks, teaching methods, curriculum planning, and teacher certification took little or no account of the convergence of two languages and of at least two cultures in the Southwest.

It became evident that the Anglo student, not to speak of his Negro peer, is also being deprived of an education consonant with his tri-ethnic environment. Worse still, the school confirms the Anglo student in an ethnocentrism that will make him view the "culturally different" as somehow humorous, deviant, and underdeveloped.

Punishment for speaking Spanish was testified to by students. Until two weeks prior to the hearing, the largest predominantly Mexican American high school in El Paso punished the speaking of Spanish on the grounds with after-school detention.

The average reading ability of predominantly Mexican-American pupils was considered low, despite the almost universally recognized fact of the inadequacy of reading tests for the "culturally different" child. The result is still a large number of

Mexican Americans being placed in slow-learner track systems and, in some cases, in classes for the mentally retarded.

PTA meetings are frequently held during working hours, thereby markedly limiting parental participation. (Yet how often have we not heard that Mexican American parents are not interested?)

This is the picture of the educational status as presented by witnesses at the U.S. Commission on Civil Rights hearings.

It is interesting to note that the Civil Rights hearings were only giving credibility to what Mexican American students have been insisting, demanding, and demonstrating about all over the nation. The past few school years have been a phenomenon of confrontation between the school and the Mexican American community in a large number of cities and towns throughout the country. This took place in the Midwest in Chicago and Kansas City; in the Southwest in Los Angeles, El Paso, Denver, Sierra Blanca, and San Antonio. The primary target is clear in all cases; the quest for "quality education" that Commissioner Howe and Dr. Estes have advocated and the development of talents to their fullest — is this not what educators tell us education is all about? Obviously the students feel now they have not been recipients of it.

What are the students saying in Los Angeles? Here are some of their demands:

1. Textbooks and curriculum revised to show Mexican contributions to society, to show the injustices they have suffered, and to concentrate on Mexican folklore.

2. Compulsory bilingual and bicultural education in Los Angeles schools, with teachers and administrators to receive training in speaking Spanish and in Mexican cultural heritage.

3. Counselor-student ratios reduced, and counselors must speak Spanish and have a knowledge of Mexican cultural heritage.

4. Students must not be grouped into slow-learning classes based on the poor tests currently in use which often mistake language problems for lack of intelligence.

5. Community parents be engaged as teacher aides.

6. The industrial arts program must be revitalized to provide training for entry into industry; modern equipment and techniques must be provided.

These are only part of thirty demands, presented in the interest of basic approaches for better education for the Mexican American. *Compare these with what was said in Chicago.*

1. Qualified bilingual Spanish-American counselors.

2. One elective year of Latin-American culture and history taught by qualified bilingual Latin-American teachers.

3. Special ESL classes for non-English-speaking students and such classes be made a part of the school curriculum.

4. A Spanish-American assistant principal at the high school with heavy Spanish-speaking population.

5. Monthly Spanish meetings of the PTA conducted by a community authorized Spanish-speaking person.

In San Antonio the demands were very similar; in fact, the list of grievances and subsequent demands, wherever they took place, were very similar. The only difference was the degree of demand, the locality, and the order in which demands were listed.

There are those who suggest that there are external forces guiding the efforts in these cities. On the contrary, it is a beautiful phenomenon of a movement that is swelling. It is a spontaneous swelling of an awakening people. The goal is quality education.

The new Republican administration under Nixon has adopted this objective of quality education as a national goal. In essence, the students have made it theirs also. That goal *will be* achieved. The only questions remaining are when and at what price?

What is the price that the young and those dedicated to them are willing to pay? No one really can say. Here are some indications. In Los Angeles one of the teachers, along with five others, who tried to give intelligent direction to the youth, is being charged with a felony. The authorities are attempting to revive an old California law which makes conspiracy to commit a misdemeanor a felony. This case is now in the courts, and it is a serious political battle. In Los Angeles, although the Mexican American community was aided by blacks and whites in protests, picketing, and walkouts, the only ones arrested were the Mexican Americans. *The question is why?*

In Santa Ana, parents and students have complained that Mexican American children in first and second grades may be arbitrarily placed in mentally retarded classes. This is the school's answer for bilingual education. The Mexican American Legal Defense Fund is presently taking the district to the federal courts, seeking damages and remedy.

In San Antonio, Edgewood School District, a young teacher who assisted the students in a protest was subsequently fired, and *publicly humiliated* by a vote of removal from the local teachers' association. In a movement, *how long will indignities such as the foregoing be tolerated?*

A recent survey of the five southwestern states was reported by the Mexican American Affairs Unit of the U.S. Office of Education. One hundred and one meetings involving 1,765 participants were held. The principal participants were state department officials, personnel from teacher training institutions, school board associations, regional laboratories, public school personnel, professional associations, and various citizen groups. The findings from that survey were as follows:

1. It is evident that there is a serious shortage of educational programs directed toward the needs of Mexican Americans in the five states surveyed.

2. There is a serious problem related to the transmission of information concerning those programs which do exist and are effective in their locations. It was observed frequently that one location would be completely unaware of a promising educational program in progress in an adjacent area.

3. School districts show a lack of imagination in devising or adopting innovative programs to meet the needs of the Mexican Americans.

4. Through the survey, in every community, there was evidenced a great interest and desire to do something about the problems which exist. However, a sense of direction was not evident, and few persons seemed to know quite what to do about the problems.

5. It is evident that very few Anglo educators are prepared to handle the educational problems of Mexican Americans.

6. There is a great desire for information on promising educational programs for Mexican Americans. Communication and dissemination seem virtually nonexistent.

7. There is a question on the part of the Mexican American community as to whether the Office of Education is seriously

concerned with doing anything to bring about an improvement of the problems in education.

8. Lack of coordination among agencies (federal, state, and local agencies) that deal with the needs of Mexican Americans is a critical problem.

9. In the *area of priorities,* a tabulation of expressions from all states ranks the first four concerns as:

a) Attention to the preschool child

b) Attention to the teacher and administrator; this includes attitudes, training, in-service education, institutes, recruitment, materials, tests, and the use of teacher aides for individual attention

c) Bilingual, bicultural educational programs

d) Vocational training, vocational and educational counseling, and placement assistance for both adults and adolescents

Finally the *Report by the National Advisory Committee on Mexican American Education* (1968) reads as follows:

The use of Spanish by some of our Mexican American leaders has depicted the international importance of bilingualism.

1. Dr. Braulio Alonza, former national president, of the NEA, representing the Department of State at an international educational conference in Mexico City, received a standing ovation by addressing the delegation (who had heard speakers in Russian and French) in Spanish, the language of the host country.

2. Dr. Hector Garcia, as alternate delegate to the U.N., addressed the United Nations in Spanish for the first time in its history. In doing so, he helped to break down barriers which existed with Spain. He also was asked to convey the condolences of the French people to Costa Rica in their language—Spanish. Can one imagine what it will be like if teachers really make the effort to conduct bilingual education in their schools? Mexican Americans cannot afford to wait any longer. Teachers must begin to pave the way!

The torch and the challenge are presented to teachers everywhere. And in accepting them, let the word go forth from this time and place that the commitment is being made and the torch is held by a new generation of people, a generation born in this century, a generation tempered by experience, disciplined by hard and bitter struggles, proud of their ancient heritage, and unwilling to witness — or permit — a slow undoing of those human rights to which this nation has always been committed and to which all Americans are committed today.

Let every man know that the time to build is now and the Mexican American will pay any price, bear any burden, meet any hardship, and oppose any philosophy which does not assure the survival and success of *La Raza*. All America must move forward together, remembering the challenge of our forefathers:

¡Viva La Causa!
¡Viva La Raza!
¡Que dios nos bendiga!
y
¡Gracias por su atención!

INDEX